PENGUIN CLASSICS

IBN FADLĀN AND THE LAND OF DARKNESS

IBN FADLĀN's account of his journey from Baghdad to the camp of the Bulghār khan, on the Volga River, in 921 is unique in Arabic literature. Sent as an emissary of the Abbasid caliph Muqtadir, his mission was to deliver a message and gifts from the caliph to the recently converted khan, who sought religious instruction for his people and wished to forge an alliance with the Abbasids to protect himself against his powerful Jewish overlords, the Khazars. The Bulghār encampment was far beyond the frontiers of the Islamic heartlands, and Ibn Fadlān faithfully recounts the customs, dress and religious beliefs of the peoples through whose territory he passed, all of whom were still pagan. In Bulghār he encountered Viking traders who were pioneering trade routes along the Russian rivers. He witnessed and meticulously describes a Viking ship burial, the only such description we have. Nothing is known of Ibn Fadlān from other sources.

ABŪ HĀMID was born in al-Andalus in 1080. In 1106, he travelled to North Africa, where he spent more than ten years, before sailing for Alexandria in 1117. En route, he passed the island of Sicily and observed Mount Etna in full eruption. Later years saw him travelling to Cairo, Damascus, Baghdad and Iran, before settling for two decades in the great trading city of Saqsīn. In 1150, Abū Hāmid went to Hungary, where he developed close ties with the king, Geza II, and was employed to recruit Pečeneg Muslims into the cavalry. He was allowed to depart from Hungary only on condition that he leave his son hostage to his return. In 1153, he returned to Saqsīn, before making the pilgrimage to Mecca. Settling in Baghdad in 1155, he composed the first of the works by which he is best known today, *al-Mu'rib 'an ba'd 'ajā'ib al-maghrib* (*Exposition of Some of the Wonders of the West*). He left for Aleppo in 1165, and five years later made the last journey of his remarkable life, to Damascus. H~ ~· ~ ~ 1170 at the age of ninety.

PAUL LUNDE spent his early years in Saudi Arabia and studied Arabic at the University of California in Berkeley and later at the School of Oriental and African Studies in London. He has travelled widely in the Middle East and spent many years researching Arabic geographical literature in the Vatican Library in Rome. He is now based in Cambridge, concentrating on the maritime history of the Indian Ocean.

CAROLINE STONE was educated at Cambridge and Kyoto University, Japan. After living many years in Rome, she currently divides her time between Seville and Cambridge, where she is editing and translating a series of travel accounts – *Travellers in the Wider Levant* – for the Civilizations in Contact Project, funded by the Golden Web Foundation. Her publications include books on North African embroideries and Manila shawls, and she worked with Paul Lunde on a selection from Mas'ūdī's *Meadows of Gold*, published by Penguin.

IBN FADLĀN

Ibn Fadlān and the Land of Darkness

Arab Travellers in the Far North

Translated with an Introduction by
PAUL LUNDE *and* CAROLINE STONE

PENGUIN BOOKS

For Gabriella and Béla Bollobás

PENGUIN CLASSICS

Published by the Penguin Group
Penguin Books Ltd, 80 Strand, London WC2R ORL, England
Penguin Group (USA) Inc., 375 Hudson Street, New York, New York 10014, USA
Penguin Group (Canada), 90 Eglinton Avenue East, Suite 700, Toronto, Ontario, Canada M4P 2Y3
(a division of Pearson Penguin Canada Inc.)
Penguin Ireland, 25 St Stephen's Green, Dublin 2, Ireland (a division of Penguin Books Ltd)
Penguin Group (Australia), 250 Camberwell Road, Camberwell, Victoria 3124, Australia
(a division of Pearson Australia Group Pty Ltd)
Penguin Books India Pvt Ltd, 11 Community Centre, Panchsheel Park, New Delhi – 110 017, India
Penguin Group (NZ), 67 Apollo Drive, Rosedale, Auckland 0632, New Zealand
(a division of Pearson New Zealand Ltd)
Penguin Books (South Africa) (Pty) Ltd, 24 Sturdee Avenue,
Rosebank, Johannesburg 2196, South Africa

Penguin Books Ltd, Registered Offices: 80 Strand, London WC2R ORL, England

www.penguin.com

This edition first published in Penguin Classics 2012

030

Part III, sections 35–7 from *Sharaf al-Zamān Tāhir Marvazī on China, the Turks and India*, translated by
Vladimir Minorsky (1942), is reprinted with the permission of The Royal Asiatic Society

Translation and editorial material © Paul Lunde and Caroline Stone, 2012
All rights reserved

The moral right of the translators has been asserted

Set in 10.25/12.25 pt Postscript Adobe Sabon
Typeset by Jouve (UK), Milton Keynes
Printed in England by Clays Ltd, Elcograf S.p.A.

Except in the United States of America, this book is sold subject
to the condition that it shall not, by way of trade or otherwise, be lent,
re-sold, hired out, or otherwise circulated without the publisher's
prior consent in any form of binding or cover other than that in
which it is published and without a similar condition including this
condition being imposed on the subsequent purchaser

ISBN: 978-0-140-45507-6

www.greenpenguin.co.uk

MIX
Paper | Supporting
responsible forestry
FSC® C018072

Penguin Books is committed to a sustainable
future for our business, our readers and our planet.
This book is made from Forest Stewardship
Council™ certified paper.

Contents

IBN FADLĀN AND THE
LAND OF DARKNESS

List of Maps
(see pp. xxxviii–xlii)

Chronology

622 Year One of the Islamic calendar. First Muslim community founded by the Prophet Muhammad in Medina.

632 Death of the Prophet Muhammad. Beginning of Arab conquests.

650 Approximate date for formation of Khazar khāqānate.

661 Umayyad dynasty takes power.

711 Islamic conquest of Visigothic Spain. Arab armies reach the Indus.

730 Khazars invade Muslim territory with army of 30,000, take Ardabil and Bardha'a, and raid as far west as Mosul and Diyarbakr.

732 Muslims defeated at Battle of Poitiers by Charles Martel. Čiček, daughter of the Khazar khāqān, married to Constantine V. Their son is Leo IV (reigned 775–780), known as 'Leo the Khazar'. The last Umayyad caliph, Marwān, leads an army of 40,000 into Khazar territory, but is driven back by torrential rains.

737 Marwān leads an army of 150,000 against the Khazars. The khāqān flees to the territory of the Finno-Ugric Burtās, but is captured and converted to Islam; 20,000 Slavs living in Khazar territory are deported. No permanent Muslim occupation results.

745 The Uighur khāqānate established.

750 The Umayyad dynasty is overthrown by the Abbasids. Around this date the Azov Bulghārs, fleeing their former Khazar masters, settle at the Samara bend of the Volga. Approximate date of the foundation of Staraia Ladoga.

758 Muslim merchants domiciled in Canton revolt.

763 The Abbasids found a new capital, Baghdad.

770 Approximate date of the foundation of the Danish Viking trading city of Hedeby.

786–809 Hārūn al-Rashīd is caliph.

793 Vikings raid Lindisfarne; the traditional date for the beginning of the Viking Age.

798 The last Khazar attack on Muslim territory. The Abbasid dynasty and the Khazars finally make peace.

800 Approximate date that the Khazar Turkish ruling elite convert to Judaism. Hārūn al-Rashīd sends the gift of an elephant to Charlemagne, who becomes Holy Roman Emperor this year. The elephant is delivered by the Aghlabid ruler of North Africa to the port of Pisa.

819 The Sāmānid dynasty creates a huge domain in Transoxania. Their capital is Bukhārā, and the rich silver mine of Panshīr in Afghanistan is in their territory. They hold power until 1005, trading throughout Central Asia.

821 Tamīm ibn Bahrī visits Balāsghūn in what is now Mongolia. His account is preserved by Ibn al-Faqīh.

838 Swedish Vikings, called *Rhos*, pass through the Carolingian capitol of Ingelheim on the Rhine on their return from Constantinople. Khazars issue the unique 'Moses' coin.

840 Hami, the capital of the Uighur khāqānate, sacked by the Kirghiz Turks.

842 The Abbasid caliph Wāthiq sends Sallām the Interpreter to 'Alexander's Wall', near Hami on the Chinese border.

844 Vikings attack Lisbon and Seville. Sallām returns from his mission.

860 Vikings attack Constantinople. Cyril and Methodius attempt to convert the Khazars to Christianity and preach at the Khazar capital. Approximate date of the foundation of Riurikovo Gorodishche by Swedish adventurer named Riurik; later grows into Novgorod.

861 Cyril and Methodius evangelize the Balkan Bulgars.

865 The Bulgarian ruler Boris forced by Byzantines to convert to Christianity.

871–899 Alfred the Great becomes king of England.

879 Muslim, Jewish, Christian and Mazdaean merchants massacred in Canton.

885 Ibn Khurradādhbih completes the final version of his *Book of Roads and Kingdoms*.

886 Danelaw established in England.

897 Death of the historian and geographer Ya'qūbī, author of *The Book of Countries*.

900 Around this date Almish, king of the Bulghārs, converts to Islam.

907 Trade agreement between Rūs of Kiev and Byzantines.

908–932 Muqtadir is caliph.

911 Vikings settle in Normandy.

912 Second trade agreement between Rūs of Kiev and Byzantines.

913 Vikings raid the Caspian.

914 Nasr ibn Ahmad becomes ruler of the Sāmānid dynasty; dies 943.

921 Ahmad ibn Fadlān sent by the caliph Muqtadir to Almish ibn (Shilkī) Yiltawār, king of the Bulghārs.

930 Approximate date of birth of Mieszko I, duke of Polons, who reigned from c. 960 until his death in 992. He is the first historically attested ruler of Poland, and is mentioned by Ibrāhīm ibn Ya'qūb.

935 Approximate date of birth of Boleslav I, duke of Bohemia. Famous for murdering his brother St Wenceslas, he ruled until his death (in 967 or 972). Ibrāhīm ibn Ya'qūb visited Prague during the last years of his reign.

942 Sviatoslav becomes king of Kiev on the death of his father Igor; his mother Olga acts as regent until 963. He is the first Rūs of Kiev to bear a Slavic name.

943 Vikings again raid the Caspian area.

944 The Byzantine emperor Constantine Porphyrogenitus writes *De administrando imperii*, containing a description of how Viking merchants negotiate the rapids on the Danube.

945 Third trade agreement between Rūs of Kiev and Byzantines.

956 Death of Mas'ūdī, author of *The Meadows of Gold and Mines of Precious Gems*.

960 Hasday ibn Shaprūt, leader of the Sephardi community of Islamic Spain, and a famous courtier and physician,

corresponds with Joseph, the Khazar *khāqān*, seeking information about his kingdom.

961 Death of the caliph 'Abd al-Rahmān III, ruler of al-Andalus, who had formed a palace guard of 14,000 Saqāliba eunuchs in Cordoba.

965 Sviatoslav of Kiev invades Khazaria, destroys the city of Sarkel, sacks Kerch in the Crimea and later destroys Itil. Ibrāhīm ibn Ya'qūb visits a number of cities in northern Europe, including Mainz, Prague and Schleswig.

965–969 Sviatoslav puts an end to the Khazar empire and attacks the Volga Bulgars, exacting tribute.

972 Sviatoslav killed by Pečenegs after invading Balkan Bulgaria.

973 Cairo founded by the Fatimids.

986 Vladimir, prince of Kiev, converts to Christianity.

1000 Leif Erikson discovers Vinland.

1016–1042 Danish kings rule England.

1040 Yahuda ha-Levi writes *The Book of the Khazars*.

1050 Death of Birūnī.

1066 Norman invasion of England. Slavs complete destruction of Hedeby, begun by the Norwegian king Harald Hardrada in 1050. The traditional date for the end of the Viking Age.

1080 Birth of Abū Hāmid al-Andalusī al-Gharnātī.

1118 The *Russian Primary Chronicle* is completed.

1130 Abū Hāmid al-Andalusī settles in Saqsīn, where he lives for twenty years.

1141–1162 Geza II of Hungary reigns.

1150 Abū Hāmid al-Andalusī travels to Hungary via Kiev and stays three years.

1155 Abū Hāmid al-Andalusī writes *Exposition of Some of the Wonders of the West*.

1161 Abū Hāmid al-Andalusī writes *The Gift of the Hearts and Bouquet of Wonders*.

1170 Death of Abū Hāmid al-Andalusī.

1237 The Volga Bulghārs conquered by the Mongols.

1258 Baghdad falls to the Mongols and the last Abbasid caliph is executed.

1283 Death of Qazwīnī, author of *The Wonders of Creation*.

Introduction

In 922, an Arab envoy from Baghdad named Ibn Fadlān encountered a party of Viking traders on the upper reaches of the Volga River, not far south of the modern city of Kazan, while on a mission to the Muslim ruler of the Bulghārs. In his subsequent report he included a meticulous and astonishingly objective description of Viking customs, dress, table manners, religion and sexual practices, as well as the only eyewitness account ever written of a Viking ship cremation. That the earliest description we have of the Viking way of life – and death – should be written in the Arabic language may seem surprising. The meeting between Viking traders and an emissary of the Abbasid caliph was not, however, as unexpected as might at first appear, and is only one of many intriguing glimpses of life in the northern world to be found in Arabic sources.

By the time of Ibn Fadlān, Vikings had been in contact with the Muslim world, both as raiders and traders, for more than a century. During the late eighth century Vikings from Sweden began trading along the Russian river systems, opening routes from the Baltic to the Black and Caspian Seas and ultimately to the two richest markets for slaves and furs in the world, Christian Constantinople and Muslim Baghdad. The Viking northern trade network overlapped with the Muslim, first at the Khazar capital of Itil,[1] at the mouth of the Volga where it flows into the Caspian, and then at Bulghār on the upper Volga at its confluence with the Kama. It is our good fortune that when the two parties met, Ibn Fadlān should have been present to record it.

The encounter between the representatives of two such disparate worlds was the result of a series of complex religious, political and economic shifts that followed the creation of the Islamic empire, which by 711 stretched from Spain to the borders of India. With the coming to power of the Abbasids in 751, a network of maritime and overland routes was established that linked Europe to China for the first time since the fall of the Roman empire. As good a symbolic date as any for its inception is 800, the year Charlemagne was crowned Holy Roman Emperor and received the congratulatory gift of an Indian elephant from the Abbasid caliph Hārūn al-Rashīd, shipped to Pisa from a North African port. Clearly, sea lanes and overland routes between east and west were already open at this early date.

The hub of the system was Ibn Fadlān's native city of Baghdad, founded in 763. It was the capital of the Abbasid empire and the largest and richest city west of China, rivalled in wealth and size only by Cordoba, the capital of Muslim Spain. As a multicultural and multilingual imperial capital, Baghdad was a clearing house for geographic, commercial and political information. News brought by merchants of the opening up of far northern lands to commercial exploitation, along with information about other distant trading partners such as India, China and the Indonesian archipelago, filtered into the works of the geographers, historians and scholars working in Baghdad and regional cultural centres.

The Routes of the Rādhānīya and the Rūs

The earliest description of the routes linking the provinces of the empire to Baghdad was written by the director of the Abbasid Bureau of Posts and Intelligence, Ibn Khurradādhbih. He completed the final version of his *Book of Roads and Kingdoms* in 885, but it contains material dating back to the early decades of the ninth century. One of these early documents is a succinct description of four routes followed by an organization of Jewish merchants called the Rādhānīya on their trading journeys from 'the land of the Franks' to China and back. They were multilingual, speaking Arabic, Persian, Greek, 'Frankish', 'Andalusian' and Slavic. They exported eunuchs, slave girls and boys, brocades, furs and swords, and brought eastern spices and aromatics back to 'Ifrānja', the land of the Franks. Ibn Khurradādhbih's document is unique evidence for the existence of organized long-distance trade between Europe and the east, both by land and sea, during a period when, it was long assumed, trade scarcely existed in Europe except on a regional basis.

Immediately after his description of the routes of the Rādhānīya, Ibn Khurradādhbih describes two northern routes followed by the Swedish Vikings, or Rūs, one leading to the Black Sea via the Dnieper, terminating in Constantinople, the other via the Volga to the Caspian, ending in Baghdad. The Rūs traded in furs and swords, and were able to communicate in Baghdad with Slavic-speaking slaves already resident there. Both the routes of the Rādhānīya and the Rūs passed through the territory of the Khazar empire. From their capital Itil in the Volga delta, the Judeo-Turkic Khazars dominated the emerging economies of the northern steppes and provided the template for the earliest Rūs and Slavic principalities.[2]

The northern trade was fuelled by Islamic silver. Silver dirham coins struck in Abbasid mints flooded west along the trade routes opened by the Swedish Vikings in their millions; hundreds of thousands have been found in Viking coin hoards. Most were obtained by Viking traders, in Bulghār and the Khazar capital of Itil, in exchange for furs, slaves, honey, wax and amber. Once again, it is Arabic sources that shed light on this lucrative trade, the profits from which led to the development of the first towns in Slavic- and Finnic-speaking regions. Kiev and Novgorod, among the earliest 'Russian' towns, were both originally founded as trading posts by the Viking 'Rūs', eventually developing into cities, losing their Viking character. By the end of the tenth century they had become Slavic-speaking and Orthodox Christian in faith.

Ibrāhīm ibn Ya'qūb

Another tenth-century Arabic source confirms the accounts of trade between early medieval Europe and the east. A Jewish merchant from Muslim Spain named Ibrāhīm ibn Ya'qūb visited a number of European cities, including Mainz, Schleswig (both in modern-day Germany) and Prague in 965, providing the first descriptions we have of these cities in any language. When he reached Mainz, Ibrāhīm was astonished to find silver dirhams struck in 913 by the Sāmānid ruler Nasr ibn Ahmad circulating in the markets; this was the same ruler who received Ibn Fadlān in 921 in his capital of Bukhārā (in what is today Uzbekistan), on his way to the land of the Bulghārs.

Ibrāhīm offers an even more surprising comment on the markets of Mainz: 'It is extraordinary that one should be able to find, in such far western regions, aromatics and spices that only grow in the Far East, like pepper, ginger, cloves, nard, costus and galingale. These plants are all imported from India, where they grow in abundance.' If it were not for his visit, we would not know that these towns were already important centres of international trade at this early period. This kind of unexpected comment, challenging the received perception of an entire period, demonstrates why the Arabic texts presented in this volume are so valuable.

The works of Arab geographers and historians contribute scattered but tantalizing information about northern lands and peoples, and the most important of these have been translated in Part III. Ibn Khurradādhbih, Istakhrī, Ibn Rusta, Ibn Hawqal, Muqaddasī and Mas'ūdī were all more or less contemporaries of Ibn Fadlān. They drew their information from travellers, merchants, soldiers and even government archives. Although sometimes difficult to interpret, these authors vividly bring to life the world of the far north. They provide striking information on everything from the institution of sacral kingship among the Khazars to Viking raids on Caspian towns, from the use of skis and dog sleds by peoples of the north to techniques for fishing sturgeon.

Gog and Magog and 'Alexander's Wall'

The regions north of the Caucasus and the peoples that inhabited them were always peripheral to Arab writers' primary concerns.

Nevertheless, the northern lands held a particular fascination for Muslims, for they played a crucial role in Islamic eschatology.

The Arab geographers placed the lands north of the Caucasus in the Sixth and Seventh Climes, the northernmost of the seven divisions into which the globe was divided. The peoples who inhabited this huge region were all considered descendants of Japheth, son of Noah, meaning that Chinese, Turks, Bulghārs, Khazars, Alans, Avars, Magyars, Slavs, Lombards, Burgundians and Franks shared a common ancestry. They comprised the majority of the world's population and their numbers were 'uncountable as the sands of the sea' (cf. Revelation 20:8). Beyond the Seventh Clime lay the Land of Darkness, a mysterious, mist-shrouded land, inhabited by the tribes of Gog and Magog. These peoples, who appear in the Qur'ān (18:92–8) under the names Yājūj and Mājūj, as well as the biblical books of Genesis, Ezekiel and Revelation, were also counted among the descendants of Japheth, and were more numerous than all the other peoples of the earth combined. They were separated from the rest of mankind by high mountains, behind which they had been penned by a rampart of brass and iron erected by Alexander the Great. It was believed that at the end of time, they would break free and spread destruction throughout the earth, heralding the Apocalypse and the final days of mankind. These conceptions reverberate throughout Islamic geographical literature, reinforced by legends of the exploits of Alexander the Great in the Land of Darkness. Echoes of them are found in western sources as well, most notably in Marco Polo and *The Russian Primary Chronicle*.

The eschatological role of the tribes of Gog and Magog was always present in the minds of the authors of the texts collected in this volume, and shaped their view of northern lands. It haunted the caliph Wāthiq (reigned 842–847), grandson of Hārūn al-Rashīd, who one night in 842, in the palace of Sāmarrā outside Baghdad, dreamed that Gog and Magog had breached the barrier behind which they were imprisoned. He was so disturbed by the dream that he immediately sent an agent, Sallām the Interpreter, who was adept in more than thirty languages, to inspect 'Alexander's Wall' and make certain the hordes of Gog and Magog were still safely imprisoned. On his return to Baghdad in 844, Sallām recounted his adventures to Ibn Khurradādhbih, who incorporated the story of his journey in his *Book of Roads and Kingdoms*. Sallām's account of his journey to Alexander's Wall, included here, is one of the earliest first-hand accounts in Arabic of the Central Asian route to China.[3] Despite its obvious folklore elements, it is clearly a description of a real journey to the Great Wall of China and additional evidence that the overland route to China was open in the mid-ninth century. The next official mission sent by a caliph to northern lands was that accompanied by Ibn Fadlān in 921, whose account is featured in this volume.

Ibn Fadlān

Ibn Fadlān's mission was dispatched in response to an envoy sent to the caliph Muqtadir (reigned 908–932) by the recently converted ruler of the Volga Bulghārs,[4] Almish ibn (Shilkī) Yiltawār. The Bulghārs were semi-nomadic, horse-riding, Turkic-speaking shamanists, who at the time of Ibn Fadlān's visit had set up their winter camp at the confluence of the Volga and the Kama rivers, close to the rich sources of valuable furs in the northern forests. Almish had asked the caliph to send someone to instruct him and his people in the Islamic faith, to help build a mosque and to construct a fortress to defend his kingdom against his enemies. These enemies were the Khazars, to whom he was a reluctant tributary.[5] By entering into diplomatic relations with the caliphate, Almish was evidently hoping to ally himself with a powerful and prestigious protector, yet one far enough away as to pose no threat to his independence. Judging by coin finds, the bulk of northern trade was already passing through Bulghār rather than Itil. Economic power was in the process of shifting from master to vassal. Since the early tenth century Almish had been coining imitation Abbasid dirhams in great quantities, and continued to do so throughout the reign of the caliph Muqtadir, who is mentioned by name on both the coins and in the *khutba*, the sermon delivered before communal prayers on Fridays.

The embassy set out from Baghdad on 21 June 921. The caliph's envoy was Sawsān al-Rassī, a freedman of Nadhīr al-Haramī, who seems to have been a sort of chief of protocol in the Abbasid bureaucracy. Two other freedmen accompanied the mission, Tikīn the Turk and Bārs the Saqlab,[6] both of whom were chosen for their knowledge of languages and the customs of the countries through which the mission would be travelling. The caravan followed the old Khurāsān road to Rayy and Nishapur, then crossed the river Oxus to Bukhārā, where the travellers were received by the Sāmānid vizier al-Jayhānī, almost certainly the famous geographer whose lost *Book of Roads and Kingdoms* was probably the main source for information on northern peoples found in the later geographers. Disappointingly, Ibn Fadlān says little of this remarkable man.

The emissaries were received by the Sāmānid ruler, Nasr ibn Ahmad (reigned 914–943),[7] and they read him the caliph's letter, which commanded him to turn over the revenues of a property in Khwārazm, owned by the disgraced Abbasid vizier Ibn al-Furāt and managed by one of his agents, to the caliph's representative, Ahmad ibn Mūsā. The revenues from this property, valued at 4,000 dīnārs, were intended to defray the costs of constructing the fortress Almish had requested. Ahmad ibn Mūsā had not left Baghdad with the rest of the caravan, but was supposed to follow five days later. However, Ibn al-Furāt's agent, loyal to his master, contrived for him to be arrested on the frontier and he was imprisoned in Merv. Unsurprisingly, the 4,000 dīnārs was never forthcoming, to the chagrin of Ibn Fadlān and the rage of Almish.

The party had spent twenty-eight days in Bukhārā and winter was setting in. They decided not to wait any longer for Ahmad ibn Mūsā to join them; they were still unaware that he was in jail. They returned to the Oxus and rented a boat to take them to Khwārazm, a distance of 200 *farsakh*s, about 600 miles. The capital was Kāth, on the eastern bank of the Oxus, not far from modern Khiva in Uzbekistan. Although geographically isolated by steppe and desert, ancient irrigation works made the area around Kāth immensely productive, and Khwārazm had long enjoyed close commercial relations with

the Khazars. The Khwārazmians were great merchants and
travellers; Ibn Hawqal says they journeyed as far as the lands
of Gog and Magog – that is, well into subarctic regions – in
their search for fine furs.

Ibn Fadlān's travelling companion, Tikīn, had at one time
lived in Khwārazm, and the Khwārazmshah regarded him with
great suspicion, accusing him of having once sold arms to the
Turkish tribes on his northern borders. As a loyal vassal of the
Sāmānid *amīr* Nasr ibn Ahmad, the Khwārazmshah also feared
that Tikīn, for reasons of his own, was trying to bypass the
Sāmānids and establish direct contact and, perhaps, trade
between Baghdad and the Bulghārs. Nevertheless, the
Khwārazmshah finally gave them permission to proceed, and
the travellers continued by river to Jurjānīya (Gurganj), a distance of fifty *farsakhs*. They intended to stay only a few days,
but the river froze and the weather became too cold to travel.
They were forced to spend three months in Jurjānīya (December to early March) awaiting the spring thaw.

The jurists and teachers who accompanied the embassy
could not face continuing, and returned to Baghdad, reducing
the party to Sawsān, Sawsān's brother-in-law, who is mentioned for the first time here, Tikīn and Bārs. Ibn Fadlān warned
his companions that if they succeeded in reaching the camp of
the king of the Bulghārs, he would immediately demand the
4,000 dīnārs promised in the caliph's letter. They dismissed his
fears, and the party set off with a hired guide on 4 March 922,
joining a caravan headed north. The travellers rode for twenty-
five days through what is now Kazakhstan, wrapped in so
many layers of clothing against the bitter cold that they could
barely move. On the far side of a mountain chain, they came to
the Ust-Yurt, the grazing lands of the Ghuzz (Oguz) Turks. Ibn
Fadlān's description of their way of life, religious practices and
customs is invaluable as it is the only eyewitness account we
have of this important people before their conversion to Islam.

The travellers pressed on, crossing seven more rivers until at
last they reached a Pečeneg camp, probably near the Ural River.
Ibn Fadlān was struck by this people's poverty in comparison
with the Ghuzz. However, the Pečenegs too were destined to

play an important role, serving the Christian rulers of Hungary as border guards in the eleventh and twelfth centuries. After only a day in the yurts of the Pečenegs, the party continued north, crossing the Jayikh (Ural River), the largest and swiftest flowing river so far encountered. One of their skin boats was lost fording the river and many men and camels drowned. They crossed seven more rivers and entered the lands of the Bāshghird, a warlike, violent and dirty people. They were clean-shaven, wore wooden phallic charms round their necks, worshipped nature gods, had clan totems representing fish, snakes and cranes, headhunted and ate lice. Despite their fearsome reputation, however, they did no harm to the travellers.

The party set off once more, forded seven more rivers, and in about a month's time reached the lands of the Bulghārs, their goal. On 12 May 922, when they were forty-eight hours from the royal camp, they were met by four 'kings' sent out with their retinues to welcome them. The next day, as they approached the camp, Almish, the 'king of the Saqāliba', as Ibn Fadlān always refers to him, rode out to meet them, dismounting and prostrating himself before them. This, of course, was extremely shocking to a Muslim, for Muslims prostrate themselves only before God. It was the custom that most upset Ibn Fadlān, and was ubiquitous among the peoples of the steppes. The king scattered dirhams over his visitors as a sign of welcome; these were probably locally-coined imitation Sāmānid dirhams, maintaining the weight and purity of the originals.

The envoys rested for four days while the king summoned the leaders of his people from outlying districts to attend the reading of the caliph's letter. When the day came, the envoys, carrying banners, presented the king with a horse and saddle which they had brought with them as a gift, and dressed him in black robes and turban, the Abbasid dynastic colour. Ibn Fadlān was in his element, for he had been appointed to read out the caliph's letter. Very much aware of his position as a visitor from a more advanced and sophisticated civilization, Ibn Fadlān insisted that everyone, including the king, who was very fat, stand while the letter was read out. When he pronounced the caliph's greeting, he paused and instructed his audience to respond, as if the caliph himself were present. A translator rendered each phrase into the Bulghār language as the letter was read, and when it was completed, the audience roared *Allāhu akbar!* An hour later they were summoned to dinner, and Ibn Fadlān describes the manner in which this was done, for everything he witnessed was new and strange. The king himself cut a piece of meat for each of the guests and served them in order of precedence. As each was served, he was brought his own individual little table. Mead was offered, and Ibn Fadlān is careful to point out that the drink was licit, since it had only been allowed to ferment a day and a night, so did not qualify as an alcoholic drink. He also noticed that at prayer time the *khutba*, or sermon by the prayer leader, which always began with a prayer for the ruler, referred to Almish as 'King Yiltawār, king of the Bulghārs'.[8] He informed Almish that only God received the title 'king', and that the *khutba* must be read in his given name and the name of his father. Almish pointed out that both his and his father's name were pagan, and asked if he could use the caliph's name, which was Ja'far. Ibn Fadlān thought this was a good idea, and chose the name 'Abd Allāh for his father. Henceforth the *khutba* was pronounced in the name of Ja'far ibn 'Abd Allāh, retroactively converting Almish's father.

Three days later, and just as Ibn Fadlān had feared, Almish demanded his money. Relations between the two were poisoned from now on, for it was clear that Almish did not believe Ibn Fadlān's version of events, and thought he was simply refusing to hand over the money. Ibn Fadlān was not only placed in an embarrassing and humiliating position, but a very dangerous one: Almish was an imposing figure, and Ibn Fadlān was a long way from home. Almish – Ja'far, as he now was – was also highly intelligent, and the psychological pressure he exerted on Ibn Fadlān, while both men outwardly observed diplomatic protocol, is recorded in fascinating detail. For example, Ibn Fadlān had noticed that the muezzin gave the call to prayer according to the Hanafī school of law, promulgated by the Sāmānid dynasty, and suggested that instead the Ash'arī form should be used, out of deference to the law school favoured by the caliph. Almish agreed, and the new call was adopted for the next few days. He continued, however, to badger Ibn Fadlān about the money, and when he saw he was getting nowhere, ordered the muezzin to resume the Hanafī call to prayer. When Ibn Fadlān protested, Almish responded with a splendid display of analogical reasoning, showing why Ibn Fadlān, by his refusal to hand over the money, had lost all authority to admonish him over matters of religion, for in refusing he was disobeying the caliph, his master. The dialogue is beautifully reported, and as Ibn Fadlān engagingly admits, reduced him to silence. He adds that henceforth Almish nick-named him Abū Bakr the Truthful (Abū Bakr al-Siddīq), after the sobriquet of the first caliph, who never told an untruth. The sarcasm was not lost on him, and it is much to his credit that he reports it.

The battle of wits between the two men continued, Almish apparently seeking to frighten his visitor by rather pointedly having his interpreter tell him the fate of a particularly intelligent visitor from Sind, who was hanged by his travelling companions as a most suitable sacrifice to Tengri, the sky god. Then Almish increased the pressure on Ibn Fadlān by taking him to a dark forest to view the remains of a giant that he had had hanged. The giant had been found swimming in the river, could not speak and was so hideous that pregnant women miscarried when they saw him. Apparently, he was from the lands of Gog and Magog, the threatening realm that featured so prominently in contemporary Islamic conceptions of the Apocalypse. The sight of the giant's remains, which included a skull the size of a beehive, must have been a sobering experience for Ibn Fadlān: 'I was astonished at the sight. Then I went away.'

Among the Rūs

It was in the Bulghār encampment that Ibn Fadlān met the party of Rūs, Viking traders who probably came from Kiev. He describes their dress, looks, sexual behaviour, customs, hygiene – or lack of it – and religious practices, and also gives a fine description of a Viking funeral. The haunting figure of the 'Angel of Death', who strangles the slave girl who volunteers to die with her master, does not occur in the Norse sagas, nor do many of the other meticulously observed ceremonies, such as the ritual fornication on behalf of the deceased with the sacrificial victim before her own death. There is no reason to question Ibn Fadlān's account, however. The Rūs had long been trading in Baltic, Slavic and Finnish lands and had evidently incorporated practices from local cultures with whom they lived and traded.[9]

Another good illustration of the 'acculturation' of the Rūs is the description of their 'king'. He was clearly a sacral ruler, modelled on the Khazar *khāqān*, suggesting the influence of the Khazars on the Rūs and on this point confirming other Arabic sources. The 'king' was installed in a palace, sat on a throne, and his feet were not allowed to touch the ground. He was surrounded by a retinue of 400 warriors, who were sacrificed when he died. In another example, a lieutenant, corresponding to the Khazar *bāk* or *beg*, led the men into battle.[10] All of this was foreign to Norse tradition, but of ancient standing among the Turcic semi-nomads of the steppes.

Wonders

Ibn Fadlān's account is remarkably free of 'wonders', the *mirabilia* so beloved of medieval readers, and always expected, almost as a guarantee of authenticity, in descriptions of unknown lands. His description of the aurora borealis, as a vision of armies battling in the heavens, follows, as James Montgomery has pointed out, a tradition of description of such phenomena that stretches back to classical times; however, he is also trying to communicate an impression of a real event.[11] Ibn Fadlān was much struck by another natural phenomenon in northern latitudes, the long summer days and long winter nights. The short days of winter posed a real problem for Muslims, for it was difficult to fit the five stipulated prayer times into winter days that lasted only 4½, or farther north, 3½ hours.

The giant from the land of Gog and Magog was certainly

wondrous, but Ibn Fadlān is careful to indicate that he is only relating what he was told by Almish. Perhaps the skeleton Almish showed him in the forest was really that of a bear. At another point in the narrative, Ibn Fadlān describes a snake he saw slithering along the trunk of a fallen tree, 'almost as thick and large as the tree itself'. This would appear to be unknown to science, for the only large snake in Russia is the Amur ratsnake, which grows to the length of 180 cm. However, the fact that Almish assured him that it was harmless shows that it probably was a ratsnake, magnified by terror. Indeed, the only 'wonder' that is difficult to rationalize is the 'rhinoceros' Ibn Fadlān mentions; however, he is only relating what he was told by his informant, rather than claiming to have actually seen one. The three plates of onyx-like material, which Almish showed him and claimed came from the horn of a rhinoceros, may have been made of the material called *khutū*, fossilized mammoth tusk; this was much sought after for making knife handles because of its durability.[12]

What is most striking about Ibn Fadlān's little book is his objectivity. Much that he saw appalled him, particularly the open sexual congress of the Rūs with their slave girls and the always shocking beliefs and practices of pagans. He nevertheless made every effort to understand, despite the language barrier, what was going on round him. His attitude is almost scientific in its detachment as he describes food, drink, dress, manners, beliefs, customs, laws, taxes and burial rites – exactly the subjects a modern anthropologist would observe. His lack of condemnatory comment is striking, for these practices surely seemed very outlandish to a Muslim from Baghdad. Viking group sex and mixed bathing must have deeply shocked him, but he gamely records what he saw. He tried and failed to get the women of the Muslim community to veil, but refrains from derogatory remarks; later travellers, like Ibn Battūta, would not show such restraint. Ibn Fadlān has a sense of humour, and can laugh at himself: after all, there was no need to report Almish's nickname for him.

At the time he wrote, there was no established genre of travel writing in Arabic, so Ibn Fadlān had no model. He seems simply to have jotted down his impressions as they occurred to him, and his book is all the better for it. He writes simply and without affectation, and most unusually in an Arabic work, never refers to written sources. Ibn Fadlān bore the hardships of his journey with great stoicism; indeed, his only complaint, on what was after all a difficult and dangerous mission, was about the bitter cold. Because the account of Ibn Fadlān's return journey has not survived, we never learn whether Almish, the Bulghār king, received the promised 4,000 *dīnārs*. Nor is the complex relationship between Almish and Ibn Fadlān resolved, as it surely must have been in the fuller version, since we know from other sources that diplomatic ties remained intact. The geographer Dimashqī (1256–1327) mentions that the caliph Muqtadir sent a *faqīh* to teach the principles of Islam to the recently converted Bulghārs, and that afterwards a party of Bulghārs came to Baghdad intending to make the pilgrimage to Mecca; this suggests that relations between the envoy from Baghdad and the Bulghārs were resolved amicably.[13]

Abū Hāmid al-Andalusī al-Gharnāṭī

The only other Arab traveller to make his way to Bulghār and write about it was Abū Hāmid al-Gharnāṭī, 'the man from Granada' (sometimes known as Abū Hāmid al-Andalusī, 'the man from al-Andalus'[14]), whose account follows that of Ibn Fadlān in this volume.

Abū Hāmid was born in 1080 and left al-Andalus in 1106, never to return. He spent more than ten years in North Africa, then in 1117 sailed for Alexandria, passing the island of Sicily on the way and observing Mt Etna in full eruption. While there he took the opportunity of visiting the famous lighthouse, the Pharos, which he describes in detail in his *Gift of the Hearts* (*Tuhfat al-albāb*). He continued his studies in Cairo, where he spent the years 1118–1121, taking time off to make a trip up the Nile to Ikhmīm and gather information about the peoples of the Sudan and beyond. In 1122 he left Cairo for Damascus, where he taught *hadīth* and continued his studies. The following year he went to Baghdad and was fortunate enough to befriend the powerful and wealthy 'Awn al-Dīn Abū Muzaffar Yahyā ibn Muhammad ibn Hubayra, who treated him as a guest and granted him access to his extensive library. Abū Hāmid left in 1127 for unknown reasons, and 1130 found him in the town of Abhar in Iran. He mentions in passing in the *Tuhfat* that he had visited Khwārazm three times; he may have made his first visit sometime this year.

The following year, 1131, found Abū Hāmid in Saqsīn, a great trading centre and the successor city to the old Khazar capital of Itil; this was to be his home for almost twenty years. He visited Bulghār in 1135, but does not tell us why or how long he stayed, and in 1150 he set out for Hungary, or as he calls it Bāshghird. He spent three years there, where he had close relations with the king, Geza II (reigned 1141-62), who at one point employed him to recruit Pečeneg Muslims to serve as light cavalry. Abū Hāmid was allowed to depart only on condition that he leave his son Hāmid, then in his thirties, hostage against his return. In 1153 he made his way back to Saqsīn via Kiev, and rejoined his wives and concubines. His stay was brief, however, for in 1154 he determined to make the pilgrimage. He crossed the Caspian and made his way first to Khwārazm, then Bukhārā, Merv, Nishapur, Rayy, Isfāhān and finally Basra, where he joined the *hajj* caravan to Mecca.

Abū Hāmid returned from Mecca in 1155 and settled in Baghdad, where he composed the first of the works by which he is best known today, *al-Mu'rib 'an ba'd 'ajā'ib al-maghrib* (*Exposition of Some of the Wonders of the West*). This is a work of popular cosmology and the 'wonders' of North Africa and al-Andalus, dedicated to his friend and patron, the vizier 'Awn al-Dīn. It includes, among many other miscellaneous topics, useful information on the calendars used by the Persians, Byzantines and Arabs; instructions for finding the direction of prayer; elements of astronomy; an explanation of latitude and longitude; and the division of the globe into Seven Climes (*iqlīm*).

Abū Hāmid's true enthusiasm was for 'wonders' (*'ajā'ib*), deviations from the natural order of things, such as unusual fish and birds, or man-made, such as the Pyramids, the Pharos of Alexandria or Alexander's Wall. Some of these wonders he saw for himself during his years of travel in unusual places, such as the giant from the lands of Gog and Magog he met in Bulghār, or the 'magic mosque' near Khwārazm; others were told to him or encountered in written sources. As with Ibn Fadlān, it is possible to rationalize some of these accounts of 'wonders'. Giant crossbills may not exist, but it is perfectly true that there is a bird with the beak Abū Hāmid describes, while the story of the swords thrown into the sea by the Yūrā (Yughra) may simply be a misunderstanding of the use of the harpoon. Abū Hāmid interpreted these wonders, as testifying to God's power over His creation and evidence of the continuing intervention of the divine in the course of nature and the affairs of man.

In 1161 Abū Hāmid left Baghdad and went to Mosul, probably at the invitation of Mu'in al-Dīn Abū Hafs 'Umar ibn Muhammad ibn al-Khidr al-Ardabilī, to whom Abū Hāmid's second book, *Tuhfat al-albāb wa nukhbat al-'ajā'ib* (*The Gift of the Hearts and Bouquet of Wonders*), is dedicated. This is a straightforward collection of 'wonders', natural and man-made. It proved immensely popular, and is frequently quoted by later authors, in particular Qazwīnī in his *'Ajā'ib al-makhlūqāt* (*The Wonders of Creation*). Abū Hāmid left for Aleppo in 1165, and five years later made the last journey of his remarkable life, to Damascus, where he died in 1170 at the age of ninety. It seems that he never returned to ransom his son Hāmid in Hungary and never rejoined his womenfolk in Saqsīn.

Abū Hāmid spent twenty-four years living and travelling in Saqsīn, Bulghār and Hungary, and was clearly an observant man, yet he is silent about much that we would like to know. Although he occasionally refers to his family, he is reticent about how he earned a living. As a learned Muslim, he was clearly in demand, and lost no opportunity to spread his faith and correct the erring. He never mentions serving in any official capacity. Perhaps like other Muslim travellers he combined his role as Muslim 'consultant' with trade, for which Saqsīn and Bulghār offered limitless opportunities, especially in slaves and furs.

Nevertheless, what he does tell us is precious, not least for what he reveals about the enormous upheavals that had taken place in the steppes since the time of Ibn Fadlān, two-hundred-forty years earlier. The once powerful Khazar khāqānate was not even a memory; the Sāmānid dynasty had come to an end in 1005; and the Rūs had long since merged with the Slavic population and become Orthodox Christians. In fact, the Volga Bulghārs were the only state from the time of Ibn Fadlān to survive, still trading at the confluence of the Volga and Kama. Some changes were particularly telling, such as the alteration in currency since the time of Ibn Fadlān. The coins in circulation at Saqsīn, Abū Hāmid tells us, were all of base metal. The fall of the Sāmānids in 1005 had resulted in a 'silver famine' that was reflected in the sudden drop in dirham hoards in eleventh- and twelfth-century Russia, Baltic lands and Scandinavia, for almost all the sources of the silver that circulated through the northern trade routes lay in Sāmānid territory.[15]

Abū Hāmid's account of Saqsīn, the Khazar capital that replaced Itil and may have occupied the same site, shows just how much had altered since the time of Ibn Fadlān. Itil had been destroyed by Sviatoslov of Kiev, the first Rūs prince to bear a Slavic name, in 965, and the Khazar khāqānate had collapsed; even the memory of the Jewish *khāqān* had vanished. The town – or perhaps city – was now entirely Muslim, the majority following the Hanafī school of law. Forty tribes of Ghuzz Turks, dwelling in round felt tents big enough to hold a hundred or more men, now inhabited the town, each with its own chief. The Ghuzz were still Shamanist when encountered by Ibn Fadlān, but by the end of the tenth century they had become Muslims. Many served the rulers of Khwārazm and Transoxania as auxiliary troops, and as so often happened, these men had soon become strong enough to seize power themselves, taking Nishapur in 1038 and Baghdad in 1055, founding the Seljuk dynasty. Ibn Fadlān could never have imagined that the herdsmen through whose territory he passed would in little more than a century come to rule the Islamic empire from his own native city of Baghdad.

When Ibn Fadlān visited Bulghār, the ruler was a vassal of

the Khazars, his son held hostage at the Khazar court in Itil. By Abū Hāmid's time, Itil had become Saqsīn and a Bulghār *amīr* was quartered in the centre of the town, supported by his tribes-men. The Volga Bulghārs, taking advantage of the destruction of the Khazar empire by the Rūs in 965, had clearly extended their political and commercial control all the way south to Saqsīn, perhaps in affiliation with the Ghuzz, on whose tents Abū Hāmid remarked.

There had also been great changes in Bulghār itself since Ibn Fadlān's day. In 922, Bulghār was a seasonal market some 3 miles from the eastern bank of the Volga. There were no permanent dwellings, simply the characteristic felt yurts of the semi-nomads. When Abū Hāmid was there in 1130, it was a 'great city' with wooden houses, walled with an oak stockade. There were villages in its environs and the king levied tribute on 'infinite peoples' to the north. Bulghār had also become the leading market for furs in the world, exporting enormous quantities of beaver, sable and mink to Islamic, Indian and Chinese markets. Nevertheless, despite these changes, some aspects of life remained constant: slaving, for example, was still a major industry. When the rivers were frozen, the king led winter raids against the pagan peoples of the far north, carry-ing off their women, children and horses. These captives were sold in Bulghār and distributed to the urban centres of the Islamic heartlands.

By the time of Abū Hāmid, the memory of Ibn Fadlān's embassy had also completely faded. According to Abū Hāmid, the conversion of the Bulghārs to Islam had occurred at the hands of a Muslim merchant with a knowledge of medicine, who agreed to cure the king and his queen, both afflicted with a serious illness, on condition that they and their people embrace Islam. The treatment was successful and the Bulghārs became Muslim. The Khazar king, furious at their conversion, invaded Bulghār territory but was defeated in battle. Pious legend, it would seem, had already overtaken history.

The topoi of descriptions of northern lands and peoples were established early in Arabic geographic literature: intense cold, long nights, bad hygiene, independent women, saunas, silent barter, fearsome giants, strange fish, pervasive idolatry and, always hovering in the background, the apocalyptic tribes of Gog Magog straining to break through Alexander's Wall. Fact was mixed with fantasy, yet as can be seen from the texts translated in this volume a surprising amount of 'hard' information was also recorded, some of it corroborated only recently by archaeological discoveries. Ibn Fadlān's gripping narrative, however, still stands almost alone in Arabic literature for its immediacy, personal flavour and balanced description of the lives and customs of the peoples of the north at a critical stage in their history. Apart from the novelistic account of Sallām the Interpreter, it is the earliest first-person travel narrative in Arabic. It had no imitators. Ibn Jubayr and Ibn Battūta, the two best-known Arab travellers, followed a different tradition and neither shared the inquiring mind and objectivity of Ibn Fadlān.

The late Michael Crichton was so struck by reading a passage from Ibn Fadlān in an anthropology course as a student that he was inspired to write his first novel, *Eaters of the Dead* (1976), an amusing and imaginative attempt to use the alleged discovery in a Greek monastery of a complete manuscript of Ibn Fadlān's journey to extend his travels to Scandinavia, where he witnessed Grendel's attack on the hall of Rothgar as recounted in the Anglo-Saxon epic *Beowulf*.[16] The imposture is made even more believable by the fact that the early chapters, up to the Viking funeral, really are a translation of Ibn Fadlān, and the rest is narrated in the same style. In the introduction, speaking in the guise of Professor Per Fraus-Dolus ('Professor Through Fraud and Trickery'), 'Professor Emeritus at the University of Oslo', Crichton wrote: 'Ibn Fadlān himself is clearly an intelligent and observant man. He is interested in both the everyday details of life and the beliefs of the people he meets. Much that he witnessed struck him as vulgar, obscene, and barbaric, but he wastes little time in indignation; once he expresses his disapproval, he goes right back to his unblinking observations. And he reports what he sees with remarkably little condescension.' The professor may have been a fraud, but his judgement of Ibn Fadlān could not be bettered.

NOTES

1. For many years it was thought that Itil had been engulfed by the Caspian Sea, but in 2008 a team of archaeologists from Astrakhan University, led by Dr Dmitry Vasilyev, announced the discovery of what may well be the site, including the remains of a triangular brick fort, near the village of Samosdelka in the Volga delta.

2. See Appendix 1 for more details on the Khazars.

3. The other account is by Tamīm ibn Bahrī, an otherwise unknown Arab, who travelled on an official mission to the Uighur *khāqān* at Khara Balghāsūn in what is now Mongolia in 821; he also visited the Kīmāk Turks on the Irtish River in Siberia. His report was preserved by Ibn al-Faqīh; it is of mainly topographic interest. The fullest version is in the same Mashhad manuscript that contains Ibn Fadlān's account. See Minorsky (1948), 275–305. On Alexander's Wall, see Part III, note 1.

4. The ruins of Bulghār are about 3 miles from the left bank of the Volga, 52 miles south of Kazan, near the village of Bolgerskoye. The Bulghārs originated in the steppe north of the Sea of Azov, but settled the Middle Volga in the eighth century. See Appendix 4 The Fur Trade.

5. The Bulghārs and Khazars also shared a common language: see also Part III, note 66.

6. See Part I, note 11.

7. See Appendix 3 for a brief history of the Sāmānid dynasty and Part I, notes.

8. It is perhaps significant that Almish is called 'king of the Bulghārs' in the *khutba*, while Ibn Fadlān uniformly refers to him as 'king of the Saqāliba'; perhaps the latter was the form of address used by the Abbasid chancery.

9. For a recent discussion of the Norse elements in the funeral rites, see Schjødt (2007).

10. For a fuller discussion of the Rūs and their relationship with the Khazars, see Appendix 2.

11. The difference between the shifting curtains of green light caused by the solar wind striking the magnetosphere and the much brighter display caused when a substorm occurs and the aurora becomes as much as a thousand times brighter than usual as high-energy electrons smash into air molecules, exciting red and

green light from oxygen molecules and blue from nitrogen. Ibn Fadlān must have been lucky enough to witness one of these striking displays. The accompanying 'tumult and noise' of battle are harder to rationalize; the hearing of sounds and even music during displays of the aurora borealis are a commonplace even of nineteenth-century descriptions; see Bates (1974), 103–8.

12. This is described by Bīrūnī. For *khutū*, see Lavers and Knapp (2008).

13. See Dimashqī (1866), 263–4. Mas'ūdī mentions a visit to Baghdad by one of Almish's sons on his way to Mecca; see Part III, 18: 137.

14. His full name was Abū Hāmid Muhammad ibn 'Abd al-Rahīm ibn Abī al-Rabī' al-Māzinī al-Qaysi al-Andalusī, al-Gharnātī al-Uqlisī. The final element of his name shows that he was originally from the town of Uclés in the province of Cuenca.

15. Lieber (1990).

16. *Eaters of the Dead* was made into a film under the title *The 13th Warrior* (1999), starring Antonio Banderas as an improbable – and clean-shaven – Ibn Fadlān.

Note on the Texts

Ibn Fadlān

The first to recognize the importance of Ibn Fadlān's account was Yāqūt, author of an immense and authoritative geographical dictionary, the *Mu'jam al-buldān* (*Lexicon of Countries*). In 1219 he visited Merv, in what is now Turkmenistan, and was granted access to two extensive private libraries; the following year found him in Jurjānīya (Gurganj), the capital of Khwārazm and the last city visited by Ibn Fadlān before setting off overland for Bulghār. It is probable that it was in one of these two places that he came across Ibn Fadlān's report on the embassy of 921, which Yāqūt always refers to by the title *risāla*, (report, letter). Yāqūt incorporated much of the work in his lexicon, arranging the relevant information under the entries for Itil, Burtās, Burghār, Bulghār, Bāshghurt, Khazar, Khwārazm, Rūs, Saqlab and Wīsū. (In the entry under Itil, he ascribes a long passage to Ibn Fadlān that is actually taken from Istakhrī.) If Yāqūt did find the manuscript in Khurāsān, it was in the nick of time. Rumours of the Mongol advance reached him while he was in Gurganj and he decided to take refuge in Aleppo, setting off in 1220. The following year the Mongol army razed Gurganj to the ground and flooded the site by diverting the waters of the Oxus.

In 1823, almost exactly 900 years after Ibn Fadlān's journey, the Russian scholar Christian Fraehn (1782–1851), professor of Arabic and Persian at Kazan University, published a brilliant study of the passages from Ibn Fadlān preserved in Yāqūt's dictionary, relating them to other Arabic and Persian sources.

Fraehn was a rigorous and careful scholar (he required his students to learn Persian, Turkish, Latin and Arabic, and expelled Leo Tolstoy for poor academic performance), and his *Ibn Fozlan's und anderer Araber Berichte über die Russen älterer Zeit* is still a mine of information. Fraehn was the first to recognize the importance of Ibn Fadlān's report for Russian history, since it pre-dates the earliest Russian written source, *The Russian Primary Chronicle* of 1113, by almost two hundred years and sheds new light on the Rūs, the Scandinavian immigrants who played an important role in the birth of medieval Russia and lent it their name. His pioneering work on Ibn Fadlān was followed by other seminal publications, particularly on numismatics, which laid the foundations for scholars studying the spread of Islam in Eurasia. Because our written sources are so fragmentary for the ninth and tenth centuries, the periods when the first principalities were formed in what is now Russia and the Ukraine, the study of numismatics has continued to be of great importance.

It fell to another scholar from Kazan, Ahmed Zeki Validi Togan (1890–1970), to make a real breakthrough in the study of Ibn Fadlān. Zeki Validi Togan was a revolutionary and Bolshevik who had grown disenchanted with Lenin's policies towards his native Tartaristan and been forced to flee the country, taking refuge in Iran in 1923. In the library of the shrine of the Imam Reza in Mashhad, he discovered a manuscript dating from the eleventh century containing a number of geographical works, including the two epistles of Abu Dulaf Mis'ar ibn al-Muhalhil, the first half of the *Kitāb al-buldān* of Ibn al-Faqīh and an account of Ibn Fadlān's journey to Bulghār. Zeki Validi Togan's translation, accompanied by exhaustive and illuminating notes, was published in Leipzig in 1939.

The Mashhad text of Ibn Fadlān is very similar, but not identical, to that preserved by Yāqūt. Some small differences in wording may be the result of editorial interventions by Yāqūt, but others are not so readily explained. The Mashhad text is also incomplete; it breaks off abruptly in the middle of a passage describing the Khazar khāqānate. Yāqūt several times mentions that the version he used included an account of Ibn Faḍlān's return journey to Baghdad; if so, he made no use of it and this portion of the manuscript has vanished. What is clear is that both the Mashhad manuscript and the text used by Yāqūt present abbreviated versions of a longer original.

This translation follows the Arabic text published by Dahhān (1959), which faithfully reproduces the Mashhad manuscript. We have compared the text throughout with the clear photographs of the manuscript reproduced by Kovalevskii (1956), occasionally differing from Dahhān's readings; these have been pointed out in the Notes. Every effort has been made to follow the original as closely as possible, consistent with readability. The headings have been inserted by the editors to help the reader navigate through the text, and are not in the original.

Abū Hāmid al-Andalusī al-Gharnāṭī

The text of Abū Hāmid's travels survives in a single source: the last nineteen folios (96a–114b) of an undated manuscript of his *al-Muʿrib ʿan baʿd ʿajāʾib al-maghrib* (*Exposition of Some of the Wonders of the West*), Gayangos Collection XXXIV, in the Real Academia de la Historia, Madrid.

The account starts in mid-sentence, and is unrelated to the preceding passage, an account of famous mountain chains. The missing beginning was almost certainly an account of Darband and the Caucasus, for it was from there that Abū Hāmid set off for Saqsīn, where he was to reside for twenty years. The narrative ends with his expression of thanks to his patron ʿAwn al-Dīn for supplying him with a letter to the ruler of Konya, allowing him to pass through his territory on his way back to Hungary.

This translation follows the edition of the Arabic text by Dubler (1953), which is accompanied by a Spanish translation and extensive commentary. The headings have been added to help guide the reader through the text, and are not in the original. The title is also our own.

Passages from Other Geographers,
Historians and Travellers

Brief biographical information and the source of the text is given in a headnote to the first extract by each author.

The Arabic definite article *al-* has been omitted from recurring personal names, hence Muqtadir, not al-Muqtadir; Mas'ūdī, not al-Mas'ūdī. Although ungrammatical, it was felt that these truncated forms were easier on the eye in a text already somewhat overburdened with transcriptions from the Arabic. Familiar place names are given in their modern form.

The Islamic *hijrī* calendar is lunar and therefore the *hijrī* year is eleven days shorter than the solar year. Year 1 of the Islamic calendar corresponds to AD 622, when the Prophet Muhammad made the *hijra*, or 'emigration', from Makka (Mecca) to Medina at the head of the early Muslim community. In the translation, Islamic dates are given first, followed by the corresponding date in the Gregorian calendar (e.g. 301/912); the abbreviations AH (= *Anno Hegirae*) and AD (= *Anno Domini*) have been thought unnecessary.

The Arabic script is ill-suited to the transcription of non-Semitic languages. The difficulty is compounded by the fact that a number of letters in the Arabic alphabet are distinguished from one another only by dots placed above or below the letter. Depending on the position of the dots, the letter form of the second letter of the Arabic alphabet, for example, can be read *b*, *t*, *th*, *n* or *y*. Scribes often simply omitted these crucial marks, relying upon the reader to supply them. Several generations of scholars have worked on the identification of the non-Arabic place names in these texts, and most have been satisfactorily identified. (See also Part III, note 50.) The texts collected here still present wide variations in their transcriptions of place names and even of well-known tribal names, such as Bāshghird and Bulghār, the former with numerous variants, the latter sometimes occurring as Bulkār and Bulqār. These variant transcriptions are significant, and have been retained, for they provide evidence of the relationships among the texts and sometimes the language of informants.

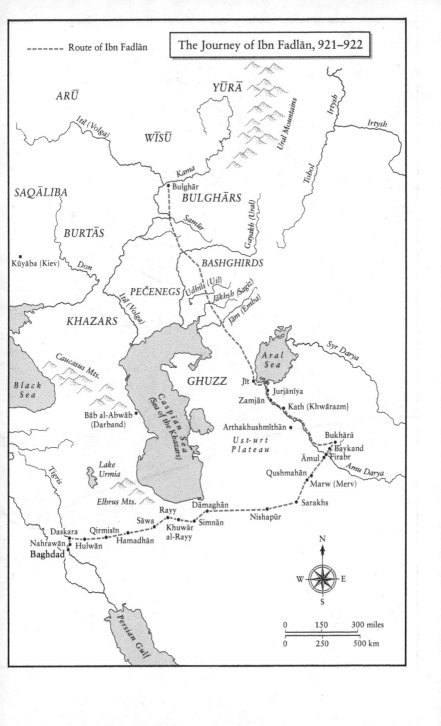

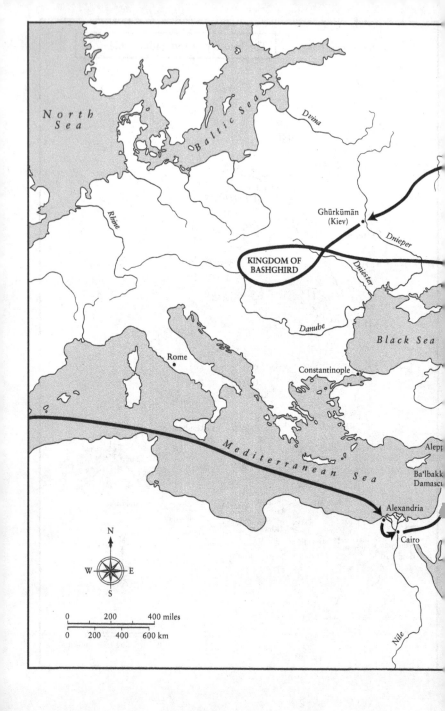

North Sea

Baltic Sea

Dvina

Rhine

Ghūrkūmān
(Kiev)

Dnieper

KINGDOM OF
BASHGHIRD

Dniester

Danube

Black Sea

Rome

Constantinople

Mediterranean Sea

Alepp[o]

Ba'lbakk
Damasc[us]

Alexandria

Cairo

N

W — E

S

0   200   400 miles

0   200   400   600 km

Nile

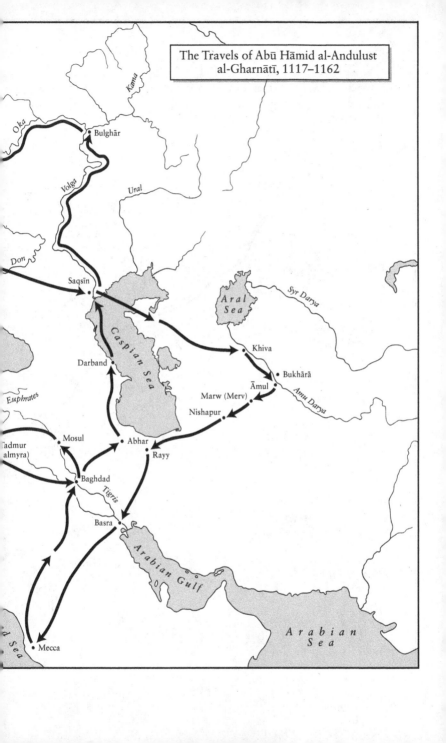

The Travels of Abū Hāmid al-Andulust
al-Gharnātī, 1117–1162

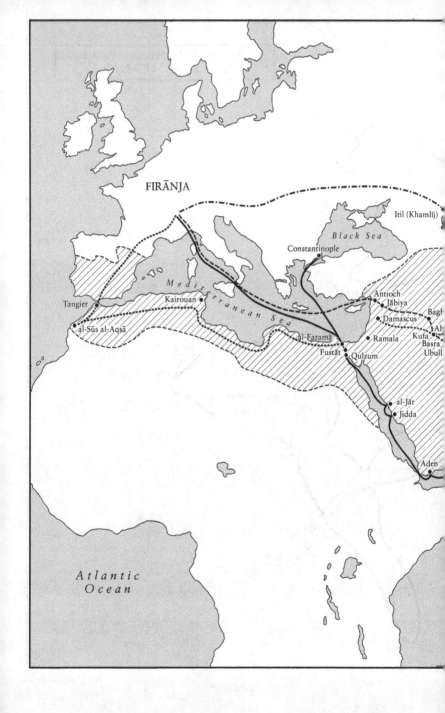

FIRĀNJA

Itil (Khamlīj)

Black Sea

Constantinople

Mediterranean Sea

Tangier

Kairouan

Antioch
Jābiya
Damascus
Bagh
[Al
al-Sūs al-Aqsā
Ramala
Kufa
Basra
Ubull

al-Farama
Fustāt
Qulzum

al-Jār
Jidda

Aden

*Atlantic
Ocean*

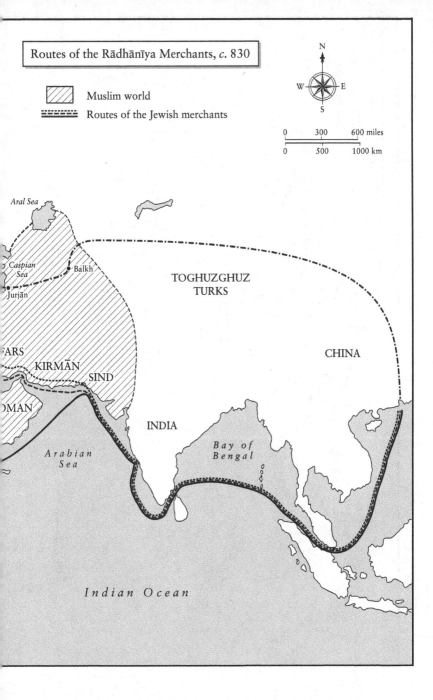

Routes of the Rādhānīya Merchants, *c.* 830

Muslim world

Routes of the Jewish merchants

N
W — E
S

| 0 | 300 | 600 miles |
| 0 | 500 | 1000 km |

Aral Sea

Caspian Sea

Jurjān

Balkh

TOGHUZGHUZ
TURKS

FARS

KIRMĀN

SIND

CHINA

OMAN

INDIA

Arabian
Sea

Bay of
Bengal

Indian Ocean

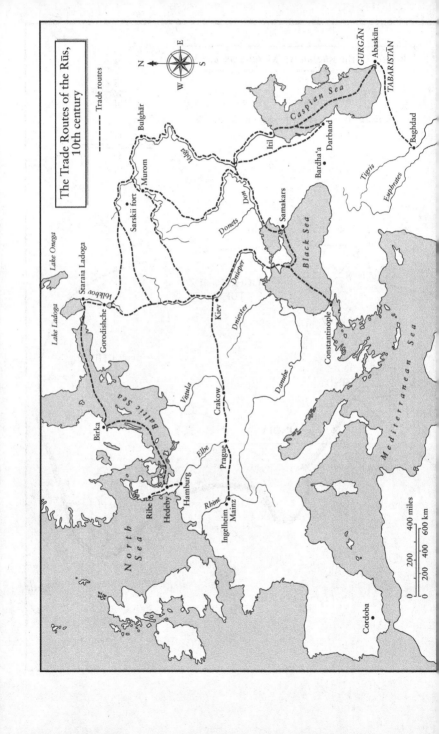

The Trade Routes of the Rūs, 10th century

- - - - Trade routes

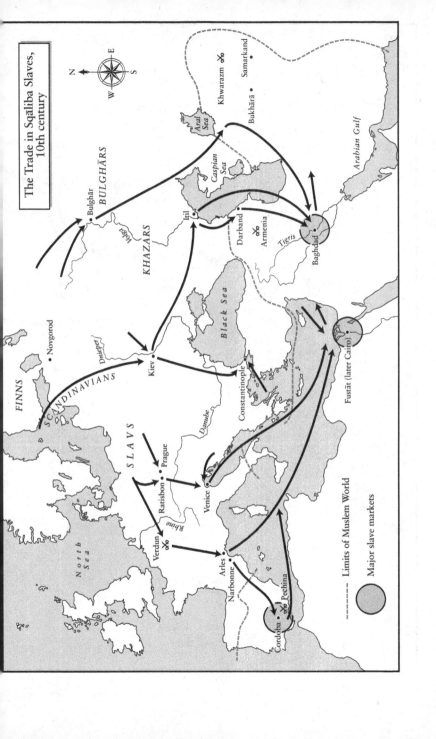

The Trade in Sqāliba Slaves, 10th century

FINNS

SCANDINAVIANS

• Novgorod

SLAVS

Prague •
Ratisbon •
Verdun ⚒
Rhine

• Kiev
Dnieper

BULGHĀRS
Bulghār •
Volga

KHAZARS
Itil •

Darband ⚒
Armenia

Khwarazm ⚒
Bukhārā •
• Samarkand

Aral Sea

Caspian Sea

North Sea

Arles •
Narbonne •

Venice •
Danube

Black Sea

Constantinople •

Baghdād •
Tigris

Arabian Gulf

Pechina ⚒
Cordoba •

Fustāt (later Cairo) •

- - - - Limits of Muslim World

⚫ Major slave markets

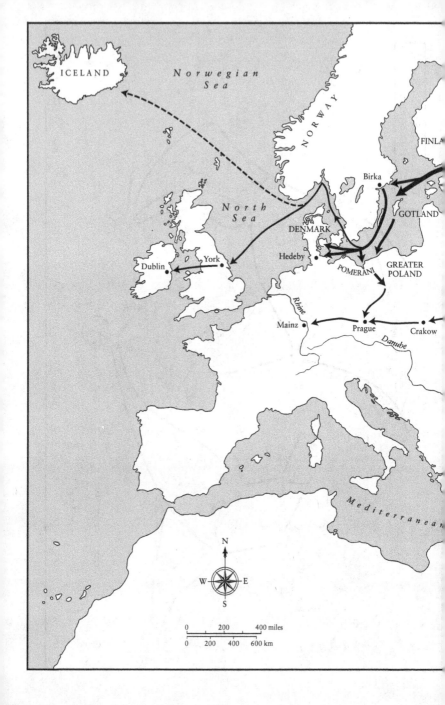

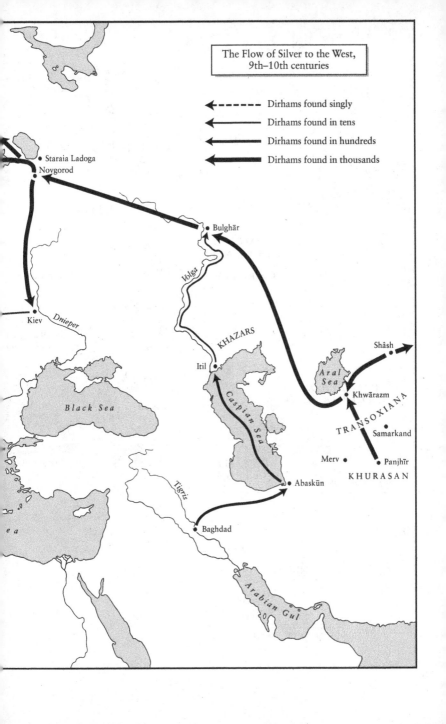

The Flow of Silver to the West,
9th–10th centuries

← - - - - - - Dirhams found singly
←——————— Dirhams found in tens
←——————— Dirhams found in hundreds
←——————— Dirhams found in thousands

Staraia Ladoga
Novgorod

Bulghār

Volga

Kiev

Dnieper

KHAZARS

Itil

Shâsh

Aral Sea

Khwārazm

TRANSOXIANA

Black Sea

Caspian Sea

Samarkand

Merv

Panjhīr

KHURASAN

Tigris

Abaskūn

Baghdad

Arabian Gulf

...ea

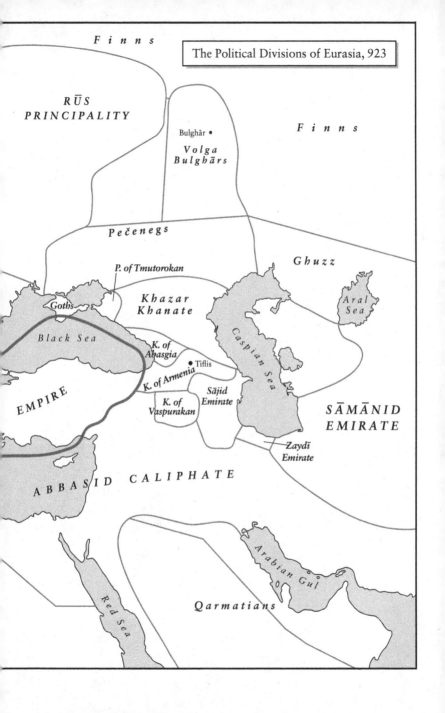

The Political Divisions of Eurasia, 923

Finns

RŪS PRINCIPALITY

Finns

Bulghār •

Volga Bulghārs

Pečenegs

Ghuzz

P. of Tmutorokan

Aral Sea

Khazar Khanate

Goths

Black Sea

K. of Abasgia

Caspian Sea

• Tiflis

K. of Armenia

Sājid Emirate

EMPIRE

K. of Vaspurakan

SĀMĀNID EMIRATE

Zaydī Emirate

ABBASID CALIPHATE

Arabian Gulf

Red Sea

Qarmatians

PART I

THE BOOK OF AHMAD IBN FADLĀN 921–922

This is the book of Ahmad ibn Fadlān al-'Abbās ibn Rāshid ibn Hammād, the client of Muhammad ibn Sulaymān, the envoy of the caliph Muqtadir[1] to the king of the Saqāliba[2] in which he tells of all he saw in the lands of the Turks, the Khazars, the Rūs, the Saqāliba, the Bāshghirds and others, their various customs, news of their kings and their current status.

Ahmad ibn Fadlān said:

When the letter arrived from Almish ibn (Shilkī) Yiltawār,[3] king of the Saqāliba, addressed to Muqtadir, the Commander of the Faithful, in which he asked for someone who could instruct him in the Faith, teach him the laws of Islam, build him a mosque and erect a *minbar*[4] so that he could have the prayers said in his name[5] in his lands and in all parts of his kingdom and also requesting that a fortress be built, for defence against the kings who were his adversaries, a favourable answer was given.

The envoy sent to him was Nadhīr al-Haramī.[6] I was given the responsibility for reading the letter to the king, making over to him the gifts that had been sent him and supervising the teachers and jurists. The king was assigned a sum of money, which was to be delivered to him, to carry out the construction work we have already mentioned and to pay the salaries of the legal scholars and teachers, from the revenues of the town known as Arthakhushmithān[7] in the lands of Khwārazm, which forms part of the estates of Ibn al-Furāt.[8]

The envoy sent to Muqtadir by the ruler of the Saqāliba was a man called Ibn Bāshtū al-Khazarī.[9] The envoy from the caliph[10] was Sawsān al-Rassī, a freedman of Nadhīr al-Haramī,

together with Tikīn the Turk and Bārs the Saqlab.[11] I accompanied them, as I have said, and delivered the gifts to the king
and his wife, children and brothers, as well as to his warlords,
including the medicine he had requested in a letter to Nadhīr.

Departure from Baghdād

We set out from the City of Peace (Baghdād) on Friday, 11
Safar 309/21 June 921. We stayed one day at Nahrawān and
set out again, marching at speed, and reached Daskara. We
stayed there three days and then continued without halting[12]
until we reached Hulwān. We stayed there for two days and set
out for Qirmisīn.[13] We stayed there for two days and then made
for Hamadhān where we spent three days.

The Road to Transoxiana

We then continued our journey and reached Sāwa. We stayed
there two days and set out for Rayy, where we spent eleven
days waiting for Ahmad ibn 'Alī, Su'lūk's brother, because he
was at Khuwār al-Rayy.[14] Then we headed for Khuwār al-Rayy
and stayed there three days. Next, we made for Simnān and
thence to Dāmaghān, where by chance we ran across Ibn Qārin,
the agent of the Dā'ī.[15] We concealed ourselves in the caravan
and hastened on our march as far as Nishapur.

Laylā ibn al-Nu'mān had just been killed. We met Hamawayh Kūsā,[16] the commander of the army of Khurāsān. Then
we set out for Sarakhs and on to Merv and then on to
Qushmahān,[17] which is the fringe of the desert of Āmul. We
stayed there for three days to allow the camels to rest before
setting out into the desert. Then we crossed the desert to Āmul.
Next, we crossed the Jayhūn (Oxus) and came to Afirabr,[18] the
ribāt of Tāhir ibn 'Alī. From there we travelled to Baykand.

Bukhārā

Then we entered Bukhārā and went to Jayhānī,[19] the secretary
of the *amīr* of Khurāsān, who was called in Khurāsān 'The Ven-
erable Support' [*al-shaykh al-'amīd*]. He gave orders that we
should be provided with a house and sent us a man to attend to
our needs and provide us with everything we might want. We
spent several days waiting and then Jayhānī requested an audience for us with Nasr ibn Ahmad.[20] We came before him and
found he was a beardless youth. We greeted him with the title
of *amīr*. He commanded us to sit down and the first thing he
asked us was:

'How did you leave our master, the Commander of the
Faithful? May God prolong his life and his good health – his
and that of his officers and ministers!'

'We left him in good health,' we replied.

'May God increase his well-being!' he exclaimed.

Next, he was read the letter [commanding him] to transfer
[the revenues of] Arthakhushmithān from al-Fadl ibn Mūsā,
the Christian, agent of Ibn al-Furāt, to Ahmad ibn Mūsā
al-Khwārazmī. He was also required to let us set out, provided
with a letter for his governor in Khwārazm, ordering him not to
hinder our mission. He was also to send a letter to the Gate of
the Turk [ordering] an escort for us and not to place any difficulties in our path.[21]

'Where is Ahmad ibn Mūsā?' asked the *amīr*.

'We left him in the City of Peace (Baghdād). He was supposed to set out five days after us,' we told him.

He replied:

'I hear and I obey the order of our lord, the Commander of
the Faithful – may God prolong his existence!'

The news reached Fadl ibn Mūsā, the Christian, Ibn al-Furāt's
agent, and he used a trick to deal with Ahmad ibn Mūsā. He
wrote as follows to the heads of Public Security along the
Khwārazm Road from the military district of Sarakhs to
Baykand:

'Keep your eyes peeled for Ahmad ibn Mūsā al-Khwārazmī in the caravanserais and customs' posts. He is a man of such and such a description. If you run across him, lock him up until you receive our letter about the matter.'

He was in fact caught at Merv and put in jail.

We stayed at Bukhārā for twenty-eight days. Fadl ibn Mūsā had come to an agreement with 'Abd Allah ibn Bāshtū and others of our companions, who said:

'If we stay any longer, winter will come and we will not be able to travel. When Ahmad ibn Mūsā gets here, he can catch up with us.'

Coinage of Bukhārā

I saw different kinds of dirhams in Bukhārā, some called *ghitrīfī* dirhams,[22] made of copper, brass and bronze. They are counted out, without being weighed, a hundred to a silver dirham. This is the way they settle the dowry of their women: so-and-so, the son of so-and-so, marries so-and-so, the daughter of so-and-so, for so many thousands of *ghitrīfī* dirhams. This is how property and slaves are sold as well. They don't use any other type of dirhams for these purposes. They also have another type of bronze dirham, of which forty make up a *dānaq*. They also have a type of bronze dirham known as *Samarqandī*, six of which are worth a *dānaq*.

Khwārazm

When I had heard the words of 'Abd Allah ibn Bāshtū and others warning me against the approach of winter, we left Bukhārā to head back to the river and hired a boat to take us to Khwārazm.[23] The distance there from the place where we rented the boat[24] is more than two hundred *farsakh*s. We only travelled for part of each day – it was impossible to travel all day because of the intense cold, which lasted until we reached

Khwārazm. We went at once to the ruler of the town, the Khwārazm Shāh Muhammad ibn 'Irāq.[25] He showed us honour, admitted us to his presence and lodged us in a house.

After three days, he summoned us to discuss the question of visiting the land of the Turks. He said to us:

'I will not give you permission to go, for it is not licit for me to allow you to risk your lives. I know that this is really all a trick thought up by this *ghulām* – that is, Tikīn – for among us, he was a blacksmith, engaged in selling iron in the land of the Infidels.[26] It was he who led Nadhīr into error and induced him to speak to the Commander of the Faithful, and it was he who arranged for the letter of the king of the Saqāliba to be delivered. The noble *amīr* – that is, the *amīr* of Khurāsān – would have more right to have the prayers read in the name of the Commander of the Faithful in that country, if he thought it advisable. Furthermore, between the country of which you speak and where you are now, there are a thousand tribes of unbelievers. The caliph has been misled in all this. I will give you a piece of good advice. You must write to the noble *amīr*, so that he can get in touch with the caliph – may God strengthen him! – by letter. As for you – you must remain here until the answer arrives.'

At that point, we left him. Later, we went back and kept trying to get into his good graces, flattering him and saying:

'Here are the orders of the Commander of the Faithful and his letter. Why refer to him again on this subject?'

Finally, he gave us permission to continue on our journey. We went from Khwārazm to Jurjānīya, which is fifty *farsakh*s away by river.

Coinage and language of Khwārazm

I noticed that the dirhams of Khwārazm are false, adulterated with lead or bronze. They call the dirham *tāzja* and it weighs four and a half *dānaq*s. The money changers sell *ki'āb*, *dāwāmāt*[27] and dirhams. The Khwārazmians are the most barbarous of people, both in speech and customs. Their language sounds like the cries of starlings. In their country there is a village one day's journey away called Ardakuwa whose inhabitants are known as Kardalīya,[28] and their speech sounds exactly like the croaking of frogs. They deny the legitimacy of the Commander of the Faithful, 'Alī ibn Abī Tālib – may God be content with him! – at the end of each prayer.[29]

The Jayhūn River freezes

We stayed at Jurjānīya for several days. The Jayhūn River froze for its entire length and the ice was seventeen spans thick.[30] Horses, mules, donkeys and carts slid over the ice as if on roads, and the ice was solid and did not crack. The river remained like this for three months.

The cold of hell

We saw a land which made us think a gate to the cold of hell had opened before us. When snow falls, it is always accompanied by a rough and violent wind. In this country, when a man wishes to make a nice gesture to a friend and show his generosity, he says: 'Come to my house where we can talk, for there is a good fire there.' But All-Powerful God has given them abundant firewood, and it is very cheap: two of their dirhams will buy a wagonload of *tāgh* wood, amounting to some 3,000 *ratl*.

It is the rule among them that beggars do not wait at the door, but come into the house and sit for an hour by the fire to warm up. Only then does the beggar say *pekend*, in other words, 'bread'.[31]

Our stay in Jurjānīya was protracted, for we remained there a few days of the month of Rajab and then the months of Sha'bān, Ramadān and Shawwāl.[32] The cold and the hardships it causes were the reasons for the length of our stay.

I was told, in fact, that two men set out with twelve camels to load wood in the forest, but they forgot to take flint and tinder with them. They had to spend the night without a fire and in the morning their camels were dead from the terrible cold. I saw how the intense cold made itself felt in this country: the roads and markets were so empty that one could wander through most of them without seeing a soul or coming face to face with another living being. Coming from the bathhouse, on returning to the house I looked at my beard. It was a block of ice, which I had to thaw in front of the fire. I slept in a house, inside which was another, inside which was a Turkish felt tent. I was wrapped in clothes and furs, but in spite of that my cheek froze to the pillow. I saw cisterns in that country lagged with sheepskins, so that they would not crack or burst, but it did no good. In truth, I saw the earth split and great crevasses form from the intense cold. I saw a great tree split in two from the same cause.

Folding boats

When we were in the middle of the month of Shawwāl 309/ February 922, the weather began to change and the ice on the Jayhūn melted. We then set about obtaining what we needed for the journey. We bought Turkish camels and had boats made out of camel skin,[33] to allow us to pass the rivers we needed to cross in the land of the Turks. We laid in three months' supply of bread, millet and dried and salted meat.

Dressing for the cold

The local people, with whom we were on friendly terms, urged us to be prudent as regards clothing and to take large quantities. They made it sound very frightening and serious. When we saw the reality with our own eyes, however, we realized that it was twice as bad as we had been told. Each of us was wearing a tunic and over that a caftan, on top of that a cloak of sheepskin and over that again a felt outer garment, with a head covering that left only the two eyes visible. Each of us wore a plain pair of trousers and another padded pair, socks, horse-hide boots and over those boots, other boots, so that when any of us mounted a camel, he could hardly move because of all the clothes he was wearing.

We now parted company with the jurist, the teacher and the *ghulām*, who had set off from Baghdād with us, because they were afraid to enter this country. I travelled with the envoy, his brother-in-law and the two *ghulām*, Tikīn and Bārs.

Ibn Fadlān warns his companions

When the day came for us to set out, I said to them: 'O people! The king's *ghulām* is with you and he knows everything that is going on. You are carrying letters from the caliph and I am quite sure that they mention the 4,000 *musayyabī dīnārs* that are intended for him. You are going to a foreign king. He will demand this money.'

'Don't worry about that,' they said to me, 'he won't ask us for it.'

I warned them and said:

'I know that he will demand it.'

But they would not listen.

The caravan to the land of the Turks

The caravan was extremely well organized. We hired a guide, called a *kilavuz*,[34] who was from al-Jurjānīya. Next we put our trust in God, mighty and powerful, and placed our fate in His hands. We set out from al-Jurjānīya on Monday, 2 Dhu al-Qaʿda 309/4 March 922. We stopped at a *ribāt* called Zamjān, which is at the Gate of the Turks.[35] Then we set out on the following morning and reached a place called Jīt. A great deal of snow fell, so that the camels were floundering in it up to their knees. We stayed at this wayside station for two days and then we entered the land of the Turks, marching on across this flat, desert-like steppe without ever turning aside from the road or meeting a soul. We journeyed for ten days, suffering from endless difficulties, from exhaustion, intense cold and the constantly falling snow. Compared to this, the days of cold in Khwārazm were like summer days. We forgot all that had happened to us in the past and almost perished.

An attempt at conversion

One day, we were suffering from the most terrible cold. Tikīn was travelling at my side and next to him a Turk, who was talking to him in Turkish. Tikīn began to laugh and said to me:

'This Turk wants to say this to you; "What does our Lord want of us? He is going to make us die of cold. If we knew what He wanted, we could bring it to Him."'

I replied:

'Tell him that what He wants of you is this: that you should say: "There is no god but God."'

He began to laugh and answered:

'If we had been taught how to say this, we would say it.'

Then, we continued on our march until we reached a place where there were great quantities of *tāgh* wood. We stopped there and the caravan lit a fire. They warmed up and stripped off their clothes to dry them. We continued on our way each night, from midnight until afternoon or midday, moving as fast as we could and over the longest stages possible. Then we would halt. After having marched like this for fifteen nights, we reached a great mountain, very rocky, through which streams fought their way, filling depressions with water and forming pools.

The Ghuzz Turks

When we had crossed that mountain we came to a tribe of Turks called Ghuzz (Oguz). They were nomads, who live in felt tents and come and go. You see their tents, first in one place, then in another, as is the way of nomads, depending on their movements. They live in poverty, like wandering asses. They do not worship God, nor do they have recourse to reason. They do not worship anything, but call their great men 'Lords'.[36] When one of them asks his leader's advice on something, he says: 'Lord, what should I do about this or that matter?'

'Their political regime is based on consultation among themselves.'[37] Nevertheless, when they have agreed on something and have decided to do it, the basest and most wretched of them can come and break the agreement. I have heard them say: 'There is no god but God; Muhammad is the Messenger of God' to make a good impression on the Muslims who stay with them, but they do not believe in this firmly. If one of them suffers an injustice, or something bad happens to him, he lifts his head to heaven and says '*bir tengri*', which means 'by the one God' in the language of the Turks, for *bir* in Turkish means one and *tengri* is God.

Filth and immodesty

They do not wash after polluting themselves with excrement and urine. They do not wash after major ritual pollution [*janāba*], or any other pollution. They have no contact with water, especially in winter. Their women do not veil themselves before their own men or strangers. Similarly, the women do not hide any part of their body. One day, we went to the home of one of them and sat down. This man's wife was with us. As we were talking, she bared her private parts and scratched while we stared at her. We covered our faces with our hands and each said:

'I seek forgiveness from God!'

Her husband began to laugh and addressing the interpreter, said:

'Tell them this: she uncovers her private parts in your presence and you see them, but she protects them and allows no one near. Better than covering them up and letting you get at them!'

The punishment for adultery

Adultery is unknown, but if they learn that someone has committed an act of that kind, they split him in two in the following way: they bend down the branches of two trees, tie him to the branches and let the trees spring back into their original position. Thus the man who has been tied to the two trees is split in two.

A theological discussion

One of them, having heard me recite the Qur'ān and liked it, went to the interpreter and said:

'Tell him not to stop!'

One day, this man said to me through the interpreter:

'Ask that Arab, whether our great and powerful Lord has a wife.'

I found this deeply shocking and pronounced the phrases:

'Glory to God!' and 'I ask forgiveness of God!'

The Turk said: 'Glory to God!' and 'I ask forgiveness of God!' just as I had done.

That is a Turkish habit. Every time he hears a Muslim pronounce the phrases 'Glory to God!' and 'There is no god but God!', he repeats them too.

Turkish marriage customs

Here are some of the Turkish marriage customs. If one of them asks another for one of the women of his family in marriage, whether it is his daughter, his sister or any other woman he possesses, in exchange for such and such a quantity of robes from Khwārazm, he carries off the woman as soon as he has paid his debt. Sometimes the bride price consists of camels, or horses, or other things. No one can get a wife if he has not paid the bride price agreed with the woman's guardian. Once he has paid for her, he comes without the slightest shame, walks into the house where the woman is and takes possession of her in front of her father, her mother and her brothers, and they do not stop him.

If a man dies leaving a wife and children, his eldest son takes her to wife, provided she is not his mother.

Taboo on washing

None of the merchants, or indeed any Muslim, can perform his ablutions in their presence after a major pollution; it must be done at night where they cannot see him, otherwise they become angry and say:

'This man wants to put a spell on us – he is practising hydromancy.'

And then they fine him.

Hospitality

No Muslim can cross their country without having made friends with one of them, with whom he stays and to whom he brings gifts from the lands of Islam – a robe, a veil for his wife, pepper, millet, raisins and walnuts. When he arrives at his friend's house, the latter pitches a tent for him and brings him as many sheep as his fortunes permit, so that the Muslim can take charge of slaughtering them, for the Turks do not cut the animal's throats, they only hit the sheep on the head until it is dead.

If one of the Muslims wants to leave and some of his camels or horses are unwell, or if he needs money, he leaves the sick camels with his Turkish friend, borrows the camels, horses and money that he needs, and sets out. When he returns from his journey, he pays off his debt and gives him back his camels and horses. Similarly, when an unknown man comes to a Turk and says to him:

'I am your guest and I want your camels and horse and dirhams', he gives him what he wants.

If the merchant dies on the journey he has undertaken, the Turk goes to the people in the caravan when it returns and says to them:

'Where is my guest?'

If they say: 'He died!', he has the man's baggage unloaded from the caravan. He then goes to the most important merchant he sees among them, opens his packs of merchandise while the merchant looks on, and takes exactly the money that is owing to him and nothing more. Similarly, he takes several of his camels and horses, and says to him:

'He was your cousin, and you are the most appropriate person to pay his debts.'

If the man has fled, the Turk does the same thing, going to the merchant and saying:

'He was a Muslim like you. Take responsibility for him!'

If he does not find his Muslim guest along the caravan route, he asks his companions:

'Where is he?'

Once he has been told where to look, he sets out in search of him, travelling for days until he finds him. He then takes back his possessions in addition to any gifts he may have given him.

Host responsible for death of his guest

This is how the Turk behaves when he enters Jurjānīya. He enquires about his guest and stays with him until he leaves. If the Turk dies in the house of his friend the Muslim and that man happens to be in a caravan going through Turkish territory, the Turks kill him, saying:

'You killed him by holding him prisoner. If you hadn't shut him up, he wouldn't have died.'

In the same way, if the Muslim has the Turk drink wine and the man falls off a wall, the Turks kill the Muslim for that.

If the Muslim in question is not in the caravan, they take the most important man in the caravan and kill him.

Pederasty

They consider pederasty a terrible thing. A man from Khwārazm went to stay with the tribe of the *kūdharkīn*,[38] the lieutenant of the king of the Turks. He stayed with a host from this tribe for a certain time buying sheep. The Turk had a son, a beardless youth. The Khwārazmian kept on making up to him and attempting to seduce him, so that finally the young man agreed to do what he wanted. The Turk arrived and found them at it. He reported the matter to the *kūdharkīn* and said to him:

'Gather together the Turks!'

So the Turks assembled.

The *kūdharkīn* said:

'Do you want a just or an unjust judgement?'

'Just,' said the Turk.

'Bring your son!' he told him.

He brought his son and the *kūdharkīn* said:

'The merchant and your son must be put to death together.'

The Turk was very upset and said:

'I will not give up my son!'

'Then let the merchant ransom himself,' said the *kūdharkīn*.

He did this and made over to the Turk a number of sheep in compensation for what he had done to his son. He gave the *kūdharkīn* 400 sheep for having changed the sentence. Then he left the land of the Turks.

A fragile conversion

The first of their kings and chiefs that we met was Ināl the Younger. He had converted to Islam. It was said to him:

'If you become Muslim, you will no longer be our leader.'

So he renounced Islam. When we came to the place where he was, he said to us:

'I will not let you pass, because this is something we have never heard of and which we thought would never happen.'

We talked to him pleasantly, until we had persuaded him to accept a caftan from Jurjān worth ten dirhams, a piece of cloth [*pay-baf*], round loaves of bread, a handful of raisins and a hundred walnuts. After we had given him these things, he prostrated himself before us, for that is their custom. When a man wants to honour another, he prostrates himself before him, and says:

'If my tents were not so far off your route, I would bring you sheep and grain.'

He left us then and we set out.

On the following day, we met a Turk. He was an ugly man, wretched looking, small and stunted in appearance, really ignoble. We had just been caught by a violent cloudburst.

'Stop!' he cried.

The whole caravan halted. It was made up of some 3,000 horses and 5,000 men. Then he said:

'Not one of you is going to get by.'

We halted, obeying his order, and said to him:

'But we are friends of the *kūdharkīn*!'

He began to laugh and said:

'What is this *kūdharkīn*? I shit on the *khūdharkīn*'s beard.'

Then he laughed and said: '*Pekend*!', which means 'bread' in the language of Khwārazm. I gave him some loaves of bread and he took them and said:

'Pass. I have taken pity on you.'

Treatment of the sick

When a man falls ill and he has male and female slaves, they serve him and no member of the family goes near him. They set

up a small tent for him at some distance from their dwellings
and he stays there until he dies or recovers. In the case of a poor
man or a slave, they cast him into the desert and ride off.

Horse sacrifices

If a man dies, they dig a great trench for him the shape of a
house and they go to him, and dress him in his tunic, with his
belt and his bow [ ],[39] then they place a wooden cup in his hand
filled with *nabīdh*[40] and leave a wooden container of it in front
of him. Then they bring everything that he possessed and put it
in this house with him and set him in a sitting position. They
put a roof on the house and above it a construction like a dome
made of clay. Next, they bring his horses, no matter how
numerous they may be, even a hundred or two hundred head,
and kill them, down to the very last one, and eat their flesh. But
they hang the head, hooves, hide and tail over wooden stakes,
and say: 'These are the horses he will ride to Paradise.' If he has
killed a man and been a warrior of note, they make as many
wooden statues as he killed men and set them up on his tomb,
saying: 'These are his attendants and they will serve him in
Paradise.' Sometimes, they delay a day or two over the sacrifice
of the horses. Then an old man, one of their elders, urges them
on, saying:

'I have seen so-and-so – that is, the dead man – in a dream
and he said to me: "You see, my companions have all gone
ahead of me and the soles of my feet are split from my efforts
to follow them, but I cannot catch up with them and I have
remained alone." '

Then they go to his horses, kill them and prop their remains
around his tomb. After a day or two, the old man comes to
them and says:

'I have seen so-and-so in a dream and he said to me: "Tell
my family and my companions that I have caught up with those
who went ahead of me and I have recovered from my great
weariness." '

Facial hair

All Turks pluck their beards, but not their moustaches. I once saw a very aged man, who had pulled out his beard, but left a tuft under his chin. He was wearing a kind of goatskin cloak, so that from a distance he looked exactly like a billy goat.

Yabghū and kūdharkīn

The king of the Ghuzz Turks is called *yabghū*, which is the title of the ruler. Each of those who has authority in this tribe is called thus, and his second-in-command is the *kūdharkīn*, and similarly all those who are second-in-command to a leader are known as *kūdharkīn*.

Atrak, son of Qataghān, and his wife

After leaving the region of these Turks, we stopped at the camp of the commander of their troops, who is called Atrak, the son of Qataghān. He had round Turkish tents pitched and settled us in them. He had followers, servants and numerous yurts.[41] He had sheep brought for us and also horses. The sheep were to slaughter, the horses to ride. He invited a large number of his family and cousins and slaughtered many sheep for them. We had sent him a present of clothing, raisins, walnuts, pepper and millet.

I saw his wife, who had been a wife of his father. She took meat, yoghurt and some of the things we had brought as presents, went away from the tents into the desert, dug a hole and buried what she had with her, and she spoke certain words. I asked the interpreter what she was saying. He answered:

'She says: "It is a gift for Qataghān, the father of Atrak, which the Arabs offer him." '

An invitation to convert and gifts from Baghdād

When night fell, I went with the interpreter to visit Atrak, who was sitting in his tent. We had with us Nadhīr al-Haramī's letter, in which he urged Atrak to embrace Islam. He sent him 50 dīnārs, among which there were many *musayyabī dīnārs*, three *mithqāl*s of musk, some pieces of well-tanned leather, two pieces of cloth from Merv, from which we cut out two tunics for him, leather slippers, a brocade robe and five silk garments. We gave him his present and a veil and a ring for his wife. I then read him the letter. He said through the interpreter:

'I do not want to say anything to you until your return. I will write to the caliph to tell him what I have decided to do.'

Clothes worn until they fall to pieces

Then, he stripped off the brocade garment he was wearing, in order to put on the robe of honour we have just mentioned. I saw the tunic he was wearing under the brocade. It was so filthy that it was in rags, for it is their custom never to take off a piece of clothing they are wearing until it falls to pieces.[42] He had plucked out all his beard and moustaches and he looked like a eunuch.

A feat of horsemanship

I noticed that the Turks spoke of him as their finest horseman and I saw what they meant one day, when he was accompanying us on horseback. As a goose flew over us, he strung his bow and spurred his horse to a gallop under the goose, shot and dropped it.

The envoys under suspicion

One day, Atrak sent for the military chiefs who served under
him. They were Tarkhān, Ināl,[43] and Baghliz. Tarkhān was the
most noble and important among them. He limped, was blind
and had a crippled hand.

Atrak said to them:

'These people are the envoys of the king of the Arabs to my
son-in-law Almish ibn Shilkī, and it did not seem advisable to
allow them to depart without consulting you.'

Tarkhān said:

'This is something we have never either seen or heard of.
Never in our whole lives, nor in the lifetimes of our fathers, has
an envoy of the caliph come to us. I can only think this is some
trick of the caliph's and that he has sent these people to the
Khazars to tell them to gather an army against us. The thing to
do is to have each of these envoys cut in two, and take everything they have with them.'

Someone else said:

'No, let's just take everything they have with them and leave
them naked to return to the place they came from.'

Another man said:

'No. The king of the Khazars holds some of our people prisoner. We will send these people as a ransom in exchange for
them.'

They continued to argue among themselves for seven days,
during which time we were at death's door, until the day they
agreed to let us continue on our way and leave.

We gave Tarkhān a robe of honour – a caftan made of cloth
from Merv – and two pieces of cotton cloth, as well as a coat
for each of his companions. We gave equivalent gifts to Ināl.
We also gave them pepper, millet and round loaves of bread.
Then they left us.

Crossing rivers

We rode until we came to the river Yaghindī. Our people got out folding boats made of camel skin and stretched them out, then they took the saddle frames[44] from the Turkish camels, because they were round and placed them at the bottom of the boats, so they would be fully stretched, then they filled them with clothes and baggage, and, when they were full, a certain number of men, five, six or four – more or less – sat in each boat. They took poles made from a wood called *khadank* and used them as oars. They continued to row like this, while the water carried them and they spun around, until we had crossed. As to the horses and the camels, they called them with loud cries and they swam across the river. It was essential to get one of the companies of men-at-arms over the river first, before any of the caravan crossed, so that they could form an advance guard to protect the others, in case the Bāshghirds fell on our people while they were crossing. We crossed the Yaghindī in the way we have just described, then a river called Jām, also by means of these boats. Then we crossed the Jākhsh, the Udhil, the 'Ardin, the Wārsh, the Akhtī and the Wabnā, which are all great rivers.[45]

The Bajanāk

At last we reached the Bajanāk (Pečenegs). They were encamped at the edge of a body of water resembling a sea, for it was not flowing. Their skins were dark brown, their chins shaved and they were poor compared to the Ghuzz. In fact, among the Ghuzz, I have seen people who possess 10,000 horses and 100,000 head of sheep. The sheep mostly graze on what lies under the snow, which they scrape aside with their hooves in order to get to the grass. When they cannot find any, they nibble snow and become very fat. When summer comes, they eat grass and grow thin. We stayed one day with the Bajanāk.

More rivers

We set out again and stopped at the river Jāyikh which was the largest we had seen, the most impressive and the swiftest. I saw a leather boat overturned in midstream and those who were in it drowned. Many of our men were carried away and a certain number of horses and camels were drowned. It cost us great efforts to get across that river. Then we marched for several days and crossed the Jākhā, after which we crossed the Arkhaz, then the Bājāgh, then the Samūr, then the Kināl, then the river Sūkh, and finally the river Kunjulū.[46] Then we halted in the lands of a Turkic people, the Bāshghirds.[47]

The Bāshghirds eat lice and fleas

We took every possible precaution against them, for they are the worst of the Turks, the dirtiest and the readiest to kill. When one of them meets another, he cuts off his head and carries it off with him, leaving the body. They shave their beards and eat lice. A man will pursue one through the seams of his coat and crack it with his teeth. We had with us a man of this people who had converted to Islam and who served us. One day, I saw him take a flea from his clothes and, after having crushed it with his fingernail, he devoured it and on noticing me, said: 'Delicious!'

The Bāshghirds carry a wooden phallus

Each of them carves a piece of wood shaped like a phallus and attaches it about his person. When he wants to start out on a journey, or when he meets an enemy, he kisses it and bows before it, and says:

'Lord, do this or that for me.'

I said to the interpreter:

'Ask one of them to explain their behaviour and why they consider such a thing to be their Lord.'

He answered:

'Because I came from such a thing and cannot imagine anything else to be my Creator.'

The twelve lords

Some of them claim that there are twelve lords, a Lord of Winter and a Lord of Summer, a Lord of Rain and a Lord of Wind, a Lord of Trees and a Lord of Men, a Lord of Horses and a Lord of Water, a Lord of Night and a Lord of Day, a Lord of Death and a Lord of the Earth. The Lord who is in the sky is the most powerful of them, but he is in concord with the others, so that each approves what his companion does. God is infinitely above the beliefs of these lost souls![48]

Snake and crane worship

We saw a clan that worships snakes and another that worships fish and another that worships cranes. These told me that one day, while they were fighting some of their enemies and were on the point of being defeated, the cranes began to give their call behind their opponents. Their enemy was frightened and turned and fled. This is why they worship cranes. They say:

'They are our Lord, because they scattered our enemies.'

And they worship them for that reason.

More rivers

We left the land of these people and crossed the river Jirimshān, then the river Uran, then the river Uram, then the river Bāynākh, then the river Watīgh, then the river Nīyāsnah, then the river Jāwshīr.[49] From one of the rivers we have mentioned to the next, there is a distance of two, three or four days, or a little more or a little less.

The king of the Saqāliba

When we were a day and a night's journey from the king of the Saqāliba, for it was to him that we were heading, he sent out to welcome us the four kings who were under his authority, accompanied by his brothers and his sons. They greeted us, bringing with them bread, meat and millet, and they rode with us. When we were two *farsakh*s away from the king, he came out to meet us in person. When he saw us, he dismounted and fell down with his face to the ground to give thanks to God, the All High, the Almighty. In his sleeve, he had dirhams which he scattered over us. He had tents pitched for us and we settled down in them.

The reading of the caliph's letter

We arrived on Sunday, 12 Muharram 310/12 May 922. The journey from Jurjānīya to the king's country took seventy days. We remained in the tents that had been set up for us for the Sunday, Monday, Tuesday and Wednesday, waiting until he had gathered the kings, military leaders and people of the country to listen to the reading of the letter. On Thursday, when they had all arrived, we unfurled the two banners that we had with us, saddled the horse with the saddle which had been sent to the king as a present and dressed the king in black[50] robes and a turban. Then I got out the caliph's letter and said:

'It is not permitted to remain seated during the reading of the letter.'

Then the king rose and the principal men of his kingdom

who were present did likewise. The king was a very fat man with a large belly. I started to read the first part of the letter. When I reached the formula:

'Peace be upon you, for in addressing myself to you I praise God, beside whom there is no god,' I said:

'Return the greeting to the Commander of the Faithful.'

He returned the greeting as did all the others, without exception. Then the interpreter continued to translate the letter for us, word for word, and when we had finished reading, they pronounced *Allāhu akbar!* so loudly the earth shook.

Rich gifts

Next, I read the letter from the vizier Hāmid ibn al-'Abbās[51] and the king listened to it standing. Then, I invited him to sit down and he sat during the reading of the letter of Nadhīr al-Haramī. When I had finished reading, members of the king's entourage scattered a large number of dirhams over him.[52] Then I got out the presents, which consisted of scent, cloth and pearls intended for him and his wife, and I presented them, one after another, until we had finished the whole business. Then, I gave his wife a robe of honour before the whole company. She was sitting beside him, for that is their custom. When I had given her this robe of honour, her women scattered dirhams over her and then we went back to our tents.

A formal dinner

An hour passed, and then the king sent for us and we went to him. He was in his tent with the kings on his right. He invited us to sit down on his left. His children were sitting in front of him. He sat on a throne covered with brocade from Byzantium. He told them to bring him a table. It had nothing on it but roast meat. He began by taking a knife and cutting a piece of

meat which he ate, then a second and a third. Then he cut a
piece which he gave to Sawsān, the envoy. When he had taken
it, a small table was brought and set down in front of him. That
is their custom; no one touches a dish until the king has served
him. As soon as he receives his share, a table is brought.

Next, he served me with a portion and I was brought a table.
[Then he cut off a piece and served the king seated on his right,
who was then brought a table. Then he served the second king,
who was in turn brought a table.]⁵³ Then he served the fourth king
and he was brought a table, then he served his children, to whom
more tables were brought. Each of us ate at his own table and no
one took anything from someone else's table. When each guest
had finished eating, he carried away what was left on his table.

When we had eaten, he had brought a kind of mead that
they call *suju*, which had only been fermented one day and one
night. He drank down a cup.⁵⁴ Then he rose and said:

'This bears witness to my joy concerning the Commander of
the Faithful – may God prolong his existence!'

The four kings rose with him, as did his children, and we too
got to our feet. When he had done this three times, we left him.

The wording of the khutba

Before I arrived, the *khutba* was read for the king from his pulpit in these words:

'O God! Preserve King Yiltawār, king of the Bulghārs.'

I said to him:

'The king is God and from the pulpit none but He, the All-
high and the All-powerful, should be called king. Your master,
the Commander of the Faithful, is satisfied that the following
should be pronounced from the pulpits in both East and West:

' "My God, preserve your slave and caliph, Ja'far, al-Imām
al-Muqtadir-billāh, the Commander of the Faithful."

'And the same was done by his forefathers, the caliphs who
reigned before him. For the Prophet – may God's prayers and
peace be upon him – said:

' "Do not address praises to me, as the Christians do to
Jesus, son of Mary, for I am only the servant of God and His
messenger." '

The king adopts a Muslim name

Then the king said to me:
'In what form may the *khutba* be read for me, then?'
'Using your name and that of your father,' I answered.
'But,' he said, 'my father was an unbeliever and I do not
want his name mentioned from the pulpit, and as for myself, I
do not want my name mentioned either, because he who gave
it to me was an unbeliever. But what is the name of my master,
the Commander of the Faithful?'
'Ja'far,' I told him.
'Am I allowed to call myself by his name?'
'Yes,' I said.
'Then I shall take the name of Ja'far and my father that of
'Abd Allāh. Give the man who pronounces the *khutba* his
orders.'
And that is what I did. He pronounced the *khutba* for him,
saying:
'O God, preserve in good health your slave Ja'far, son of
'Abd Allāh, *amīr* of the Bulghārs, client of the Commander of
the Faithful.'

The king demands his money

Three days after the reading of the letter and distribution of
presents, the king sent for me. He had heard the story of the
4,000 *dīnārs* and the trick that the Christian had played to defer
payment. On my entering, he invited me to sit down. I did so,
and he threw me the letter of the Commander of the Faithful.
'Who brought this letter?' he asked.

'I did,' I replied.

Then he threw me the vizier's letter and said:

'And this one, too?'

'Yes,' I said.

'And what has happened to the money mentioned in these two letters?'

'It was impossible to collect it,' I answered. 'There was not enough time and for fear of missing the season for reaching your country, we left it to be brought later.'

'You all came together and my master [the caliph] paid all your expenses, and the only reason was so that you could bring me this money to have a fortress built to protect me from the Jews, who have tried to reduce me to slavery. As regards the presents, my *ghulām* could perfectly well have brought them.'

'That is quite true,' I said, 'but we did what we could.'

Then the king said to the interpreter:

'Tell him that I do not recognize these people. I only recognize you [i.e. Ibn Fadlān], for these other people are not Arabs. If the caliph[55] – may God aid him! – had thought that they could have obtained the same results as you could, he would not have sent you to protect my interests, read my letter and listen to my answer. I shall not demand one single dirham from anyone else but you. Hand over the money; it will be better for you.'

I left him and went out in consternation and much saddened. He was a good-looking man, stout and full bodied, who inspired respect. He was like a great barrel speaking.

I left his presence, gathered together my companions and told them what had passed between the king and myself.

'I warned you about this,' I told them.

A disagreement on the call to prayer

The king's muezzin repeated the phrases of the *iqāma* twice when he gave the call to prayer.[56] I said to him:

'In his dominions your master, the Commander of the Faithful, only has them said once.'

Then the king told the muezzin:

'Accept what he tells you and don't contradict him!'

For several days, the muezzin observed the rule. Meanwhile, the king asked me questions about the money and argued with me about it, but I made him despair of winning the debate by providing most excellent arguments. When he realized that he was not going to get the better of me, he ordered the muezzin to repeat the phrases of the *iqāma* twice. The muezzin obeyed, for the king wanted to use this as a way of starting up the discussion again. When I heard the repetition of the phrases, I ordered the muezzin to stop doing it and shouted at him.

The king heard of this and summoned me to appear before him with my companions. When we had all assembled, he said to the interpreter:

'Ask him' – meaning me – 'What would you say of two muezzins, one of whom repeated the formulae of the *iqāma* only once, the other twice, if afterwards each performed the prayer with his congregation? Would the prayers be licit or not?'

I replied: 'The prayers would be licit.'

He continued: 'Would there be divergent opinions, or would the agreement be unanimous?'

'Unanimous,' I answered.

Then he said to the interpreter:

'What would you say of a man who gave to others money intended for poor people, people who were suffering a blockade and reduced to servitude, and then was cheated out of that money?'

'It is not permitted,' I said, 'and such people would be evil-doers.'

'Unanimously agreed, or with differences of opinion?'

'Unanimously,' I answered.

Then he said to the interpreter:

'Say to him: Do you think that if the caliph – may God prolong his days! – sent an army against me, he could prevail over me?'

'No,' I said.

'Or over the *amīr* of Khurāsān?' he continued.

'No.'

'Is that not because of the great distance that separates us and the number of infidel tribes between his lands and mine?'

'Clearly!' I said.

Then he said to the interpreter:

'Tell him this: By God, although I live in a remote place, as you see, I still fear my Master, the Commander of the Faithful. I fear that he will learn something about me that will displease him, that he will call down God's wrath upon me and destroy my country without even leaving his kingdom, despite the great distance between us. But you – you eat his bread, you wear his clothes, you see him every hour of the day, and yet you have betrayed him on the mission upon which he sent you to me, to a weak people! And you have betrayed the Muslims! I shall accept no admonishments from you in matters of religion until someone comes to me who speaks with a sincere tongue. When such a man comes to me, I will accept what he says.'

We were at a loss for words. There was nothing we could answer, so we left his presence.

Even after this conversation, he continued to favour and honour me, although he kept my companions at a distance. He called me Abū Bakr the Truthful.[57]

Northern lights

In his country I saw uncounted marvels. Thus, the first night that we spent in this land, before the light of the sun faded, [a full hour before sunset,] I saw the horizon turn a brilliant shade of red and in the upper air there was great noise and tumult. I raised my head and saw a red mist like fire close to me. The tumult and noise issued from it and in the cloud were the shapes of men and horses. These spectral men held lances and swords. I could see them clearly and distinguish them. Then suddenly another bank of mist appeared, just like the first, in which I saw men, horses and arms; it advanced to charge the first, as one cavalry detachment falls upon another. Frightened, we began to pray and beseech God most humbly, while the locals laughed at us and were astonished at our behaviour. We watched the two armies charging. They clashed for a moment and then parted, and so it continued for an hour after nightfall. Then they vanished.

We questioned the king on this subject. He claimed that his ancestors said:

'They are the believing and the unbelieving Jinn. They fight every evening and have not failed to do so every night since they were first created.'[58]

Prayer times during the white nights

One day I went into my tent to talk for a while with a tailor belonging to the king, who was from Baghdād and had come to this region by chance. We talked for the amount of time it would take to read less than half of a seventh part of the Qur'ān,[59] while we waited for the call to evening prayer. Suddenly we heard it and went out of the tent. Day was breaking. I asked the muezzin:

'To which prayer have you called us?'

'The dawn prayer,' he said.

'And the evening prayer?'

'We say it with the sunset prayer.'

'And during the night?'

'The night is as you see. They have been even shorter than now, for already they are beginning to lengthen.'

And he said that a month earlier, he had not slept at night, for fear of missing the dawn prayer. For if a pot is put on the fire at sunset, there is no time for the water to boil before the dawn prayer.

I observed that in their lands the days are very long and remain so for a certain part of the year and the nights are short. Then the nights lengthen and the days shorten. On the second night of our stay, I sat outside the tent and watched the sky. I saw only a few stars. I think there were about fifteen [scattered across the sky. The red glow that one sees before the evening prayer never fades],[60] and the night was not dark – a man can recognize another from a bowshot's distance. I saw that the moon did not reach the middle of the sky, but lingered above the horizon for a while. Then dawn broke and the moon vanished.

The king told me that beyond his country, three months' march away, there is a people called the Wīsū[61] (Ves) among whom the night lasts less than an hour.

I saw the landscape dyed red at sunrise, everything – earth, mountains, all that one sees when the sun rises is like a great cloud and the red glow stays thus until the sun has reached its zenith. The locals told me that when winter comes, the nights go back to being the length of the [summer] days and the days become as short as the [summer][62] nights. Thus, if one of us were to set out at dawn for the place they call Itil,[63] which is only one *farsakh* away, when he arrived, night would already have fallen and all the stars have risen and covered the sky.

We did not leave the country until the nights had become long and the days short.

Howling of dogs a good omen

I noticed that the people of that land consider the howling of dogs as a great blessing and they rejoice on hearing it, saying: 'A year of plenty, blessings and peace!'

Snakes

I observed that snakes[64] are very numerous in that land, so that there may be more than ten of them twisted about a single branch of a tree. The people do not kill them and the snakes do them no harm. In one place, I saw a tree more than a hundred cubits high that had fallen. Its trunk was enormous. I stopped to look at it, when suddenly it moved. Frightened, I examined the tree more carefully. I noticed that there was a snake on it, almost as thick and large as the tree itself. When it saw me, it dropped off and slithered away among the trees. In a panic, I hastened back and told the king and his council what I had seen, but they paid no attention. The king said to me:

'Don't be frightened, they won't hurt you.'

Wild berries, green apples and hazelnuts

One day when we were with the king we made camp and I went in among the trees with my companions, Tikīn, Sawsān and Bārs, and one of the king's followers, who showed us the stem of a plant. It was small and green, like a spindle in thickness, but longer and at the base, a large leaf spread out on the ground which was carpeted with new shoots which bore a berry.[65] If you tasted them you would think they were seedless pomegranates. We tasted them and found them incredibly delicious, and spent our time hunting for them and eating them.

I also saw that they have apples of a very brilliant green, with a taste more acidic than wine vinegar. The slave girls eat them and get plump.

I never saw more hazelnut trees than in their country. I saw forests of them, 40 *farsakh*s in area.

Tree sap,[66] meat and grain

I also noticed that they had trees that I do not know. They are extremely tall and the trunk is leafless, while the crowns are like those of a palm tree. They have narrow leaves like palms, but grouped together. The people of the region go to a place they know where such trees are, make a cut and with the help of a container collect the sap which is sweeter than honey. If someone drinks too much of this liquid, he becomes drunk as if with wine, or even more so.

They eat millet and horse meat, although there is also an abundance of wheat and barley. All those who sow, harvest for themselves. The king has no rights whatsoever over their crops, but every year they give him a sable skin for each household. When the king orders them to form a raiding party for an expedition against another country and they bring back loot, he gets one share, like the rest of the troop. All those who give a wedding feast, or give a banquet are required to reserve a share for the king, proportionate to the importance of the occasion. They must also provide a measure of mead and a quantity of spoiled wheat, for their earth is black and stinking and they have no place to store their food, so they dig pits in the ground and put the food in them, with the result that within a few days it rots and becomes disgusting and is no longer of any use.

Cooking with fish oil

They have neither olive oil nor sesame oil; in place of these, they use fish oil, so that everything they make with it smells bad. They make a kind of porridge with barley that the young slaves eat, both girls and boys. Sometimes they cook barley with meat. The masters eat the meat and give the barley to the slave girls, but if the meat is goat's head, they give them some of the meat.

Doffing hats

They all wear tall pointed hats. When the king mounts his horse, he rides alone without a *ghulām* or anyone accompanying him. As he goes past in the market, there is no one who does not rise and doff his hat and put it under his arm. When he has ridden past, the people put their hats back on. It is the same whenever anyone visits the king, whether great or small, including his children and his brothers. As soon as they see him, they take off their hats and put them under their arms, then they make a sign with their heads in his direction and sit down, then they stand up again until he invites them to sit

down. Everyone who sits down before the king does so by
squatting on his heels and does not take his hat out from under
his arm, nor show it until he has gone out.

The king's tent

They all live in tents, but that of the king is very large, large
enough for 1,000 people or more, and it is spread with Armenian carpets. In the centre is a throne covered with brocade
from Byzantium.

The grandfather raises his grandson

One of their customs is that when a man's son has a child, it is
the grandfather and not the father who takes the child, saying:
    'I have more right than his father to raise him until he
becomes a man.'

Fraternal inheritance

When a man dies, his brother inherits from him, to the exclu-
sion of his sons.
    I told the king that this was not allowed and explained to
him how inheritance should work until he understood.

Lightning

I have never seen more lightning than in their country. When it
strikes a tent, they do not go near it again, but leave it as it is,
together with anything that is inside it – men, goods or other

things – until time has destroyed them. They say that it is a tent upon which the wrath of God has fallen.

The punishment for murder

If one man kills another deliberately, they execute him, but if he has killed by accident they make a box for the killer out of *khadank* wood, put him inside with three loaves of bread and a jug of water, and close it with nails. Then they set up three wooden poles, rather like the supports of a camel's saddle, and hang the box from them. They say:

'We place him between the sky and the earth, exposed to the rain and the sun – perhaps God will have mercy upon him.'

And he remains there until time has caused him to rot and the winds have dispersed his bones.

The sacrifice of the intelligent

If they see a man whose mind is lively and who knows many things, they say:

'This man deserves to serve our Lord.'

And they take him and put a rope round his neck and hang him in a tree until he falls to pieces.

The king's interpreter told me that a man from Sind had come to this country by chance and remained for a time in the service of the king. He was skilful and intelligent. A number of people from that country wanted to set out for reasons of trade. The man from Sind asked the king for permission to leave with them, but the king forbade him to go. The man insisted so much that the king gave him permission to go and he set off with them in a boat. The people saw that he was quick-witted and intelligent, and they discussed it among themselves and said:

'This man is fitting for the service of our Lord, so let's send him to Him.'

As their route took them near a forest, they took him there, placed a rope about his neck and hung him from the top of a tall tree. Then they left him there and went away.

Taboo against urinating while armed

When they are on the road and one of them has to urinate and does so while carrying his weapons, they will rob him [of his weapons][67] and clothes. That is their custom. But if he sets down his arms to one side and then urinates, they will not attack him.

Mixed bathing

Men and women go down to the river together to wash completely naked, no one concealing their body from anyone else. Under no circumstances do they fornicate.

The penalty for adultery

If somebody, no matter who he is, commits adultery, they set out four iron stakes, attach the guilty person by their hands and feet, and cut them in two from the nape of the neck to the thighs with an axe. They do the same to the woman. Then they hang the pieces of both bodies from a tree.

Ibn Fadlān fails to impose the veil

I tried ceaselessly to induce the women to veil before men[68] but I did not succeed.

Punishment for theft

They put thieves to death in the same way as adulterers.

Honey

There is much honey in their forests, in beehives, and they know where to find them. They set out to search for it, but sometimes a band of their enemies falls upon them and kills them.

Furs

There are many merchants among them who go to the lands of the Turks and bring back sheep, and to a land called Wīsū, from which they bring the skins of sable and black foxes.

Converts to Islam

We saw a kin group among them numbering 5,000 members, counting men and women, and they had all converted to Islam. They were known by the name of al-Baranjār. They had built themselves a wooden mosque to pray in, but did not know how to say the prayers. So I taught the whole group how it should be done.

One man called Tālūt converted to Islam through my agency and I called him 'Abd Allāh. He said to me:

'I would like you to call me by your name, Muhammad.'[69]

I did what he asked. I also converted his wife, mother and children and they all took the name Muhammad! I taught him how to say: 'Praise be to God!' and: 'Say, He is God, the One.' His joy at knowing these two verses was greater than if he had been made king of the Saqāliba.

The market on the Volga

When we caught up with the king, we found him encamped by a body of water called Khallaja. It consists of three lakes, two large and one small, but there is nothing that can plumb their depths. A *farsakh* separates this place from the great river called Itil that flows from their country to the land of the Khazars. On this river is the site of a great market[70] which is held frequently and where all kinds of precious merchandise is to be had.

A giant

Tikīn told me that in the king's lands there was a man of extraordinary size. When I arrived in that country, I asked the king about him.

'Yes, he was living in our country,' he told me, 'but he is dead. He was not one of our people, nor was he an ordinary man. His story is as follows. One day some merchants set out in the direction of the Itil River,[71] as they were in the habit of doing. The river was in flood and had broken its banks. A day had scarcely passed when a group of these merchants came to me and said:

' "O king, we have seen swimming on the waters a man of such a kind that if he belonged to a people dwelling near us there would be no place for us in these lands, but we would have to emigrate."

'I set out on horseback with them and reached the river. I found myself face to face with the man. I saw that judging by the length of my own forearm, he was twelve cubits tall. He had a head the size of the biggest cooking pot there ever was, a nose more than a span long, huge eyes, and fingers each more than a span in length. His appearance frightened me and I had the same feeling of terror as the others. We began to speak to him, but he did not speak to us and only stared. I had him

taken to my residence and I wrote to the people of Wīsū, who
live three months' distance from us, to ask for information
about him. They wrote to me, informing me that this man was
one of the people of Gog and Magog.[72]

Gog and Magog

'They live three full months from us. They are naked,[73] and
the sea forms a barrier between us, for they live on the other
shore. They couple together like beasts. God, All-high and All-
powerful, causes a fish to come out of the sea for them each
day. One of them comes with a knife and cuts off a piece sufficient for himself and his family. If he takes more than he needs,
his belly aches and so do the bellies of his family and sometimes
he even dies, with all his family. When they have taken what
they need, the fish turns round and dives back into the sea.
They do this every day. Between us and them, there is the sea
on one side and they are enclosed by mountains on the others.
The Barrier also separates them from the gate by which they
leave. When God, All-high and All-powerful, wants to unleash
them on civilized lands, He causes the Barrier to open and the
level of the sea to drop and the fish to vanish.'

I questioned the king further about this man and he told me:
'He stayed with me for a time, but no child could look at
him without dropping dead and no pregnant women without
miscarrying. If he took hold of a man, his hands squeezed him
until he killed him. When I realized that, I had him hung from
a high tree until he died. If you want to see his bones and his
head, I will go along with you and show them to you.'

'I would like very much to see them,' I answered.

He rode with me into a great forest filled with immense trees
and shoved[74] me towards a tree under which had fallen his
bones and head. I saw his head. It was like a great beehive. His
ribs were like the stalk of a date cluster and the bones of his legs
and arms were enormous too. I was astonished at the sight.
Then I went away.

Local politics

The king set off from the stretch of water called Khallaja to a river called Jāwshīr, where he stayed for two months. Then he wanted to leave and sent a messenger to a people called Suwāz, commanding them to march with him, but they refused and divided into two groups, one headed by his son-in-law. His name was Wīragh,[75] and he ruled over them. The king sent them the following message, saying:

'God, All-mighty and All-powerful, has granted me the blessing of Islam and the rule of the Commander of the Faithful. I am his slave. This people[76] has recognized my authority, and if someone opposes me, I shall meet him with the sword.'

The other group was headed by a king of a tribe, named king Askal. He obeyed the ruler, but had not entered the faith of Islam.

When the king sent them this message, they were afraid of what he might do and all set out with him for the river Jāwshīr, which is a narrow watercourse, some five cubits across. The water only comes up to the navel, but in other places it reaches the collarbone. Generally, however, it is more than a man's height. All around, there are many *khadank* and other trees.[77]

Rhinoceroses

Near this river there is a great stretch of desert land where it is said that animals are found, smaller than a camel in size, but broader than a bull. Their heads are like those of camels and their tails are those of the bull. Their bodies are the bodies of mules and their hooves are those of bulls. In the centre of their heads, they have a thick round horn. This horn grows thinner and thinner until it becomes like the point of a lance. Some of them are between three and five cubits in length, some more, some less. This creature grazes on the leaves of certain trees that are very green. When it sees a man on horseback, it charges him. Even if the horseman has an excellent mount, he still finds it hard to get away safely. If the beast catches him, it lifts him from the back of the horse with its horn, tosses him in the air, and then catches him on its horn and continues to do this until it has killed him. But under no circumstances does it harm the horse. They hunt it across the countryside and through the forests until they kill it. They do this by climbing the tall trees among which it lives. They gather together a certain number of archers shooting poisoned arrows and when the beast is in their midst, they shoot at it until they wound and kill it. In the king's possession I saw three great plates of a material resembling Yemeni onyx, and he told me that they were made with the base of the horn of this animal. Some of the people of the country told me that this creature was a rhinoceros.[78]

The sickliness of the people

I have never seen any man among them with a ruddy complexion. Most of them are ill and many of them often die of colic, so that even babies at the breast suffer from this complaint.

Muslim burial rites

If a Muslim dies there among them and if a woman from Khwārazm[79] is present, then they wash the body after the Muslim fashion, load it on to a wagon and walk before it with a banner until they come to the place where they bury him. When they arrive, they take him from the wagon and lay him on the ground. Then a line is traced round him and they move him away and dig his grave within the line, hollowing out a lateral niche for the body. Then they bury him. They do the same with their own dead.

Pagan burial rites

The women do not weep for the dead, but the men weep over him on the day of death. They stand at the door of his tent and sob, making the most hideous and savage noise. This is how it is done by free men. When their lamentations are over, the slaves come with plaited leather thongs and weep continually as they strike their sides and any uncovered parts of their bodies with the straps, until their bodies are marked as if by the blows of a whip. They must set up a banner before the door of the tent. They bring the dead man's weapons and set them around his tomb. They continue these lamentations for two years.

When the two years are over, they lower the banner and cut their hair, and the close relatives of the dead man offer a feast to mark the end of mourning. If the dead man had a wife, she can then remarry. This is the custom among the great men of that land. The common people only perform a part of these ceremonies for their dead.

Taxes and custom duties

The king of the Saqāliba is required to pay a tax to the king of the Khazars. He gives a sable skin for each household in his kingdom. When a boat arrives in the land of the Saqāliba from Khazar territory, the king rides out and checks what is in each boat and levies a tithe on everything. When it is the Rūs or people of other races, who come with slaves, the king has the right to take for himself one head in ten.

Marriage of a Jewish prince and a Muslim princess

The son of the king of the Saqāliba is a hostage to the king of the Khazars. This last, having learned that the king of the Saqāliba had a beautiful daughter, asked for her in marriage.

But the king of the Saqāliba made excuses and refused. The king of the Khazars sent men and had her carried off by force. Now, he was a Jew and she was a Muslim. She died there with him and he demanded another daughter in marriage. As soon as this request reached the king of the Saqāliba, he hastened to marry his daughter to king Askal, who was subordinate to him, for fear that the king of the Khazars should carry her off by force as he had her sister.

A fortress for the Saqāliba

The king of the Saqāliba, fearing the king of the Khazars, wrote to the caliph and asked him to build him a fortress.

One day I questioned him, saying:

'Your kingdom is vast, you have great wealth, the taxes you raise are considerable, so why did you ask the caliph to build you a castle from his own, admittedly unlimited, funds?'

'I thought,' he answered, 'that the empire of Islam is prosperous and that its revenues come from licit sources. For this reason, I made my request. If I had wanted to build a fortress with my own money, silver or gold, it would not have been impossible for me. But I wanted to have the blessing which is attached to money coming from the Commander of the Faithful, and so I asked him for it.'

The beauty of the Rūs

I saw the Rūs, who had come for trade and had camped by the river Itil. I have never seen bodies more perfect than theirs. They were like palm trees. They are fair and ruddy. They wear neither coats [qurtāq] nor caftans, but a garment which covers one side of the body and leaves one hand free. Each of them carries an axe, a sword and a knife and is never parted from any of the arms we have mentioned. Their swords are broad bladed and grooved like the Frankish ones. From the tips of his toes to his neck, each man is tattooed in dark green[80] with designs, and so forth.

Brooches, torques and beads

All their women wear on their bosoms a circular brooch[81] made of iron, silver, copper or gold, depending on their husband's wealth and social position. Each brooch has a ring in which is a knife, also attached to the bosom. Round their necks, they wear torques of gold and silver, for every man, as soon as he accumulates 10,000 dirhams, has a torque made for his wife. When he has 20,000, he has two torques made and so on. Every time he increases his fortune by 10,000, he adds another torque to those his wife already possesses, so that one woman may have many torques round her neck.

The most desirable ornaments they have are green ceramic beads they keep in their boats.[82] They will pay dearly for them, one dirham for a single bead. They thread them into necklaces for their wives.

The uncleanliness of the Rūs

They are the filthiest of God's creatures. They do not clean themselves after urinating or defecating, nor do they wash after having sex. They do not wash their hands after meals. They are like wandering asses.

The Rūs have sex with their slave girls in public

When they arrive from their land, they anchor their boat on the Itil, which is a great river, and they build large wooden houses on the banks. Ten or twenty people, more or less, live together in one of these houses. Each man has a raised platform[83] on which he sits. With them, there are beautiful slave girls, for sale to the merchants. Each of the men has sex with his slave, while his companions look on. Sometimes a whole group of them gather together in this way, in full view of one another. If a merchant enters at this moment to buy a young slave girl from one of the men and finds him having sex with her, the man does not get up off her until he has satisfied himself.

Disgusting habits

Every day without fail they wash their faces and their heads with the dirtiest and filthiest water there could be. A young serving girl comes every morning with breakfast and with it a great basin of water. She proffers it to her master, who washes his hands and face in it, as well as his hair. He washes and disentangles his hair, using a comb, there in the basin, then he blows his nose and spits and does every filthy thing imaginable in the water. When he has finished, the servant carries the bowl to the man next to him. She goes on passing the basin round from one to another until she has taken it to all the men in the house in turn. And each of them blows his nose and spits and washes his face and hair in this basin.

Offerings to the idols

As soon as their boats arrive at this port, each of them disembarks, taking with him bread and meat, onions, milk and *nabīdh*, and he walks until he comes to a great wooden post stuck in the ground with a face like that of a man, and around it are little figures. Behind these images there are long wooden stakes driven into the ground. Each of them prostrates himself before the great idol, saying to it:

'Oh my Lord, I have come from a far country and I have with me such and such a number of young slave girls, and such and such a number of sable skins . . .' and so on, until he has listed all the trade goods he has brought. [Then he adds:] 'I have brought you this gift.' Then he leaves what he has with him in front of the wooden post [and says:]

'I would like you to do the favour of sending me a merchant who has large quantities of *dīnārs* and dirhams and who will buy everything that I want and not argue with me over my price.'

Then he departs.

If he has difficulty selling and his stay becomes long drawn out, he returns with another present a second and even a third time. If he cannot get what he wants, he brings a present for each of the little idols and asks them to intercede, saying:

'These are the wives of our Lord and his daughters and sons.'

Thus he continues to make his request to each idol in turn, begging their intercession and abasing himself before them. Sometimes the sale is easy and after having sold his goods he says:

'My Lord has satisfied my needs and it is fitting that I should reward him for it.'

Then he takes a certain number of sheep or cows and slaughters them, distributing part of the meat as gifts and carrying off the rest to set before the great idol and the little figures that surround it. Then he hangs the heads of the sheep or cows on the wooden stakes which have been driven into the ground. When night falls, the dogs come and eat all this, and the man who has made the offering says:

'My Lord is pleased with me and has eaten the gift that I brought him.'

The sick abandoned

If one of them falls ill, [the others pitch a tent for him] in a place distant from them. They leave him some bread and water, but they neither go near him nor speak to him. [They do not even come to visit him] during all the days of his illness, particularly if he is a poor man or a slave. If he recovers and gets well, he comes back to them; if he dies, they burn him. If he is a slave, they leave him where he is, and the dogs and birds of prey devour him.

The punishment of thieves

If they catch a thief or a brigand, they lead him to a great tree, tie a stout rope round his neck and hang him [from the tree, and there he remains] until he drops to pieces [from exposure] to the wind and the rain.

The burial of a great man

They say that when their great men die, they do all kinds of things to them, of which burning is the least. I wanted to have certain knowledge of this [but did not] until one day I learned of the death of one of their great men. They placed him in his grave which they covered with a roof and they left him there for ten days, waiting while they finished cutting and sewing his garments.

The burial of a poor man

If the dead man was poor, they build him a small boat and place him in it and set it on fire. If he was wealthy, they gather together his fortune and divide it into three parts, one for his family, one to have clothes cut out for him and another to have the *nabīdh* prepared that they will drink on the day that his slave girl kills herself and is burned with her master. For they drink *nabīdh* unrestrainedly, night and day, so that sometimes one of them dies with his wine cup in his hand.

Funeral of a noble

When a great man dies, the members of his family say to his
slave girls and young slave boys:

'Which of you will die with him?'

One of them replies:

'I will.'

Once they have spoken, it is irreversible and there is no turning back. If they wanted to change their mind, they would not
be allowed to. Usually, it is the slave girls who offer to die.

When the man whom I mentioned above died, they said to
his slave girls:

'Who will die with him?'

One of them answered:

'I will.'

Then they appointed two young slave girls to watch over her
and follow her everywhere she went, sometimes even washing
her feet with their own hands.

Everyone busies himself about the dead man, cutting out
clothes for him and preparing everything that he will need.
Meanwhile, the slave girl spends each day drinking and singing, happily and joyfully.

When the day came that the man was to be burned and the girl
with him, I went to the river where his boat was anchored. I saw
that they had drawn his boat up on to the shore and that four posts
of *khadank* or other wood had been driven into the ground and
round these posts a framework of wood had been erected. Next,
they drew up the boat until it rested on this wooden construction.

Then they came forward, coming and going, pronouncing
[words that I did not understand, while the man was still in his
grave, not yet taken out].

The 'Angel of Death'

Then they brought a bed and placed it on [the boat and covered
it with a mattress] and cushions of Byzantine silk brocade.

Then came [an old woman whom they call] the 'Angel of Death' and she spread the bed with coverings we have just mentioned. She is in charge of sewing and arranging all these things, and it is she who kills the slave girls. I saw that she was a witch, thick-bodied and sinister.

When they came to the tomb of the dead man, they removed the earth from on top of the wood, and then the wood itself and they took out the dead man, wrapped in the garment in which he died. I saw that he had turned black because of the coldness of the country. They had put *nabīdh* in the tomb with him, and fruit and a drum. They took all this out. The dead man did not smell bad and nothing about him had changed except his colour. They dressed him in trousers, socks, boots, a tunic and a brocade caftan with gold buttons. On his head, they placed a brocade cap covered with sable. Then they bore him into the pavilion on the boat and sat him on the mattress, supported by cushions. Then they brought *nabīdh*, fruit and basil which they placed near him. Next they carried in bread, meat and onions which they laid before him.

Sacrificial animals

After that, they brought in a dog, which they cut in two and threw into the boat. Then they placed his weapons beside him. Next they took two horses and made them run until they were in lather, before hacking them to pieces with swords and throwing their flesh on to the boat. Then they brought two cows, which they also cut into pieces and threw them on to the boat. Finally they brought a cock and a hen, killed them and threw them on to the boat as well.

The slave girl has sex with those present

Meanwhile, the slave girl who wanted to be killed came and went, entering in turn each of the pavilions that had been built, and the master of each pavilion had intercourse with her, saying:

'Tell your master that I only did this for your love of him.'

The slave girl gazes on Paradise

On Friday, when the time had come for the evening prayer, they led the slave girl towards something which they had constructed and which looked like the frame of a door. She placed her feet on the palms of the hands of the men, until she could look over this frame. She said some words and they let her down. They raised her a second time and she did as she had the first and then they set her down again. And a third time and she did as she done the other two. Then they brought her a chicken. She cut off its head and tossed it away. Then they took the chicken and threw it on to the boat.

I asked the interpreter what she had been doing. He replied:

'The first time they lifted her up, she said:

[' "There I see my father and my mother."]

'The second time, she said:

' "There [I see] all my dead relatives [sitting]."

'And the third time she said:

' "There [I see my master sitting in] Paradise and [Paradise is green and beautiful.] There are men with him and [young people, and he is calling me.] Take [me to him." ' They went off with her] towards the boat. She took off the two bracelets that she was wearing and gave them both to the old woman who is known as the [Angel of Death – she] who was to kill her. Then she stripped off her two anklets and gave them [to the two young girls who served her. They were the daughters] of the woman called the Angel of Death. Then the men lifted her on to the boat, but did not let her enter [the pavilion].

Next, men came with shields and staves. They handed the girl a cup of *nabīdh*. She sang a song over it and drank. The interpreter translated what she was saying and explained that she was bidding all her female companions farewell. Then they gave her another cup. She took it and continued singing for a long time, while the old woman encouraged her to drink and then urged her to enter the pavilion and join her master.

I saw that the girl did not know what she was doing. She wanted to enter the pavilion, but she put [her head] between it and the boat. Then the old woman seized her head, made her enter the pavilion and went in with her. The men began to bang on their shields with staves, to drown her cries, so that the other slave girls [would not be frightened] and try to avoid dying with their masters. Next, six men entered the pavilion and [lay with] the girl, one after another, after which they laid her beside her master. Two seized her feet and two others her hands. The old woman called the Angel of Death came and put a cord round her neck in such a way that the two ends went in opposite directions. She gave the ends to two of the men, so they could pull on them. Then she herself approached the girl holding in her hand a dagger with a broad blade and [plunged it again and again between the girl's ribs],[84] while the two men strangled her with the cord until she was dead.

The burning of the boat

Next, [the closest male relative of the dead man] came forward and [took a piece of wood] which he lit at a fire. He then walked backwards towards the boat, his face turned [towards the people] who were there, one hand holding the piece of flaming wood, the other covering his anus, for he was naked. Thus he set fire to the wood that had been set ready under the boat, [after they had placed the slave girl beside her master.] Then people came with wood and logs to burn, each holding a piece of a wood alight at one end, which they threw on to the wood. The fire enveloped the wood, [then the boat, then the tent,] the man, the girl and all that there was on the boat. [A violent and frightening] wind began [to blow, the flames grew in strength] and the heat of the fire intensified.

Why the Rūs burn their dead

[One of the Rūs was standing beside me] and I heard him speak to my interpreter. I asked the latter [what he had said.] He replied:

'You Arabs are fools!'

['Why is that?' I asked him.]

He said:

'Because you put the men you love most, [and the most noble among you,] into the earth, and the earth and the worms and insects eat them. But we burn them [in the fire] in an instant, so that at once and without delay they enter Paradise.'

Then he began to laugh in a very excessive way. I asked him why he was laughing and he said:

'His Lord, for love of him, has sent a wind that [will bear] him hence within the hour.'

And indeed, not an hour had passed before ship, wood, girl and master were no more than ashes and dust.

Raising the grave mound

Next, at the place where this boat had been drawn out of the river, they build something like a round hill and in the middle they set up a great post of *khadank* wood, inscribed with the name of the man and that of the king of the Rūs. Then they departed.

The king of the Rūs

One of the customs of the king of the Rūs is to have 400 men in his palace, who are the bravest of his companions, men upon whom he can count. These are the men who die when he dies and allow themselves to be killed for him. Each of them has a slave girl who serves him, washes his head and prepares everything that he eats or drinks, and then there is another slave girl with whom he sleeps. These 400 men sit below the king's throne, which is immense and encrusted with the finest gems. Forty slave girls destined for his bed sit by him on the throne. Sometimes he has sex with one of them in front of the companions whom we have just mentioned, without coming down from his throne. When he wants to perform his natural functions, he does so in a basin. If he wants to ride, his horse is led right up to the throne and he mounts. If he wants to dismount, he has the horse move forward so that he can get down directly on to the throne. He has a lieutenant who commands his troops, fights his enemies and represents him in dealings with his subjects.

The king of the Khazars

The king of the Khazars, whose title is *khāqān*, only appears in public [once every four months]. He is called the Great Khāqān, whereas his lieutenant is known as *khāqān beg*.[85] It is he who leads the armies, directs the affairs of the kingdom, appears in public and receives the allegiance of neighbouring kings. [Every[86] day, he enters the presence of the Great Khāqān with a humble mien and words indicating submission and modesty. He only enters the presence barefoot, holding a piece of firewood in his hand. Once he has greeted the Great Khāqān, he ignites this piece of wood before him. When it has burned away, he sits beside the king on his throne, to the right of him.[87] He has as his second in command a man called *kundur khāqān*, who has in his turn a lieutenant known as *jawshīghīr*.[88]

It is the custom of the Great King never to give public audience and never to speak to the people. No one, except for those whom we have mentioned, has access to him. It is up to his lieutenant, the *khāqān beg*, to nominate officers for all positions of authority, to inflict punishments and to take charge of the government.

The hidden tombs of the Khazar kings

When the Great King dies, it is customary to build him a house composed of twenty chambers and in each chamber to hollow out a tomb for him. They break up stones until they become like powdered antimony. They spread a layer of this powder and then throw quicklime on top of the body. Beneath this house there is a river, a great river that flows rapidly, which they divert over the tomb.

They say: 'This is so that no devil, or man, or maggot, or reptile can reach it.'

Once the king has been buried, they cut off the heads of those who buried him, so that no one knows in which of the chambers he lies. They call his tomb 'Paradise' and they say:

'He has entered Paradise.'

All the chambers are decorated with silk brocade woven with gold.

The harem of the king of the Khazars

It is the custom for the king of the Khazars[89] to have twenty-five wives, each of whom is the daughter of the king of a neighbouring country. He is given them freely or he takes them by force. He also has slave girls as his concubines for his bed, sixty in number, every one of them extremely beautiful. All these women, whether free or slave, are kept in an isolated castle, where each of them has her own alcove roofed with teak, and each alcove is surrounded by a pavilion. Each of them has with her a eunuch who protects her from all eyes. When the king wishes to sleep with one of them, he sends a messenger to the eunuch who guards her and he arrives with her quicker than the blink of an eye to put her in his bed, and then he remains standing at the door of the king's alcove. When the king has finished with her, the eunuch takes her by the hand and leads her back, without leaving her for a single moment.

When this Great King goes riding, all the troops set out with him as an escort, keeping the distance of a mile between him and them. None of his subjects sees him without prostrating themselves face to the ground, and they only lift their heads again after he has passed by.

The length of the reigns of their kings is forty years. If one of them oversteps this time even by a single day, his subjects and courtiers kill him, saying:

'His reason has diminished and his opinions are confused.'

The fate of cowards

If he sends out a detachment of his forces on an expedition, never under any circumstances or for any reason will they turn their backs on him. If they are routed, those who flee in the king's direction are killed. If his lieutenant or any of his military chiefs are put to flight, the king has them brought into his presence with their wives and children, and their wives and children are given away to others before their very eyes. The same is done with their horses, their possessions, their arms and their houses. Sometimes they are cut in two and sometimes crucified. Sometimes, the king has them hung from a tree by their necks. Sometimes, if he wishes to be kind to them, he employs them as grooms.

The Khazar city on the Itil

The king of the Khazars has a great city on the River Itil, on both banks of the river. The Muslims live on one bank and the king and his followers on the other. The head of the Muslim community is one of the king's officers and is known as *khaz*,[90] and he is a Muslim. All legal decisions concerning Muslims living in the land of the Khazars, or visiting the country on business are referred to this Muslim officer. He is the only person with the authority to examine their affairs or judge their quarrels.

Revenge for the destruction of a synagogue

The Muslims in this town have a congregational mosque where they perform the Friday prayers. It has a tall minaret and a certain number of muezzins. When the king of the Khazars learned in the year 310/922 that the Muslims had destroyed the synagogue that was in Dār al-Bābūnaj,[91] he ordered the minaret to be destroyed and the muezzins put to death.

'If I did not fear that not a synagogue would be left standing throughout the lands of Islam,' he said, 'I would have destroyed the mosque.'

The Khazars and their king are all Jews. The Saqāliba and all the neighbouring peoples are subject to him and he speaks to them as if they were slaves and they obey him most humbly. Some go so far as to say that Khazars are Gog and Magog.]

PART II

THE TRAVELS OF
ABŪ HĀMID AL-ANDALUSĪ
AL-GHARNĀTĪ, 1130–1155

Abū Hāmid[1] *al-Andalusī says: 'I saw in this sea [the Caspian] a mountain of black clay like tar, surrounded by the sea. On the summit of the mountain was a long crevice from which water flows, and with the water come pieces of sulphur the weight of a* dānaq, *more or less. People collect them and transport them everywhere as a curiosity.'*

In this sea is the Island of Snakes. Abū Hāmid says it is near the black mountain just mentioned: 'It is an island covered with snakes,[2] *slithering all over one another. The sea birds come and lay their eggs in the middle of them, but the snakes don't harm them at all. I saw men carrying strong canes or staffs in their hands, clearing the snakes from the ground so they could walk through them and collect the eggs of the sea birds and their chicks. The snakes did no harm to anyone.'*

There is also the Island of the Jinn. Abū Hāmid says it is an uninhabited island, with no wild animals. The people said the Jinn had taken it over and that they could hear their voices. No one dared approach it.

There is also the Island of Siyāh Kūh. Abū Hāmid says it is a big island with springs and trees and vegetation and sweet water. There are wild four-footed animals as well. They gather madder there and export it to other countries. It is near the eastern shore of the sea. One of the tribes of the Ghuzz (Oguz) Turks has settled there because of a quarrel among the tribes, so they separated and came to this island.

There is also the Island of Sheep. Sallām the Interpreter, the envoy of the Commander of the Faithful, al-Wāthiq, to the

*king of the Khazars, said: 'We saw an island between the lands
of the Khazars and the Bulghārs in which were mountain sheep
(as numerous) as locusts. They were unable to flee, there were
so many. When ships came to that island, they hunted as many
as they wished. They were all ewes and fat lambs. I saw no
other animals on that island. It has springs, grass and many
trees. Praise be to Him whose blessings are past counting!'*

Lodgings

... there is a great hospice intended for illiterate foreign visitors, but they take men of learning to their houses. I stayed
with one of the *amīr*s known as Abū al-Qāsim. Every day his
slaves slaughtered a sheep for me.

'Aren't there any leftovers from yesterday?' I asked them.

'Yes,' they answered, 'but this is what our master has ordered.'

The amīr

This *amīr* read a legal work, the *Kitāb al-Muqni'* of al-Mahāmilī,[3]
with me. He spoke – may God have mercy on him! – various
languages, among them: Lakzān, Tabbalān, al-Fīlān, al-Zaʿqalān,
al-Khaydāq, al-Ghamīq, al-Sarīr, Alān, Arsā, al-Zaqhakārān,
the language of the Turks, Persian and Arabic.[4] He used to
receive men from different nations in my presence and speak to
each one in his own language.

The amīr's sister asks for legal advice

One day, when I was the guest of the sister of this *amīr*, she said
to her brother:

'Lying with my husband, he ejaculated in his sleep. Ask this man if I ought to perform the ritual ablutions.'

I was amazed and said to the *amīr*:

'Tell her the following. A woman of the *ansār* asked the Messenger of God – may God bless him and save him! – this very question, and the Prophet replied:

' "If you see water, wash yourself."

'Then the Messenger of God added – may God bless him and save him! – "How excellent are the women of the *ansār*! Modesty does not prevent them from making a study of the law if that will lead them to a more perfect observation of their faith." '

Saqsīn

I set sail on the Caspian Sea and reached a mighty river like a sea, many times larger than the Tigris, and from it flow other large rivers.

On its banks is a city called Saqsīn,[5] inhabited by forty tribes of the Ghuzz, each of which has its own independent *amīr*. Their dwellings are large and each of them is a huge tent, like a dome, covered in felt, with room for a hundred men or more. There are also within the city communities of merchants, both foreigners and westerners who have come from the Maghrib in uncountable thousands.[6]

There are mosques in the city, where the prayers are said on Fridays for the Khazars, who likewise are divided into various tribes. In the centre of the town lives an *amīr* of the Bulghārs, who has a great mosque in which to say the Friday prayers, and round about live the different tribes of Bulghārs. A people called the Suwār, also very numerous, pray in yet another mosque. On feast days they set up many pulpits and each *amīr* prays in front of many different nations. Each different group has its own judges, religious scholars and preachers. They all follow the law school of Abū Hanīfa, except for the descendants of the

Maghribīs,[7] who follow that of Mālik, and a few foreigners who
are Shāfiʾī.

My home is now, in fact, among them and there I keep those
of my concubines who have borne children, my sons and my
daughters. This country is extremely cold.

Sturgeon and other fish

In this river are a number of kinds of fish that I have never seen
in any other part of the world. There is one kind which weighs
as much as a large man and another sort that weighs as much
as a large camel. There are smaller ones, too. They have no
bones or skulls, and no teeth; they are like the fat tail of a sheep
stuffed with chicken. They are even better and sweeter than fat
lamb. This fish is grilled and served with rice and it is better
than lamb or chicken. Each fish – and they weigh about a hundred *mann* – can be bought for half a *dānaq*. Enough oil comes
out of their belly to provide lighting for a month and similarly
half a *mann* or more of roe. They are preserved in strips dried
in the sun, and this is the most delicious thing in the world. It
is a pure reddish gold in colour, like amber, and it is eaten with
bread; there is no need to bake or fry it.

Currency and prices

For currency, they use white lead, valued at one dīnār for eight
Baghdadi *mann*. They cut it into little bits and use it to buy the
fruit, bread and meat they want.

Meat is cheap when sheep are available. They are usually
brought by the infidel caravans. One sheep costs half a *dānaq*
and a lamb costs a *tussūj*.

There is a great variety of fruit, among them a supremely
sweet melon and another kind of melon that is harvested in
winter.

Wooden houses

The winters there are very cold and while they last, they make use of houses built out of pine, using great trunks placed one upon the other, with roofs and terraces of wooden planks. They light fires in these houses, which have small doors protected by sheepskins with their fleece. Inside the house it is as warm as a bathhouse. They have an abundant supply of firewood.

Frozen rivers

The river freezes until it is like land, and horses and animal carts can travel along it. They even fight on the ice. I crossed the whole river when it was frozen and it was more than 1,840 of my paces wide, excluding the tributaries.

The works of the Jinn

Beside this great river, the Jinn dug Solomon a thousand canals, each a mile long. They piled the earth which they dug out beside each canal, forming a mound alongside the canal, about a bowshot high, so that there are, as it were, a thousand hills and a thousand canals.

The abundance of fish

These deep canals are filled with water from the great river. So many fish breed in them that they seem like dry land. Any boat that comes to one of these canals can cast its net at its mouth and the fish pour into the boat until it is completely full. Even if there were a hundred boats, they could all be filled with every

kind of fish from one single canal. These canals have no outlet.
There is nothing like them.

Coloured snow

Beyond these rivers and mountains, there is a land, several
days' journey away, where there is snow of red, white and blue
and other colours.[8] Ships are filled with it, and it is taken down-
river to Bulghār.

The distance from Saqsīn to Bulghār by river is forty days.

Bulghār

Bulghār is also a great city, all built of pine. Its walls are of oak.
Round about it, there are an infinite number of peoples. It lies
beyond the Seventh Clime.[9]

The climate

When the days are long, they have twenty hours and the nights
four, but on the other hand in the winter, it is the nights that
last twenty hours and the days but four. In summer, at midday,
it is very hot, hotter than anywhere else in the world; but at
sunset and throughout the night it is cold, so that one needs
much clothing.

*In Bulghār, a city of the north, located at the extreme limit of
the Islamic world, forty days upriver from Saqsīn, the days in
summer are twenty hours long and the nights four hours long.
In the winter it is the reverse, the nights are twenty hours long
and the days four hours long. The cold is so great at this time
that if someone dies it is impossible to bury them until six*

months later, for the earth freezes as hard as iron and it is impossible to dig a grave. One of my sons died there and I could not bury him. His body had to wait six months until this could be done. The bodies of the dead are frozen hard as stones.[10]

I tried to fast in this city during the month of Ramadān, which fell in the summer, but I had to give up and take refuge underground in a room where there was a spring.

In the winter, the cold is so intense that wood splits. It is at this season of great cold that the king sets out on raids against the infidel and captures his women, his sons, his daughters and his horses.

Honey

The people of Bulghār are more resistant to the cold than anyone else, and this is because their food and drink largely consists of honey, which is very cheap there.

The bones of 'Ād

In this country are found the bones of the people of 'Ād.[11] A single tooth is two palms wide and four long. The distance from the head to the shoulder is four arms in length. The head is like a great dome. Many of these are found here.

Mammoth ivory

Under the earth, elephant tusks are to be found. They are as white as snow and as heavy as lead. Each one weighs 200 *mann*, more or less. No one knows from what beast they come. They are exported to Khwārazm and Khurāsān. Combs, little

boxes and other objects are made from them, just as they are
from ivory, but this material is stronger than ivory and does not
break.[12]

The origin of the name Bulghār

North of this country, there are numerous peoples who pay
tribute to the king of Bulghār.

The word *Bulghār* means 'wise man'. And the reason is as
follows:

A Muslim merchant came to this country on business. He
was a jurisconsult and learned in medicine. The wife of the
king and the king himself were stricken with a very serious illness. They were treated with all the remedies known to them,
but the sickness only increased, until they feared that they
would die. Then the Muslim merchant said to them:

'If I were to cure you and you were to recover your health,
would you accept my faith?'

'Yes,' they replied.

So he gave them medicines and cured them, and they, and all
their people, embraced Islam. Then the king of the Khazars
came to attack them with a great force and said to them:

'Why have you embraced this religion without my permission?'

But the Muslim said to them:

'Do not fear. Say: "God is great!"'

They said:

'God is great! God is great! God is great! Praise be to God.
Bless, oh my God, Muhammad and the family of Muhammad!'

Then they fought with the said king and defeated his army,
so that the king offered them peace and embraced their religion. Then the Khazar king said:

'I saw enormous men, mounted on whitish horses, slaughtering my host and putting it to flight.'

And the *faqīh* confirmed this, saying:

'These are the troops of God – may He be honoured and exalted!'

Since among them a wise man is called *bular*, that land was called 'Bular', which means 'a sage'. The Arabs adapted it to their own tongue, so that it became 'Bulghār'. I have read it thus in the *History of Bulghār* set down in the qādī al-Bulghārī's own hand.[13] He was one of the followers of Abū al-Maʿālī al-Juwaynī[14] – may God have mercy upon him!

Beavers

Bulghār exerts its dominion over a people called Wīsū (Ves) who pay taxes, even though they live a month's march away. Another people is called Arū.[15] They live where very good beaver, ermine and grey squirrel are hunted. There, in summer, the day is twenty-two hours long. The best and highest-quality beaver pelts come from those parts.

The beaver is a wonderful animal. It lives in the great rivers and builds houses on land, at the edge of the water. It makes a kind of high platform for itself and to the right another, less high, for its wife and to the left another, for its children. Below, there is a place for its slaves. The house has a door which gives on to the river and another, higher up, on to the land. Sometimes, it eats the wood known as *khalanj*;[16] at other times it eats fish. Some beavers are jealous of others, and make them prisoners.

Those who trade in those lands and through the country of Bulghār have no trouble in distinguishing the fur of slave beavers from those of the masters. This is because the slave beaver cuts the wood of the *khalanj* and other trees with its teeth, and as it gnaws them, they rub its sides and its hair falls off right and left. Hence they say, 'This pelt is from the servant of the beaver.' The fur of the beaver who owns slaves, on the other hand, is perfect. God Almighty has said: 'And He inspired it (both) with lewdness and with godfearing.'[17]

The Sea of Darkness

Beyond Wīsū, there is a region known as Yūrā,[18] on the Sea of Darkness. The day there is very long in summer, so the merchants say that the sun does not set for the space of forty days. In winter, on the other hand, the nights are equally long. The merchants say that the Darkness is very close to this place, so that the people of Yūrā enter the Darkness provided with torches. In the Darkness there is a tree as big as a large village and on it perches an enormous creature, some say a bird.

Silent barter

They take different kinds of goods with them. Each merchant sets his wares out in a particular place, marked with his sign. Then they all withdraw and when they come back again, everyone finds something left beside his goods. If he approves the exchange, he takes these wares. If not, he picks up his own merchandise and leaves the other things, without ever transgressing or cheating. No one knows who it is that exchanges goods with them.

Imported swords

People bring swords from the lands of Islam, made in Zanjān, Abhar, Tabrīz and Isfāhān, but only bare blades without pommel or decoration; simply the iron blank as it comes from the furnace, after being tempered in water for a considerable time, until when it is hung from a string and struck with the fingernail or with some object of wood or iron, it resonates for a long time.[19] These are the swords suitable for transport to Yūrā.

Honey, bones and fur

The Yūrā do not make war and have no horses or beasts of burden. They have nothing but huge trees and forests, in which honey is gathered. They also have great numbers of sable, the flesh of which they eat. The merchants take to them the swords just mentioned and the bones of cows and sheep in exchange for sable skins, and so make great profits.

Skis

The way to these places crosses country permanently covered in snow. The people fasten specially smoothed boards on their feet. Each board is a fathom long and a palm wide, and both the front and the back curve up from the ground. In the middle of the board, there is a place for the person to put his foot, which consists of an indentation with very strong leather straps, by which the feet are attached. Both boards, one on each foot, are yoked together by long thongs, like the reins of a horse, which the man holds in his left hand. In his right, he carries a stick, the height of a man, which has at the bottom a ball of cloth filled with a large quantity of wool, the size of a human head, but weighing very little. The man leans on this stick as he walks over the snow, pushing with it until it is behind his shoulder, like a boatman poling a boat. In this way, he moves over the snow at speed and if it were not for this ingenious contrivance, it would be absolutely impossible to walk, for the snow lies on

the earth like sand and never hardens. Thus, any animal that walks across it sinks in and dies, except for dogs or other very small creatures, such as hares and foxes, because they run fast and lightly. The coats of the foxes and hares in this country turn white like cotton, and in the region around Bulghār during the winter so does the coat of the wolf.

Swords traded for furs and slaves

Now, these swords are exported from the lands of Islam to Bulghār with great profit for the merchants. Then the people of Bulghār take them to Wīsū, the place of the beavers, and the people of Wīsū take them to Yūrā, where they sell them for sable pelts, slave girls and young boys.

Swords thrown in the sea

In Yūrā, every human being needs a sword each year to throw into the Sea of Darkness, for only when they throw in swords does God make a great fish like a vast mountain come out of the sea for them. This fish is pursued by another fish, many times greater, which seeks to devour it. The smaller fish, fleeing the greater, comes close to land and stops in a place from which it cannot return to the open sea. Therefore, it stays there, while the greater fish, since it cannot reach the smaller one, goes back to the sea.

Then the people of Yūrā get in their boats and, heading for the smaller fish, cut the flesh from its sides, without the fish moving or heeding them. They fill their houses with its flesh and climb up on its back, which is like a huge mountain. It stays with them for some time, during which they continue slicing off its flesh. All those who have thrown a sword into the sea take their share of the fish. When the water of the sea rises and the fish is lighter, it returns to the deep, having filled one hundred thousand houses or more with its flesh.

The girl who came from a fish's ear

I was told in Bulghār that one year, they pierced the ear of one of these fish and, inserting a cable through the hole, drew it to land. Then they opened the ear of the fish and from within emerged a kind of girl, who looked like a human – white, with pink cheeks, black hair and plump buttocks, like the most attractive of women.

The people of Yūrā took her and drew her to land, while the creature struck her face, tore her hair and screamed. God had created for her in the middle of her body a kind of white skin like a thick, strong cloth, which went from her waist to her knees, covering her private parts and it was like a veil attached to her waist to hide her nakedness. They kept that girl among them until she died. Truly, the power of God on High knows no limits!

The Yūrā

They say:

'If the Yūrā do not throw the swords that we have mentioned into the water, no fish come out and they die of hunger.'

The people of Wīsū and Arū do not let the Yūrā enter the lands of Bulghār during the summer, because if any of them enters that territory during the hot weather, it grows cold, the water freezes as in winter and the people's crops are ruined. This is something that has been proved.

I saw a group of these people in Bulghār in the winter. They are reddish in colouring with light-blue eyes and hair like linen, almost white. They wear linen clothes, despite the cold, and some of them have cloaks of the most magnificent beaver skins, worn fur side out. They drink barley water, as sharp as vinegar, which suits the heat of their constitutions, for they eat the flesh of beavers and squirrels, as well as honey.

Giant birds

In their country, there are giant birds with very long beaks.[20] The beaks of these birds are twisted to the right and to the left; the upper part, six palms to the right and six palms to the left, in the shape of the letters *lam–alif*, like in this picture. If the bird needs to eat or drink, it shuts its beak and eats and drinks.

The flesh of this bird is good for those who suffer from kidney or bladder stone, and they take it to Bulghār in slices dried in the sun, which have to be hacked into pieces. If the egg of this bird falls on ice or snow, it melts as if in the fire. They can only be preserved if laid on earth or wood.

The river of the Saqāliba and its snakes

When I entered the country of the Saqāliba, I left Bulghār and travelled by boat down the river of the Saqāliba.[21] The water is as black as that of the Sea of Darkness, and looks like ink. It is, however, sweet, pleasant and clear.

In this river, there are no fish, but only great black snakes, one on top of the other. They are far more numerous than fish and do no one any harm. There is also an animal like a small cat with a black pelt, called the 'water sable'.[22] Its fur is taken to Bulghār and Saqsīn. It lives in this river.

Produce of the lands of the Saqāliba

When I reached the land of the Saqāliba, I saw that it was very large and rich in honey, wheat and barley. They have big apples; nothing could be finer. The cost of living is low.

Squirrel skins used as currency

For their dealings among themselves, they use old squirrel skins with no hair, that cannot be used for anything and are absolutely worthless even though there is still fur on the heads and paws. They reckon eighteen old skins to be worth a silver dirham and they tie them up in bundles called a *juqn*.[23] With one of these skins, you can buy a great loaf of magnificent bread, large enough to sustain a big man; and they can be used to buy slave girls, young boys, gold, silver, beaver skins and other merchandise, in spite of the fact that in any other country, a thousand loads wouldn't buy you a bean and would be totally valueless.

When the skins are completely worn out in a household, they put them in sacks, once they have been cut, and take them to a particular market, where there are men supervising the workers. The workers string eighteen skins together with strong thread, forming a single bundle. At the end of the thread, they attach a piece of black lead, sealed with a die stamp bearing the image of the king. They charge a single skin out of the bundle in order to seal up the rest. No one may refuse to accept them, either when buying or selling.

Justice

The Saqāliba have very strict norms of behaviour. If anyone dares to touch another man's slave girl, or his son, or his horse, or commit any kind of crime against him, he is obliged to pay a sum of money. If he does not have it, his sons are sold, then his daughters and his wife, to pay for his offence. And if he has neither family nor descendants, he himself is sold. He never ceases to be a slave, serving his purchaser, until he dies or returns the sum for which he was sold. Nothing whatever is given to him for any of the work he does for his owner.

Security for Muslim traders

It is a safe country. When a Muslim has business dealings with a local and that Saqlabī[24] goes bankrupt, his sons and house are sold to pay the merchant what he is owed.

The Saqāliba are Nestorians

The Saqāliba are brave. Like the Byzantines, they are Nestorian Christians.[25]

Witch trials

There are a people around there who live in the woods and shave their beards. They live by a great river and hunt beavers.

I was told that every ten years, witchcraft increases and the old witches begin to lead the women astray. So they round up all the old women in their territory, tie their hands and feet and throw them in the river. They let the old women who sink live, because they realize that they are not witches, but those who float on the water are burned alive.

I travelled among them with the caravan for a long time. Their country is safe. They pay taxes to Bulghār. They have no revealed religion and worship a kind of tree before which they bow down. So I was told by those who know them well.

Ghūrkūmān (Kiev)

I came to one of the cities of the Saqāliba called Ghūrkūmān, where there are thousands of descendants of the Maghribīs.[26] They look like Turks, and they speak Turkish and shoot arrows in the Turkish manner. They are known there by the name of HNH (Hun?).

I met a man from Baghdād named 'Abd al-Karīm ibn Fayrūz al-Jawharī, who had married into the Muslim community there.

Ignorance of Friday prayer

I established the custom of public prayer on Friday among the Muslims there and taught them about the khutba, since they did not know about praying together on Fridays.

On the way to Bāshghird

One of my companions stayed there with them to instruct them, and I went on to Bāshghird, which is forty days above the lands of the Saqāliba, passing through infidel peoples from innumerable different lineages. They live among tall trees and gardens. I have never seen such trees anywhere in the world; they do not bear fruit.

A beautiful lizard

One day, at the foot of a tree, I saw a creature like the lizard called 'izāya. It had two hands and two feet. You would think that God most high had brought it from Paradise. It seemed as if it were made of the purest red jacinth, so translucent that you could see through it, and pure polished gold, the like of which I have never seen in this world, as if it were crafted with the greatest art and skill. I was amazed when I saw it. My companions, mounted on their horses, surrounded it. It gazed at us with eyes that seemed to be weaving a spell and turned its head towards us, right and left, but it did not move and paid no attention to us whatsoever.

Hungary

Then I reached the country of Hungary [Anqūrīya], where the people called Bāshghird live. They are descended from the first tribes that came from the lands of the Turks and entered the lands of the Franks. They are brave and their numbers are beyond counting.

Their land, which is known as Hungary, consists of seventy-eight cities, each of which has many fortresses, hamlets, farmsteads, mountains, forests and gardens. Uncountable thousands of the descendants of the Maghribīs live there and thousands, likewise uncountable, of the descendants of the people of Khwārazm.

The people of Khwārazm serve the kings and pretend to be Christians, although they practise Islam in secret. The descendants of the Maghribīs, on the other hand, do not serve the Christians, except in war, and openly practise Islam.

Hungarian Muslims

When I made contact with the descendants of the Maghribīs, they treated me with great honour. I taught them some basic religious knowledge and even induced some of them to attempt to speak Arabic. I made a great effort to have them repeat and practise the ritual prayers and other observances. I summarized the duties of pilgrimage for them and the principles of the division of inheritances, which they began to follow.

The value of book-learning

One of them said to me:

'I want to copy the Qur'ān and learn from it.'

Since he spoke Arabic well, I answered:

'Make an effort to learn it by heart and to understand it well, and never talk about what the Qur'ān says without an *isnād*. If you do this, you will achieve what you desire.'

He replied:

'But did you not say that the Prophet – may God bless him and save him! – said: "Bind learning with writing"?'

'In a book,' I said, 'there is no knowledge, there is only writing that guides us to knowledge. It only becomes knowledge when you harbour it in your memory, for knowledge is the attribute of the wise man.'

And I recited to him this verse of mine:

> Science is in the heart, it is not in books.
> Do not immerse yourself in frivolities and games.

Then I also recited these lines of mine:

If you write knowledge down, it is like putting it in a basket;
If you don't learn it by heart, you will never succeed.
The only one who triumphs is he who commits it to memory
After hearing it, and so guards against error.

'When you know something by heart, then write it down from memory, and then that will be knowledge that you have bound with writing. But if you copy it from a book, it will just be a copy, and will not be knowledge at all. Get this quite straight.'

They did not know about congregational prayer on Fridays and they learned how to perform it and to have the obligatory sermon. I explained to them:

'The Prophet – may God bless him and save him! – has said:

' "Friday prayer is the pilgrimage of the poor. He who cannot go on pilgrimage, but attends the Friday prayers, will receive the reward of those who go on pilgrimage." '

Today, the Friday sermon is preached, publicly or secretly, in at least ten thousand places, for the country is very extensive.

The size of Hungary

I remained among them for three years, but I could not visit more than four cities. Their country stretches from Rome the Great to the frontiers of Constantinople. There are mountains there from which they extract gold and silver.

Prices

This country is cheaper and more prosperous than any other. Twenty sheep cost a *dīnār* and for the same price you can buy thirty lambs or kids. Five hundred *ratl* of honey also cost a *dīnār*. A beautiful slave girl can be had for ten *dīnārs* and during the raiding season, a fine slave girl or a Greek lad can be had for as little as three *dīnārs*.

A slave girl

I bought a slave girl who had already borne a child, and whose father, mother and brothers were still alive; I bought her from her owner for ten *dīnārs*. She was fifteen years old and as beautiful as the moon, with black hair and eyes, and skin as white as camphor. She knew how to cook, sew and embroider.

I also bought, for five *dīnārs*, another Greek slave girl, eight years old. One day I bought for half a *dīnār* two jars full of honeycomb with its wax and I said to her:

'I want you to purify this honey and extract the wax.'

Then I went out and sat on a bench at the door of the house, where people were gathered. After sitting with them for a while, I went back into the house and saw five disks of wax as pure as gold and two jars full of liquid honey that seemed like rose water. The honey had been purified and returned to the two jars, all within an hour.

She had a child, but it died. I freed her and gave her the name Maryam.

I wanted to take her with me to Saqsīn, but I was afraid of the way she might be treated by the Turkish concubines who had borne children to me and whom I kept in Saqsīn.

Raids against Byzantium

The king of Bāshghird[27] continually devastated the lands of the Byzantines. I said to those Muslims:

'Make every effort to go on *jihād* with this king, for thus God will set down the merit of Holy War to your account.'

So they set out with this king to the territory of Constantinople and put twelve armies of the king of Byzantium to flight. They came back with a band of Turcomen from the army of Konya. I asked some of them:

'How is it that you have come here in the army of the king of Byzantium?'

'They hired us,' they replied, 'for two hundred *dīnārs* each and we didn't know that there were Muslims in this country.'

I arranged for them to leave for Byzantine territory, so that they could make their way back to Konya.

The Byzantine emperor sues for peace

The lord of Constantinople[28] came to sue for peace, bringing with him great riches and many Muslim prisoners whom he had in his power. One of these Muslim captives, who had been in Constantinople, told me that the king of the Byzantines asked:

'Why does the king of Bāshghird come into my lands and destroy them, when before he did no such thing?'

'It is,' they replied, 'because the king of Bāshghird has an army of Muslims whom he allows to practise their religion publicly, and they are the ones who have urged him to invade your territory and devastate your dominions.'

The king of the Byzantines replied:

'I also have Muslim subjects, but they do not fight for me.'

'That is because you,' they said, challenging him, 'force them to become Christians.'

The king replied:

'From now on I will not force any Muslim to embrace my faith and I will build them mosques so that will they fight for me.'

The king of Bāshghird

The king of Bāshghird is called *kirālī*[29] and his kingdom is much larger than that of the lord of Byzantium. His armies are without number. His territory is greater than that of Byzantium by a matter of twenty days' march, or more. The king follows the religion of the Franks, because he married their women. Nevertheless, he raids Frankish lands and captures all he can. Every country fears his attack, because of the many armies he has at his disposal and his great courage.

Muslim and Christian attitudes to wine

When he heard that I had forbidden the Muslims to drink wine and had allowed them to have slave concubines, as well as four legal wives, he said:

'This is not reasonable, for wine strengthens the body, whereas women weaken the body and the sight. The religion of Islam is not rational.'

I then said to the interpreter:

'Say to the king:

'The religious law of the Muslims is not like that of the Christians. The Christian drinks wine with his food, instead of water, without getting drunk and this increases his strength.

'The Muslim, on the other hand, drinks wine only in order to get as drunk as possible. He loses his reason, goes mad, commits adultery, kills, blasphemes and commits acts of impiety. There is nothing good about it. He hands over his horse and arms, and wastes all he has, simply in order to seek pleasure.

'The Muslims here are your soldiers. If you send them out on campaign, they will have no horses, arms or money, because they will have thrown them all away on drink. And you, when you learn of it, will have to kill them or beat them or drive them out, or give them new horses and weapons, which they will lose in the same way.

'As regards slave concubines and legitimate wives, sexual intercourse suits the Muslims because they are of a passionate temperament. Furthermore, given that they make up your army, the more sons they have, the more soldiers for you.'

At this the king said:

'Listen to this sheikh! What a wise man he is. Marry as often as you like and do what he says.'

In this way, the king, who loved the Muslims, clashed with the Christian priests and allowed the taking of slave concubines.

The author's son

I left my eldest son, Hāmid, there among them. When I left him, he was more than thirty years old. He married two women, the daughters of respectable Muslims, and was blessed with children. He was brave and generous. When he was a child, I gave him half a *dānaq* for each precept that he learned by heart.

Wild cows

In Bāshghird there are wild cows as big as elephants. It takes two strong mules to carry the skin of one and a head makes up a full cartload. They hunt them and call them *thaytal*.[30] They are marvellous animals. Their flesh is fat and excellent; their horns as long and large as an elephant's tusks.

The bones of giants

I also saw in those lands many tombs of the people of 'Ād. They dug out half the root of one middle incisor for me and it measured a palm in width and weighed 1,200 *mithqāl*s. They also got me the knob of a wrist bone from another tomb, and I could not lift that bone from the earth with one hand.

The building of Iram and the ten thousand giants

In his book, entitled *Siyar al-mulūk* [*Lives of the Kings*], al-Shu'bī[31] says that when Shaddād ibn 'Ād built the city of Iram Dhāt al-'Imād, he sent his cousin al-Dahhāk ibn 'Alwān ibn 'Ād ibn Iram ibn Sām, accompanied by ten thousand giants, to Iraq and Khurāsān.

With them went a believer, a disciple of Hūd – may peace be upon him! – called Lām ibn 'Āmir ibn 'Ād ibn Iram. But al-Dahhāk intimidated him and Lām was afraid of him, for he had urged him to cease his tyranny, impiety and corruption. Al-Dahhāk said to him:

'You have disobeyed the king and you have embraced the religion of Hūd.'

Then Lām, through fear of al-Dahhāk, departed and wandered far to the north of Rome the Great, until he came to steppes where there was not one human soul. There he found a mine of lead with which he built himself a domed tomb, 4,000 cubits in circumference and 1,000 cubits high, in which he was buried.

Meanwhile, al-Dahhāk, when he realized Lām was missing, sent two of his commanders to search for him, each with an army of followers. One of the commanders reached Bulghār and the other Bāshghird, seeking throughout the countries of the north, but without finding any trace of him.

Al-Dahhāk was assassinated and the giants remained in Bulghār and Bāshghird, where their tombs are to be found. As to the dome of lead that Lām ibn 'Āmir built over his tomb, it bears a stone tablet with these verses written on it:

> I am Lām ibn 'Āmir, he who replaced
> The darkness of polytheism with purity,
> Saying: 'There is no God but He,
> My Lord, Who is my refuge.'
> Al-Dahhāk and the infidels demanded
> That I should follow them, erring and in blindness,
> But I left the land with all my people and abandoned
> My walled courtyards and campsites.
> I believed in God, the Lord of Idrīs
> And of Noah, and I was certain divine vengeance was to come.
> I lived long years in the wilderness,
> Afraid and fleeing from those who rebelled against God.
> This tomb that you see before you, I built
> With the help of God, the Powerful, of sheets of lead.
> I ordered that my sons should bury me,

Here within, clad in my tunics and robes.
In future ages, there will come to me an envoy,
One of the noblest of the Banū Hāshim.
You are merciful, generous and compassionate
With the orphans and the hungering poor.
Would that I might have lived to see him
To fulfil my desires and the merit of the elect.

A giant in Bulghār

In Bulghār, I saw a man of the race of 'Ād, more than seven cubits tall. I came up to his waist. He was so strong that he could take the leg of a horse that had just been slaughtered, and in a moment, at great speed, break the bone and cut through the skin and nerves. Even with an axe, I would not have been able to do it so quickly.

The king of Bulghār had a cuirass made for him, which he carried to battle with him in a cart, and an iron helmet like a great cauldron. He fought with a great wooden mace, thick and long, made from a massive oak which no man could lift, but in his hand it was like a stick would be in ours. The Turks respected and went in awe of him, and when they saw him coming towards them, they gave themselves up, saying:

'Our lord is angry with us.'

Nevertheless, he was amiable, modest and in no way quarrelsome. In the whole of Bulghār there was no bathhouse in which he would fit, except one, that was very spacious with high doors.

In Bulghār in the year 530 (1136) I saw a man of the race of 'Ād, more than seven cubits tall. He was called Danqa. He was so strong that he could carry a horse under his arm as if it were a goat. He could also crush the leg of a horse and cut through its nerves with his hand, as if it were a bundle of herbs. The king of Bulghār ordered a cuirass made for him, which he used

*to transport in a cart, and a helmet the size of a huge cauldron.
He fought with the trunk of an oak, which he brandished in his
right hand as if it were a walking stick. He could have killed an
elephant with a single blow. Despite all this he was an extremely
modest person. When we met – and my head didn't even reach
his belt – he used to greet me, make me welcome and heap
honours upon me – may God have mercy upon him!*

*There wasn't a bathhouse in the whole city big enough for
him to enter, except one, which had very big doors.*

*He was the most extraordinary man I have seen in my life.
He had a sister as big as he was, whom I saw several times in
Bulghār. In that city the* qādī *Ya'qūb ibn Nu'mān informed me
that this woman, so exceedingly tall, had killed her husband,
who was named Adam and was one of the strongest men in the
country. Clasping him to her bosom, she broke his ribs, killing
him instantly.*[32]

The author leaves Bāshghird

I asked the king of Bāshghird if he would let me go to the land
of the Muslims, to Saqsīn, saying:

'I have my children there, and my family and I will return to
you, if God wills.'

He replied:

'You will leave your eldest son Hāmid here and I will appoint
a Muslim envoy to go with you, to collect and bring back poor,
humble people, Muslims and Turks, who are good at shooting
arrows.'

And indeed, he wrote me a letter for the king of the Saqāliba
and sealed it with a seal of red gold that bore his effigy.

The person who was sent with me was a man called Ismā'īl
ibn Hasan, who had been one of my students and was the son
of one of those brave Muslim commanders who did not hesitate publicly to practise their religion. A group of his servants
and friends went with him.

Return to the land of the Saqāliba

When I reached the land of the Saqāliba, the king received us very well, thanks to the letter from the king of Bāshghird, of whom he was much afraid. We spent the winter there, and in spring set out for the land of the Turks heading in the direction of Saqsīn. 'Abd al-Karīm ibn Fayrūz al-Jawharī left with me, along with his wife and her children, who were from the land of the Saqāliba. He left her in Saqsīn and returned alone to the country of the Saqāliba.

Recruiting archers

I gathered a group of Muslims skilled at shooting arrows for the envoy of the king of Bāshghird. I sent along with them one of my students who already knew something of religious law and said to him:

'I am going to go on pilgrimage and, if God wills, I shall return to you by way of Konya.'

When they had left for Bāshghird, I set out on a month's voyage to the Caspian Sea heading for Khwārazm, where I had been before.

The fruits of Khwārazm

The country of Khwārazm extends for a hundred *farsakh*s. There are many cities, villages, farmsteads and fortresses. In some of them there are fruits, the like of which I have not seen in any of the other countries I have visited. There is a kind of watermelon sweeter and more delicious than sugar with honey, and another variety with a green rind speckled with black. The flesh inside is brilliant red, like a carnelian, and extremely sweet, firm and consistent. These melons weigh about ten *mann* each, more or less. They keep them in the houses during the winter and sell them in the markets.

Similarly, there are grapes, both red and white, as large as dates. They are picked in winter and are cheap. There are also apples, pears and pomegranates. They decorate the shops with these fruits at all seasons, but especially in the spring, and you would think they had just been picked in the orchard.

Encounters in Khwārazm

The people of Khwārazm are generous, good poets and noble-minded. Their *khatīb* was al-Muwaffaq ibn Ahmad al-Makkī, who told me that he had met the vizier 'Awn al-Dīn.

'I have never,' he said 'among all the viziers and people of worth, met anyone as deserving, pious and generous as the vizier 'Awn al-Dīn.'

Someone else who came to see me and frequented my house, was a man called 'Abd al-Wāhid ibn Fayrūz al-Jawhari,[33] who had been in the service of the vizier and was deeply grateful to him.

Again, the sheikh and religious scholar Mahmūd al-Shāfi'ī, the imam of the *sunni* community, told me the following story:

'I was in Baghdād with the *khatīb* and we went to see 'Awn al-Dīn, the vizier, with a poem in praise of the Commander of the Faithful, and entered his presence. In the *dīwān*, they said to him:

'"You must stand while you read your poem in praise of the Commander of the Faithful."

'So the *khatīb* and I remained standing until he finished reading the poem that he had composed in praise of the Commander of the Faithful in the presence of 'Awn al-Dīn – may God prolong his glory!'

The enchanted mosque

In the region of Khwārazm, on the road to Saqsīn, some eight *farsakhs* from the city there is a marvel. There is a deep canyon in the mountains at the bottom of which is an artificial mound surmounted by a structure like a mosque, with a dome and four entrances with high porticoes. The mosque is covered with tiles of gold, clearly visible to anyone who stops to gaze at it. The mound is surrounded on all sides by stagnant water, fed by the rain or the snow in winter. Below the water, the bottom is clearly visible.

The water is roughly two cubits deep, judging it by eye. The surface is covered with pondweed and it smells bad. No one dares enter the water, or dip in a hand or foot, since anything which touches the surface of that water disappears and vanishes, and no one can see where it goes. The width of the expanse of water, again judging by eye, is about a hundred cubits.

Mahmūd, the lord of Ghazna, who was a powerful and victorious king, came to this place[34] and stayed there for some time. He had rowing boats brought, but when they were placed on that water, they disappeared. Then he ordered his troops to bring earth, canes, wood and stones, loading all the beasts of burden and the camels, and to throw it all into the water. But it all vanished. Then, he ordered them to inflate skins, animal hides and bladders of cows and sheep with air, but they too disappeared in the water without leaving a trace.

The king of Khwārazm, 'Alā' al-Dawla Khwārazmshāh[35] – may God have mercy on him! – also made every possible effort to reach the treasure, but achieved nothing.

They say that if an animal falls into this water, it never emerges again; even though men tie ropes to it and try to haul it out, they never succeed and it vanishes. On the other hand, if a strong man looses a wooden arrow, it can hit the gold. There is so much gold that it can never be counted and it is in full view; all the people who come there from Khwārazm can see it, and so can travellers and infidels, when they go to that place. But there is no stratagem to get hold of it, unless God wishes to allow it. It is one of the marvels of the world.

A jurisconsult from Khwārazm told me how a certain peasant entered the city and in the marketplace took out a bowl of green emerald, the like of which had never been seen. Taken into the presence of the Khwārazmshāh, the latter asked him:

'Where did you find this?'

'I went to see the treasure,' answered the peasant, 'and there I saw a great green dome, like this bowl. Under the dome, there was a tomb and the sarcophagus too was green, like this. Above the sarcophagus, there were great bowls, but I could not carry any of them, because of their size and weight, except for this one, which was the smallest I could find. I marked the door, leaving some stones as a sign.'

The Khwārazmshāh rode at once with his troops to the place the peasant had described, but he found nothing and said:

'These are the works of the Jinn!'

He gave the peasant some money, rewarded him and exempted him from taxes. That bowl was without price. Only God knows the truth!

The same Khwārazmshāh gave orders to dig a canal from the Oxus to reach that place, but he died before it was finished.

The author's apology

I have only mentioned, in a very abbreviated fashion, something of what I have seen, since if I had elaborated in any detail, it would have made the book much longer and this epitome is quite sufficient. If it had not been for the noble imams asking and begging me to gather the information together, I would not have undertaken this book, for I do not consider myself a writer.

Return to Baghdād

I left Bāshghird in the year 1153, and set off from Saqsīn for Khwārazm in 1154. I left Khwārazm to go on the pilgrimage in Rabī' I of the year 1155, in Shawwal ... [lacuna] I made the pilgrimage and returned to Baghdād, where my lord the vizier 'Awn al-Dīn, the glory of Islam, purest imam, the honour of mankind, support of the dynasty, the shield of the people, the crown of kings and sultans, the lord of all viziers, the foremost of East and West, the chosen of the caliphate, the right hand of the Commander of the Faithful – may God with His favour make eternal the suppression of the enemies of his government! – showed me favour and bestowed upon me so many robes of honour, so much money and other favours, that they can be neither counted nor set down.

He also obtained a letter for me from the caliph – may God prolong his protecting shadow over the two worlds, the East and the West, and overthrow and humiliate his enemies! – to the lord of Konya, the son of king Mas'ūd[36] – may God have mercy upon him! He in turn wrote a letter allowing me to pass through his territory on the way back to Bāshghird – if God on High should allow me to return and be reunited with my family,[37] something not difficult for God, indeed most easy, for He is All-Powerful.

Praise be to God, Lord of the Worlds! May God bless our Prophet Muhammad, seal of the Prophets, and all his friends, companions, wives and descendants. God suffices us, for He is the most excellent Protector!

PART III

PASSAGES FROM OTHER GEOGRAPHERS, HISTORIANS AND TRAVELLERS

1. Qudāma ibn Jaʿfar on Alexander in China 928–932

Qudāma (c. 883–948) was the author of a number of works on history and criticism. This extract is from Kitāb al-kharāj wa sināʿat al-kitāba *(The Book of the Land Tax and the Art of the Secretary), a handbook for government officials written 928–932.*

This account of Alexander/Dhū al-Qarnayn is typical of the Arabic versions of the Alexander Romance that occur in tenth-century histories, even to the alternation in the same text of the Qurʾānic Dhū al-Qarnayn, 'Possessor of the Two Horns', with Iskandar, 'Alexander'. The anachronisms need no comment. The historical Alexander (356–323 BC) 'contemporary with the Warring States period of Chinese history (475–221 BC) 'never reached China, while Qudāma describes the Tang (AD 618–907). The Turkic title tarkhān, *here used for the Tibetan nobility, occurs in the story of Sallām the Interpreter as the title of the 'king' of the Khazars.*

After Dhū al-Qarnayn had vanquished and killed Porus, king of India, he remained in India for seven months, but dispatched his armies to Tibet and China. Some of those he sent returned to tell him that all the kings of the east had agreed to submit to him and pay him tribute, having learned of his victories over Darius and Porus, the kings of Persia and India, and of his justness and noble conduct.

So he left one of his most loyal generals as his viceroy in India with 30,000 men and set off with the rest of his army for

Tibet. The king of Tibet came out to meet him, accompanied by his *tarkhān*s, and saluted him, saying:

'Oh king, I have learned of your justness and good faith towards your enemies after your victories over them, and this has proved to me that you are following God's will. I have been inspired to take your hand and not to fight you or defy you, convinced that anyone who opposes you opposes God, and will be vanquished. That is why I and my people and my empire submit to you. Tell us what you desire.'

Alexander [Iskandar] answered with kindness: 'Whoever acknowledges the rights of God obliges us to acknowledge his rights. I hope you will be pleased with our justness and good faith.'

He then asked to be guided to the Turks who inhabited the steppes, for the settled Turks had already submitted to him. The king of Tibet hastened to obey and offered gifts. Alexander only accepted them after much urging. They consisted of 4,000 ass-loads of gold, and the same amount of musk. Alexander gave a tenth part of the musk to his wife Roxana, the daughter of Darius, king of the Persians, and distributed the rest among his friends. The gold was deposited in the treasury.

Then Alexander asked the king of Tibet to precede him with his army on the road to China. The king of Tibet left his son Madābīk to govern his kingdom during his absence. Alexander also left him one of his generals with 10,000 men.

When they arrived on the border of China, the king of Tibet in the vanguard and Alexander following with the bulk of his army, the king of China came out to meet them at the head of ten battalions, each one numbering 100,000 men. He sent a message to Alexander, telling him that he had been informed of his good faith and noble actions, and because of this had no desire to fight, although he felt quite prepared to do so if Alexander wanted war. He asked Alexander to let him know which he preferred.

Alexander replied that the king of China must pay one-tenth of the revenues of his empire, just as the rulers of other countries had agreed to do when they submitted. If he refused,

Alexander would not quail before the armies of the king, but put his trust in God, who had the power to make a small army triumph over a large. Along with this message he sent a number of Indians and Persians, whom he asked to bear witness to his justness and good treatment.

The king of China immediately made his submission and asked Alexander if he could pay the tribute in white and coloured silk and other manufactured goods. Alexander agreed, and the king sent him 1,000,000 pieces of coloured silk and the same of white, 500,000 of damask silk [*kīmkāwa*], 10,000 saddles with stirrups, bridles, cinches and so forth, along with 1,000,000 *mann* of silver.

Alexander stayed in the country until he had finished building a city, called Stone Tower [Burj al-Hijāra]. He garrisoned it with 5,000 Persians under the command of one of his generals named Neoclides.

Then he turned to the north, still accompanied by the king of China, and conquered the land of Shūl. Then he turned his attention to the Turks of the steppes, who submitted. There he learned that there was a very numerous Turkic people to the north-west, who were harassing neighbouring countries with their invasions. Alexander consulted the king of China about them, and the king told him that the only booty worth taking from them were herd animals and iron. He said their country was a remote corner of the earth with the Green Sea, which no one can sail, to the north and very high and inaccessible mountains to the west and south. In fact, there was only one way out, a narrow defile like a corridor. If this corridor could be closed, they couldn't get out, and the world would be spared their ravages. Alexander immediately recognized the truth of this, and closed the defile with the wall[1] spoken of in the Qur'ān.

After having completed this task, Dhū al-Qarnayn returned by way of the land of the pagan Turks who live in towns and arrived in Soghdia, where he founded the cities of Samarqand, Dabūsīya and Alexandria the Farther. Continuing on this route, he came to Bukhārā, where he founded the city of the same name, then to the country of Merv, where he built the capital, then he founded the cities of Herat and Zarānj. He then passed through Jurjān and ordered the foundation of the cities of Rayy, Isfāhān and Hamadhān. He then went to Babylon, where he stayed for several years.

Qudāma ibn Ja'far (1889), 263–5

2. Ibn Khurradādhbih on Sallām the Interpreter and Alexander's Wall 844

Ibn Khurradādhbih (c. 820–c. 911) served for many years as director of the barīd, *the Abbasid postal and intelligence service. He was a friend the caliph Mu'tamid (reigned 870–892) and wrote on musical theory, literature and geography. His* Kitāb al-masālik wa'l-mamālik *(Book of Roads and Kingdoms) is the earliest surviving work of descriptive geography in Arabic. Later geographers, including Istakhrī, Ibn Hawqal and Muqaddasī, augmented and perfected this form by incorporating their own observations and those of knowledgeable travellers. We know from citations by later authors that we possess only an abridgement of his great work.*

This is what Sallām the Interpreter told me:

The caliph Wāthiq, having seen in a dream that the barrier raised by Dhū al-Qarnayn (Alexander the Great) between our lands and those of Gog Magog had been breached, sought for a person capable of going to that place and discovering what state it was in. Ashnās[2] said to him:

'No one is so suitable for the task as Sallām the Interpreter, who speaks thirty languages.'

Wāthiq summoned me and said:

'I want you to go to the barrier and examine it and tell me what you find.'

He gave me an escort of 50 strong young men, 5,000 dīnārs and 10,000 dirhams as the price of my blood. Each man received a personal allowance of 1,000 dirhams and a year's provisions. On the orders of the caliph, felt jackets covered

with leather were prepared for us, fur-lined boots and wooden
stirrups. Two hundred mules carried the provisions and water
necessary for the journey.

We set out from Samarra bearing a letter from Wāthiq
addressed to Ishāq ibn Ismā'īl, the governor of Armenia resid-
ing at Tiflis, asking him to help us on our journey. Ishāq gave
us a letter for the 'Master of the Throne'.[3] The latter wrote concerning us to the king of the Alans, and this king wrote to the
Fīlān-shāh, and he in turn to the *tarkhān*,[4] king of the Khazars.
Having reached the *tarkhān*, we stopped for a day and a night
and then we set out again, accompanied by five guides whom
this king gave us.

After having travelled for twenty-six days, our company
entered a land where the earth was black and gave off a rank
smell. Luckily, we had taken the precaution of providing ourselves with vinegar to combat the bad air. After ten days' march
across this country, we spent another twenty days passing
through ruined towns. We were told that they were the remains
of the towns previously invaded and devastated by the people
of Gog and Magog.

At last, we reached a number of fortresses built close to the
mountains, in one chain of which stands the Barrier. We found
people who spoke Arabic and Persian. They are Muslims and
know how to read the Qur'ān, and they have schools and mosques.
They asked us where we came from. On learning that we were the
envoys of the Commander of the Faithful, they exclaimed in
surprise:

'The Commander of the Faithful!'

'Yes,' we replied.

'Is he old or young?'

'He is young.'

Their amazement increased and they added:

'Where does he live?'

'In Iraq, in a city named Samarra [Surra-man-ra'a].'

'We have never heard of it,' they answered.

The distance between these fortresses varies from one to two
*farsakh*s.

Next we reached a city named Īkah (Hami), which is ten

*farsakh*s in circumference and has gates of iron which are closed by lowering them. Within the confines of this city there are fields and windmills. It is in this city that Dhū al-Qarnayn camped with his army. It is three days' march from there to the Barrier. Passing fortresses and small towns, on the third day one reaches the Barrier. The chain of mountains forms a circle. It is said that Gog and Magog are enclosed within. The people of Gog are taller than those of Magog; their heights vary between a cubit and a cubit and a half.[5]

Then, we reached a high mountain surrounded by fortifications. This is the Barrier of Gog Magog. There is a ravine 150 cubits wide through which these people used to sally forth to infest the earth, until it was sealed by Dhū al-Qarnayn. The Barrier was built in the following manner. First the earth was excavated to the depth of 30 cubits and foundations were laid, built of brass and iron, up to the level of the ground. Then, two enormous piers were raised, 25 cubits wide and 50 cubits high; at the base a projection jutted out 10 cubits beyond the gate, one on each slope of the mountain, to the right and the left of the ravine. The whole construction is made of iron bricks sheathed in brass, each of which is 1½ cubits long and 4 fingers thick. An iron lintel 120 cubits long and 5 wide rests on the two great piers, and its ends extend 10 cubits beyond them. This lintel supports masonry built of iron bricks sheathed in brass that rises out of sight to the summit of the mountain. I estimate the height to be roughly 60 cubits. It is crowned with thirty-seven iron crenellations, each armed with two horns that curve inward towards each other. Each crenel is 5 cubits long and 5 wide. The portal itself has double doors of iron, 50 cubits wide and 50 high and 5 thick. The uprights of the doors swivel on an axis that is in proportion to the lintel. The whole structure is so solid that not a breath of wind is felt either through the door or from the mountainside, as if it had been made in one single piece. On the portal, 25 cubits from the ground, there is a bolt 7 cubits long and a fathom round, and 5 cubits above the bolt there is a keyhole, even longer than the bolt itself, and the two wards are each 2 cubits long. Above the lock hangs a key 1½ cubits long and 4 spans in circumference, with

twelve iron teeth, each the thickness of a pestle. The chain
holding it is 8 cubits long and 4 spans round, and the ring by
which it is attached to the door is like the rings on a piece of
siege machinery. The threshold of the door is 10 cubits wide
and 100 cubits long, not including the part that runs under the
pillars. The part that juts out is 5 cubits wide. All these meas-
urements are given in the cubits known as 'black cubits'.

Near the gate there are two forts, 200 cubits square. To the
right and the left of their gates two trees have been planted and
a stream of fresh water runs between the two forts. The instruments that were used in the building of the wall are preserved in
one of the forts: enormous iron cauldrons, like those used for
making soap, iron ladles and tripods, each of which can support
four of these cauldrons. There are also the iron bricks left over
from the construction of the wall, fused together by rust.

The responsibility for guarding this gate is hereditary, like
the caliphate, and runs in the family of the commander of these
fortresses. He rides out every Monday and Thursday in the
early morning, followed by three men, each equipped with a
hammer. One of them climbs a ladder, which is leaning against
the door, and when he reaches the top step, he strikes the bolt
with his hammer. Then, if one applies one's ear to the door, one
hears a muted sound like a nest of wasps. Then everything falls
silent again. Towards midday, a second blow is given and the
same sound heard, but a little louder. In the afternoon, they
strike the bolt again, with the same result. The commander
only retires at sunset. The point of these blows is to tell those
on the other side of the door that the guards are at their posts
and to let them know that Gog and Magog have made no
attempt against the door.

Near this place there is a large fortified area, 10 *farsakhs*
wide and deep, in other words an area measuring 100 *farsakhs*
square.

Sallām said:

'Having accompanied the commander on one of these sorties,
I asked whether the gate had ever suffered any kind of damage.
I was told that there was only one small crack no bigger than a
thread.

' "Have you no fears concerning the door?"

' "None," they said. It is 5 Alexandrian cubits thick, each of which equals 1½ "black cubits".

'I took a knife from my boot and began to scratch the crack, from which I obtained half a dram of dust, which I tied in a handkerchief to show Wāthiq.

'On one of the panels of the door, there is an inscription in letters of iron, which gives the following words in the original language:

' "When the promise of my Lord comes, He will make it powder, and the promise of my Lord is true."[6]

'The general appearance of the building is strange, because the yellow layers of brass alternate with the black layers of iron, so that for the most part it is striped horizontally.

'It is still possible to see on the mountain the mould made for casting the doors; the place where the furnaces stood for blending the brass; the place where the tin and the copper were melted together; the cauldrons, apparently made of brass, each with three handles, together with their chains and hooks for the purpose of hauling the brass up to the top of the Barrier.

'We asked the guardians of the gate whether they had ever seen anyone of the race of Gog and Magog. They told us that one day they had seen several of them on top of the mountain, but a violent wind had thrown them back to their side. Seen at a distance, their height did not appear to be more than a span and a half.

'Seen from the outside, the mountain has no plateau or downward slope; it has absolutely no vegetation; there are no trees or plants to be seen; it stretches into the far distance, steep, smooth and white in colour.

'On our departure, we were escorted by guides who led us in the direction of Khurāsān. We crossed a country whose king is called al-Lub and then the kingdom of Tabānūyan, which pays taxes to the governor of Khurāsān. We spent several days at the residence of this prince. Then we continued on our journey. It took eight months to travel from the Barrier to Samarkand. On the way, we passed through Isbīshāb, Ushrūsana,[7] Bukhārā and Tirmidh, where we crossed the river of Balkh (Oxus). By the time we arrived at Nishapur, there were only fourteen of us left, having lost, either through death or sickness, twenty-two men on the way out and fourteen on the way back.

'We had been obliged to abandon the sick in villages along our route and bury the dead in their clothes. As regards provisions for the return journey, the garrisons of the forts had supplied us with everything we needed. At Nishapur, we went to 'Abd Allāh ibn Tāhir, who gave me 8,000 dirhams and distributed 500 to each of my companions. Furthermore, he allotted 5 dirhams a day to each horseman and 3 dirhams to each foot soldier, until we reached Rayy. We only had 23 mules left.

'When we reached Samarra, I presented myself before Wāthiq to tell him of our adventures and I showed him the iron dust that I had extracted from the door. The caliph gave thanks to Allāh and large sums were distributed in alms. Each of my men received a reward of 1,000 *dīnārs*. Our journey to the Barrier had taken sixteen months and the return had taken twelve months and odd days.'

First Sallām the Interpreter gave me a short summary of his journey, then he dictated the account in the form that he had presented to Wāthiq.

Ibn Khurradādhbih (1885), 162–70

3. Ibn Hayyān on the Viking attack on Seville 844

The chronicler Ibn Hayyān (987–1076) wrote the fullest and most reliable history of al-Andalus that we have. His Kitāb al-muqtabis, from which the following passage is taken, is based on earlier sources, carefully credited. Ahmad ibn Muhammad al-Rāzī (888–955) and his son ʿĪsā (d. 980), his sources for the Viking attack of 844, are among the earliest historians of al-Andalus. Their work survives largely because Ibn Hayyān incorporated passages in Muqtabis; the title means 'brands plucked from the fire', that is, selections from earlier authors, saved from oblivion.

News of the appearance of the fleet of the *majūs*, of the Norsemen[8] – may God curse them – from the Mediterranean[9] off the western coast of al-Andalus in the time of the *amīr* ʿAbd al-Rahmān ibn al-Hakam,[10] and their attack on his people and the great harm they did to his cities and to the Muslims, and how the *amīr* came to their aid and brought reparation, and what happened during this attack, insofar as we have been able to learn, for full knowledge belongs only to God, Whose ways are glorious.

Ahmad ibn Muhammad al-Rāzī said:

'At the end of the year 229/844, the ships of the Norsemen [*al-Urdumānīyīn*], who were known in al-Andalus as *majūs*, appeared off the western coast of al-Andalus, landing at Lisbon, their first point of entry to the forbidden lands. It was a Wednesday, the first day of Dhū al-Hijjah [20 August] in that year, and they remained there thirteen days, during which time they engaged in three battles with the Muslims. Next, they went on to Cádiz and after that to Medina Sidonia. There a battle took place with the Muslims, at which Lubb ibn Mūsā was present, having received a safe-conduct from the *amīr* 'Abd al-Rahmān. He had received a letter from Wahb Allāh ibn Hazm, the governor of Lisbon, telling him that along his stretch of coast 54 ships of the *majū*s had appeared, with 54 smaller craft and their crews, and that the *amīr* had immediately sent out letters to the governors of the coastal regions so that they might be warned to be on their guard.

'On Wednesday, after the fourteenth night of the month of Muharram in the year 230/1 October 844, the ships of the Norsemen halted at Seville, which was undefended. That day they plundered all they could, taking advantage of the negligence of its inhabitants. As soon as the news reached the *amīr*, 'Abd al-Rahmān immediately sent his cavalry to the river,[11] led by 'Abd-Allāh ibn Kulayb, Muhammad ibn Sa'īd ibn Rustum and 'Abd al-Wāhid bin Yazīd al-Iskandarānī. They occupied the Aljarafe[12] and camped there. Later they were reinforced by 'Abd Allāh ibn al-Mundhir and 'Isa ibn Shuhayd with a party of men who had joined them. They sent letters to the governors, telling them to proclaim a general call to arms to the Muslims to fight off these unexpected tyrants, whose unprovoked attack on a defenceless region was without precedent. People gathered from all sides and rallied at Cordoba. At their head was the eunuch Abū al-Fath Nāsir, the favourite of the *amīr* 'Abd al-Rahmān, who hastened out with a great multitude and a very great show of force.

'Meanwhile, the Norsemen – may God curse them! – had arrived, ship after ship, and occupied the city of Seville. They spent seven days there, killing the men and enslaving the women and children, until the commanders arrived and clashed with them again and again, causing more and more casualties, until the death toll began to have an effect on them and it became clear that they had been defeated.

'The greatest battle against them took place on a Wednesday, when there were five nights left of the month of Safar in the year 230/11 November 844 at the village of Tejada, near

Seville. God destroyed many of them and they died there, and 30 of their ships were burned and many of the dead were hung from posts and others from the trunks of the palm trees of Seville. From the day that they entered Seville and overcame its inhabitants to the day of their defeat and the final departure of the survivors was 40 days. God caused their leader to die and reduced their numbers and news of the victory was sent to the provinces, not only in al-Andalus, but also to the Berber *amīr*s of the North African coast, to 'Aflah ibn 'Abd al-Wahhāb, the lord of Tahert and client of the Umayyads, and to others. They were sent the heads of the leader and his two hundred paladins. God calmed the agitation of al-Andalus, which had shuddered at such audacity against its people and the defiance of its power, and dispelled its fear.'

'Īsā ibn Ahmad al-Rāzī, remarking on this news, said:

'The fleet of the Norsemen – may God destroy them! – coming from the Western Sea, which is adjacent to them, seized Seville at the beginning of the year 230/September 844.

'The first point at which they disembarked was the Island of Qabtīl (Isla Menor), some way up the river, a place dedicated to horse breeding. They disembarked on the Sunday, 12 nights after the beginning of Muharram, in the year 230/29 September 844, and their ships were 80 in number. On the second day after their arrival, four ships were sent off to Coria (del Rio), which stands on the banks of the river, to the west of the city, inhabited by Yemeni Arabs from Yahsub, known as the Banī Ma'dī, four miles from the place where they disembarked at Qabtīl. They immediately sacked the village and killed everyone they encountered there in a great attack, the first that they carried out against the Muslims. This village has continued to be a *ribāt* and during the reign of the caliph 'Abd al-Rahmān III,[13] a congregational mosque was built there, because formerly it did not have a place for prayers.

'Then, on Wednesday, the third day after their arrival, the Norsemen – may God curse them – left the village of Qabtīl and set out in the direction of the city of Seville. When they reached the Church of the Water [*Kanīsat al-Mā*], two *farsakh*s from the city, and were already close, the Muslims of the city and others who joined them decided to fight off the infidels. They sallied out against them, filled with great courage and determination, but without discipline. They had no designated leader, not even a standard-bearer, because the governor had deserted and fled to the city of Carmona, leaving them with no support on which they could rely. When the Norsemen approached the town from the river, the weakness of the people and their diminishing numbers were clear to them, so they set out in their ships after them, shooting flight after flight of arrows against them, so that they scattered. Then they disembarked and fought them on the river-bank, most vigorously and with relentless pressure, so that the Sevillians were put to flight and none of them stood their ground. Most of them fled back to the city, each going his own way, trying to escape, for the Norsemen burst upon them, attacking any who remained, people who were weak or stubborn, and the wives and children of those who fled, killing, seizing and enslaving. They remained in the city seven days, looting and showing no respect for what is sacred.

'Then, when eight nights of the month of Muharram remained [9 October], they set out, laden with their booty and loaded it on to their ships. They returned to their original encampment on the Island of Qabṭīl, where they remained for several days. They allowed the ransom of prisoners and children, but at the same time they were enraged against the inhabitants of the city who had fled, so they returned to the attack, determined to exterminate them. The people, however, were prudent and did not return, nor appear at all. When the Norsemen got to the city, they found not a soul there, except for a small number of fugitives who tried to defend themselves in a mosque. They were surrounded and all were killed, for which reason it came to be known thenceforth as the "Mosque of the Martyrs".

'News soon reached the *amīr* 'Abd al-Rahmān. He was very angry and sent letters to the districts and frontiers, telling them to mobilize their people and hasten to come from all parts. The first measures were taken by Muhammad ibn Saʿīd ibn Rustum, who set out for Seville with a troop of horsemen, who quickly reached the district where the Norsemen were established and began to set traps for them. They set up an ambush at a place called Tablada, two miles south of Seville, next to the river. Ibn Rustum sent some of his swiftest men, chosen from among the frontier guards and others to head for the city and provoke skirmishes with the Norsemen, who were occupying it. This was on a Friday, when nine nights remained of the month of Safar in the year 230/7 November 844. The Norsemen, seeing that the attackers were few in number, hurled themselves against them; they moved their ships down the river in parallel and disembarked in great numbers to fight and pursue them until they reached the village of Tejada, where the commander Muhammad ibn Saʿīd ibn Rustum and the bulk of his troops lay in ambush.

'When the Norsemen had gone past them, the Muslims sallied out against them. The Muslims who were fleeing suddenly turned back against their pursuers, who gave up the chase, dismayed at what had happened. They suffered a terrible defeat, in which God awarded their heads to the Muslims. More than a thousand barbarians were killed and four hundred captured. Only those who hastened to the ships, fleeing and terrified, escaped. They embarked and defended themselves from on board, abandoning 30 ships, left undefended by their crews, who were either dead or captive. Ibn Rustum halted before them, ordering that the captives should be beheaded in front of their companions, which increased their terror. Meanwhile, the Muslims took possession of their empty ships and burned them all.

'The enemies of God, shamefully defeated, withdrew. Thanks be to God!'

Ibn Hayyān (1999), 185v–186v

4. Zuhrī on Viking ships c. 1160

Abū 'Abd Allah Muhammad ibn Abī Bakr al-Zuhrī (d. between 1154 and 1161) was an Andalusian cosmographer about whom almost nothing is known. He was a contemporary of al-Idrīsī (d. 1165) and Abū Hāmid al-Gharnātī (d. 1169). His Kitāb al-ja'farīya (Book of Geography) is based on earlier written sources, some of which have not survived. This passage describes a Viking longboat.

There used to come from this sea [the Atlantic] large ships which the people of al-Andalus called *qarāqīr*. They were big ships with square sails, and could sail either forwards or backwards. They were manned by men called *majūs*, who were fierce, brave and strong, and excellent seamen. When they attacked, the coastal peoples fled for fear of them. They only appeared every six or seven years, never in less than 40 ships and sometimes up to 100. They overcame anyone they met at sea, robbed them and took them captive.

Zuhrī (1968), 215 [§ 240]

5. Ibn Khurradādhbih on the routes of the Rādhānīya and the Rūs c. 830

For Ibn Khurradādhbih, see headnote to III: 2. This passage is the earliest description of the sea and land routes linking Europe with China, and the Jewish and Scandinavian merchants who engaged in long-distance trade in the ninth century. Ibn Khurradādhbih wrote between 846 and 885, but it is possible that this account dates from the first decades of the ninth century. As it reads like an intelligence report, it may come from the archives of the barīd.

The routes of the Jewish merchants called al-Rādhānīya:

These merchants speak Arabic, Persian, Greek, Latin, Frankish, Andalusian and Slavic. They journey from west to east, from east to west, travelling by land and by sea. From the west they export eunuchs, young girls and boys, brocade, beaver pelts, marten and other furs and swords.

They set sail from the Mediterranean coast of the land of the Franks [Firānja] and head for Faramā in Egypt. There they transfer their merchandise to the backs of camels and travel to Qulzum on the Red Sea, a distance of 25 *farsakh*s. They sail down the Red Sea to al-Jār, the port of Medina, and to Jiddah, the port of Mecca. Then they continue on to Sind, India and China.

They return from China with musk, aloe wood, camphor, cinnamon and other eastern products, docking at Qulzum, then proceed to Faramā, whence they once more set sail on the Mediterreanean Sea.

Some head for Constantinople to sell their goods to the Byzantines. Others go to the palace of the king of the Franks.

Sometimes these Jewish merchants set sail on the Mediterranean from the land of the Franks to Antioch. They then proceed overland to al-Jābiya (al-Hānaya) on the Euphrates, a journey of three days. They sail down the Euphrates to Baghdād, then down the Tigris to al-Ubulla, whence they sail down the Arabian Gulf to Oman, Sind, India and China.

The routes of the Rūs merchants are as follows:

The Rūs, one of the Saqāliba people, journey from the farthest reaches of the land of the Slavs [Saqlab] to the eastern Mediterranean and there sell beaver and black fox pelts, as well as swords. The Byzantine ruler levies a ten per cent duty on their merchandise. On their return they go by sea to Samkarsh,[14] the city of the Jews, and from there make their way back to Slavic territory.

They also follow another route, descending the River Tanais (Don), the river of the Saqāliba, and passing by Khamlīj,[15] the capital of the Khazars, where the ruler of the country levies a ten per cent duty. There they embark upon the Caspian Sea, heading for a point they know. This sea is 500 *farsakh*s long. Sometimes they transport their merchandise on camel back from the city of Jurjān to Baghdād. There, Slavic-speaking eunuchs interpret for them. They pretend to be Christians and, like them, pay the poll tax.

The overland routes of the Rādhānīya are as follows:

The Jewish merchants also follow a land route. Merchants departing from Spain or France sail to southern Morocco and then to Tangier, from where they set off for Ifriqiyya and then the Egyptian capital. From there they head towards Ramla, visit Damascus, Kufa, Baghdād and Basra, then cross the Ahwaz, Persia, Kirman, Sind and India, and finally arrive in China.

Sometimes they take a route north of Rome, heading for Khamlīj via the lands of the Saqāliba. Khamlīj is the Khazar capital. They sail the Caspian Sea, make their way to Balkh, from there to Transoxiana, then to the *yurt*[16] of the Toghuzghuz, and from there to China.

Ibn Khurradādhbih (1885), 153–5

6. Ibn al-Faqīh on the Rādhānīya 903

Nothing is known of this author except that he was born in Hamadan. The passage is taken from his Kitāb al-buldān (Book of Countries), *which from internal evidence can be dated to 903. The surviving manuscripts, one of which is the Mashhad manuscript which also contains* Book of Ibn Fadlān, *are all abridgements of a much longer original. Although Ibn al-Faqīh is clearly following Ibn Khurradādhbih here, there are significant differences between their accounts of the Rādhānīya merchants, most notably Ibn al-Faqīh's replacement of* Rūs *by* Saqālib.

Someone relates that it is stated in the Torah: 'Rayy is one of the ports of the earth and the place of commerce for mankind.'

According to Muhammad ibn Ishāq,[17] Rayy has a fine climate and its buildings are marvellous. It is the gate of commerce, the refuge of libertines, the bridegroom of the earth, the highway of the world. It lies mid-way between Khurāsān, Jurjān, Iraq and Tabaristān. It is the most beautiful creation on earth. It has the Surr and Sarbān quarters, and to it flows merchandise from Armenia, Azerbaijan, Khurāsān, Khazaria and the country of the Burjān (Bulghārs).

Merchants sail from east to west and west to east, carrying brocades [*dībāj*] and fine quality silk [*khazz*] from the land of the Franks[18] [Firanja] to al-Faramā. Then they sail from Qulzum and cross the sea to China, carrying these products. Then they carry cinnamon and celadon [*māmīrān*] and all the products of China until they come back to Qulzum and cross [the isthmus of Suez] to al-Faramā.

These are the Jewish merchants called Rādhānīya.[19] They speak Persian, Greek, Arabic and Frankish. They embark from al-Faramā and sell the musk and aloes wood as well as everything they have brought with them from the kingdom of the Franks. Then they come to Antioch, then go to Baghdād and then to al-Ubulla.

As for the Saqālib merchants, they bring fox and beaver pelts from the depths of their country to the Mediterranean, where the Byzantine king imposes a ten per cent tax on them. Then they go by sea to Samkarsh of the Jews. From there, they either go on to the Saqāliba or take the way from the sea of the Saqāliba to the river of the Saqāliba (Volga), until they come to the gulf of the Khazars, where the ruler imposes a tax of ten per cent. Then they go to the sea of Khurāsān (Caspian), usually disembarking at Jurjān, where they sell all their goods, which are then sent to Rayy, and the most amazing thing is that this is the emporium of the world.

Ibn al-Faqīh (1885), 270–71

7. Ibn Khurradādhbih on exports from the western Mediterranean 885

For Ibn Khurradādhbih, see headnote to III: 2.

The goods that are exported from the western Mediterranean are Saqālib eunuchs and Roman, Frankish and Langobard slaves, and Roman and Andalusian slave girls, and beaver pelts and other furs, aromatics such as storax, and drugs such as mastic. From the sea floor near France comes the substance called *bussadh*, commonly known as coral.

Ibn Khurradādhbih (1885), 92

8. Ibn Rusta on the
Khazars 903–913

Ibn Rusta was a native of Isfāhān and made the pilgrimage to Mecca in 903. He wrote a seven-volume encyclopedia of historical and geographical knowledge, completed in 913, of which only one volume survives. Ibn Rusta seems to have had access to a more complete version of Ibn Khurradādhbih than any that we have, and it is possible that the material here comes from that or perhaps from the lost work of Jayhānī. The information Ibn Rusta gives on the Khazars and other peoples north of the Caucasus is thought to come from an anonymous source probably composed c. 860.

Between the Pečenegs and the Khazars is a journey of ten days through steppe lands and forests. There is no main road or beaten track between them and the Khazars; there is only this route through forests and thickets, until they reach the country of the Khazars.

The country of the Khazars is extensive. On one side is a great mountain [chain: Caucasus] and it is the same mountain [chain] that slopes down, at its far end, to Tūlās and Abkhaz. This mountain [chain] reaches to the region of Tiflis.

They have a king called the *īshā*,[20] and a greater king called Khazar *khāqān*. Though he has this name, the Khazars do not take orders from him. The *īshā* has the power to command and the control of the army, and answers to no higher authority. Their supreme authority [the Khazar *khāqān*] is Jewish, and so is the *īshā* and those commanding officers and important men who support him. The rest of them follow a religion like the religion of the Turks.

Their city is Sārighshin and nearby is another city called [Khanbaligh?].[21] The inhabitants dwell in these two cities during the winter, but in the spring go out to the steppe and stay there until the onset of winter.

There are Muslims in these two cities. They have mosques, imams, muezzins and Qur'ān schools.

Their king, the *īshā*, imposes a levy of cavalry on the people of power and wealth, in accordance with their wealth and means. They raid the Pečenegs every year. This *īshā* leads the expedition himself, going with his men on raids. They present a handsome spectacle. When they go out in any direction, they go out fully armed, with banners, lances and strong coats of mail. He rides with 10,000 horsemen, some regular troops, others levied on the wealthy. When he goes in any direction, a sort of disk, like a drum, is carried in front of him. A horseman bears it before him and he follows leading the army, who can see the light reflected from the disk. When they take booty, it is gathered together in his camp and the *īshā* takes what he likes for himself, leaving the rest to be divided among the troops.

Ibn Rusta (1892), 139–40

9. Ibn Rusta on
the Burtās 903–913

For Ibn Rusta, see headnote to III: 8.

The lands of the Burdās (Burtās) are located between the lands of the Khazars and those of the Bulkār (Bulghār). They are fifteen days' march from the land of the Khazars.

They obey the king of the Khazars and supply him with 10,000 horsemen.

They recognize the authority of no chief. Instead, in each community are found one or two old men whose opinion they seek when quarrels arise. In principle, however, they submit to the king of the Khazars.

Their lands are vast and they live in forests. They periodically raid the territories of the Bulkār and the Pečeneg. They are valiant and brave.

Their religion is like the religion of the Ghuzz (Oguz).

They are handsome, good-looking and well-built.

If one of them quarrels with another, or suffers an injustice or an intentional or unintentional wound, no reconciliation between them is possible until the injured party has taken vengeance.

When a girl reaches marriageable age, she is no longer under the authority of her father and can choose any man she wants. The man comes and asks the father for her hand, and her father says yes or no according to the wishes of his daughter.

They have camels and cattle and lots of honey. Most of their wealth comes from marten pelts [*dalaq*].

They are divided into two types, one of which burns their dead and the other inters them.

Their lands are flat and most of their forests are *khalanj* trees. They cultivate fields, but most of their wealth comes from marten pelts and wool [*wabar*].

Their territory is seventeen days' march in length and breadth.

Ibn Rusta (1892), 140–41

10. *Ibn Rusta on the Bulkārs 903–913*

For Ibn Rusta, see headnote to III: 8. See also headnote to III: 11.

The Bulkārs (Bulghārs) border the lands of the Burdās (Burtās). They are camped on the bank of a river that flows into the Khazar Sea (Caspian) and is called the Itil (Volga). They live between the Khazars and the Saqāliba. Their ruler, called Alm-ish, is a Muslim. The region is marshy and thickly forested, in the middle of which camps the population.

They are composed of three hordes, the Barsūlā, the Isghil (Askel) and the Bulkārs, all living together in one place. They trade with the Khazars and the Rūsīya (Rūs), who bring their merchandise to them. The Bulkārs, who live on both banks of the Itil, offer various products in exchange, such as the pelts of sable, ermine and grey squirrel and other furs. They are an agricultural people, who grow all sorts of grain, wheat, barley and millet. The majority are Muslim and there are mosques and Qur'ān schools in their inhabited places. They have muezzins and imāms.

The infidels have the custom of prostrating themselves when they meet their friends.

These Bulkārs are camped three days' march from the Burdās, whom they raid frequently and bring back as captives. They have horses and coats of mail and their arms are superb. They pay tribute to their ruler in the form of horses and the like. When a man marries, the king takes a horse. When Muslim ships come to them, a tax of ten per cent is levied on the merchandise.

They dress like the Muslims and their tombs are constructed like those of the Muslims.

Their wealth consists above all of marten pelts [*dalaq*]. They don't use hard cash [*amwāl al-sāmita*], since their unit of exchange is the marten pelt, which is worth 2½ dirhams. Sometimes they use round silver dirhams, which they receive from Muslim lands, in exchange for their wares. [Then they in turn use those dirhams to pay the Rūs and Saqāliba, for these peoples will only sell their goods for hard cash.][22]

Ibn Rusta (1892), 141–2

11. *Ibn Rusta on the Magyars 903–913*

For Ibn Rusta, see headnote to III: 8. Despite the variant spelling, the 'country of Iskil' must be the same as 'Isghil' in III: 10.

Between the country of the Pečenegs and the country of Iskil (Askel), which belongs to the Bulkārs (Bulghārs), lies the first of the Magyar frontiers. The Magyars (Majgharīya) are a race of Turks. Their chief rides at the head of 20,000 horsemen. He is named *kundah*, but the one who actually rules them is called *jilah*.[23] All the Magyars implicitly obey this ruler in wars of offence and defence.

They dwell in tents and move from place to place in search of pasturage. Their territory is vast, extending to the Black Sea, into which two rivers flow, one larger than the Oxus. Their campsites are located between these two rivers. During the winter, everyone camps by the nearest river. They stay there, living by fishing, because this is the best place to spend the winter.

The Magyar country is rich in wood and water. The land is well watered and harvests abundant. They lord it over all the Slavs who neighbour them and impose a heavy tribute on them. These Slavs are completely at their mercy, like prisoners.

The Magyars are pagans, worshipping fire. They make piratical raids on the Slavs and follow the coast [of the Black Sea] with their captives to a port in Byzantine territory named Karkh (Kerch).

It is said that the Khazars used to be protected from attack by the Magyars and other neighbouring peoples by a ditch.

When the Magyars bring their prisoners to Karkh, the Greeks go there to trade. The Magyars sell their slaves and buy Byzantine brocade, woollen rugs and other products of the Byzantine empire.

Ibn Rusta (1892), 142–3

12. Ibn Rusta on the Saqāliba 903–913

For Ibn Rusta, see headnote to III: 8.

It is ten days' march from the lands of the Pečenegs to the lands of the Saqāliba. The first town encountered after crossing the frontier is Wabnīt.²⁴ To reach it, one crosses steppe and trackless wilderness, with springs and thick forest. The country where the Saqāliba dwell is flat and heavily forested. There are no vineyards or cultivated fields. They have a sort of wooden box, provided with holes, in which bees live and make their honey; in their language they are called *ulīshaj*. They collect around ten jars of honey from each box. They herd pigs as if they were sheep.

They burn their dead. When a woman dies, they cut her hands and face with a knife. The day after the funeral of a man, after he has been burned, they collect the ashes and put them in an urn, which is buried on a hill. After a year, they place twenty hives, more or less, on the hill. The family gathers and eats and drinks there and then everyone goes home. If the dead man had three wives, and one of them says she loved him, she raises two posts near the tomb, and sets another horizontally across them. To this cross beam she attaches a rope and ties the other end round her neck. When these preparations have been made, they remove the stool she has been standing on and she strangles. Her body is then thrown in the fire and burnt.

They all worship fire. Their chief crop is millet. At harvest time, they place a few grains in a dish and hold it up to the sky, saying: 'Lord, it is you who give us our daily bread; continue to show us your benevolence.'

They have different kinds of lutes, pan pipes and flutes a cubit long. Their lutes have eight strings. They drink mead. They play their instruments during the incineration of their dead and claim that their rejoicing attests the mercy of the Lord to the dead.

They have very few mules, and even notables possess very few horses. Their arms are javelins, shields and lances; they have no others.

They obey a chief named *sūbanj*[25] and carry out his orders. He dwells in the middle of the land of the Saqāliba. Their supreme lord, called 'chief of chiefs', however, is named Svetopolk.[26] The *sūbanj* is his lieutenant and viceroy. This king has many cattle and lives exclusively on their milk. He has splendid, finely woven and effective coats of mail. The name of the town in which he lives is Graditsa.[27] For three days every month a great market is held there and every sort of commercial transaction takes place.

The extreme cold which afflicts the country is so harsh that the inhabitants are forced to construct underground dwellings, roofed with wood like a church and completely covered with earth. The head of the family builds one of these for his family and relatives. They bring firewood and stones, light the wood until the stones turn red hot and then throw water on them. The steam released warms the room and the inhabitants take off their clothes and live in this shelter till spring.

The ruler levies fixed taxes every year. Every man must supply one of his daughter's gowns. If he has a son, his clothing must be offered. If he has no children, he gives one of his wife's or concubine's robes. In this country thieves are strangled or exiled to Jīra (Yūrā?), the region most remote from this principality.

Ibn Rusta (1892), 143–5

13. Ibn Rusta on the Rūs 903–913

For Ibn Rusta, see headnote to III: 8.

The Rūs [Rūsīya] live on an island in a lake.[28] This island is three days' march across and consists of forest and thickets. It is pestilential and the soil is so damp that when a man steps on it, it quivers underfoot.

They have a ruler called *khāqān* Rūs. The Rūs raid the Saqāliba, sailing in their ships until they come upon them. They take them captive and sell them in Khazarān[29] and Bulkār (Bulghār). They have no cultivated fields and they live by pillaging the land of the Saqāliba.

When a son is born, the father throws a naked sword before him and says: 'I leave you no inheritance. All you possess is what you can gain with this sword.'

They have no dwellings, villages or cultivated fields. They earn their living by trading in sable, grey squirrel and other furs. They sell them for silver coins which they set in belts and wear round their waists.

Their clothing is always clean. The men wear gold bracelets. They treat their slaves well and dress them suitably, because for them they are an article of trade.

They have many cities. They are generous hosts, treating their guests well. Strangers who take refuge with them or visit them receive a warm welcome, and no one is allowed to harm them or treat them unjustly. A stranger who has a complaint or who has suffered an injustice is certain to find protectors and defenders.

They use 'Sulaymān' swords.[30] If an enemy makes war against them, they all attack together, and never break ranks. They form a single fist against the enemy, until they overcome them.

If one of them has a quarrel with another, it is referred to the ruler, who settles it as he sees fit. If they do not agree with his settlement, he orders the difference to be settled by single combat. The man with the sharpest sword wins.[31] The companions of the two adversaries come out and stand [watching] with their arms. The two men fight, and the winner imposes his will on his adversary.

In their lands they have medicine men who have power comparable to the gods, for they can order the sacrifice of women, men or horses to their creator. Anything ordered by these medicine men must faithfully be executed. Any medicine man can seize a man or animal, put a rope round his neck and hang him until he dies, saying that he is a sacrifice to God.

They have great stamina and endurance. They never quit the battlefield without having slaughtered their enemy. They take the women and enslave them. They are remarkable for their size, their physique and their bravery. They fight best on shipboard, not on horseback.

They use up to a hundred cubits of cloth to make their trousers. The man must wrap himself in the cloth and fasten it between his knees.[32]

They never go off alone to relieve themselves, but always with three companions to guard them, sword in hand, for they have little trust in one another. Treachery is endemic, and even a poor man can be envied by a comrade, who will not hesitate to kill him and rob him.

When a leading man dies, they dig a hole as big as a house in which they bury him dressed in his clothes and wearing his gold bracelet, accompanying the corpse with food, jars of wine and coins. They bury his favourite woman with him while she is still alive, shutting her inside the tomb and there she dies.

Ibn Rusta (1892), 145–7

14. Mas'ūdī on the Iron Gates 943

Mas'ūdī (d. 957) was born in Baghdad. He travelled widely, finally settling in Egypt in 941, where he completed the first draft of his universal history, Murūj al-dhahab wa ma'ādin al-jawhar *(The Meadows of Gold and Mines of Precious Gems) in 943, revising it in 947 and in 956. All surviving manuscripts are from the 947 edition, but the passages below were written in 943. See also headnote to III: 25.*

The Caucasus [Jabal al-Qabkh] is a great chain of mountains. This huge area contains a large number of kingdoms and peoples. There are no less than seventy-two different peoples, each with their own king and speaking a language different from their neighbours. The mountains are seamed with valleys and ravines. At the head of one of these passes is the city of Darband,[33] built by Chosroe Anushīrwān in a place between the mountains and the Sea of the Khazars (Caspian Sea). The same ruler built the wall of which one end extends for a mile into the sea and the other reaches into the Caucasus, following the rise and fall of the mountain crests and descending into the valleys for a distance of some forty *farsakh*s until it terminates at a fortified point called Tabarsarān. Every three miles or so, depending on the importance of the route upon which it opens, he placed an iron gate; nearby, inside the walls, guards were stationed to protect and watch that portion of the wall. This rampart formed an impassable barrier against the evil intentions of the peoples inhabiting the mountains, the Khazars,

Alans, various Turkish peoples, Avars [Al-Sarīr] and other infidel tribes.

The high peaks of the Caucasus cover such a large area that it would take two months or more to traverse their length or breadth. Only the Creator can number the peoples that live there. One of the passes through these mountains near Darband leads to the Sea of the Khazars, as we have said. Another, discussed earlier in this book, leads to the Black Sea, into which flows the channel of Constantinople. Trebizond is located on this sea. Every year many markets are held there, frequented by a large number of Muslim, Byzantine, Armenian and other merchants, without counting those who come from Circassia.

If God, Mighty and Exalted, had not, in His wisdom and great power and compassion for the perilous situation of His servants, aided the rulers of Iran in founding the city of Darband and constructing these ramparts, which extend both into the sea and over the mountains as we have said, and in building castles and establishing colonies ruled by properly constituted kings, there is no doubt that the rulers of Georgia, the Alans, the Avars, the Turks and other nations we have named would have invaded the territories of Bardha'a, Arrān, Baylaqān, Azerbaijan, Zanjān, Abhār, Qazwīn, Hamadān, Dīnawār, Nihāwand and the frontiers of the dependencies of Kūfa and Basra, thereby reaching Iraq, had God not blocked their advance in the way we have described.

This is especially true now that Islam has weakened and declined. The Byzantines are making inroads against the Muslims, the Pilgrimage is in peril,[34] Holy War has ceased, communications have been interrupted and roads are insecure. Every local military chief has taken power in his region and made himself independent, just as the 'Party Kings'[35] did after the death of Alexander the Great, until Ardashīr ibn Bābak, the Sāsānian, re-established political unity and put an end to endemic warfare, restoring security to the people and cultivation to the land. This lasted until Muhammad – may prayers and peace be upon him – received his mission from God and effaced the vestiges of unbelief and the traces of other doctrines. Islam has

always been triumphant, until this year 332/943, when under
the caliphate of the Commander of the Faithful Muttaqī,[36] its
supports are shaking and its foundations crumbling. We seek
help from God for the state we find ourselves in.

Mas'ūdī (1966), §§ 442–3, 504

15. Mas'ūdī on the Khazar capital 943

For Mas'ūdī, see headnote to III: 14.

The inhabitants of Darband are bordered by a people called Khaydhān, who form part of the Khazar nation. Their capital was formerly called Samandar, and lay eight days from Darband. It is now inhabited by Khazars, but when it was conquered in the early days of Islam by Salmān ibn Rabī'a al-Bāhilī,[37] the king moved the capital to Itil, seven days' journey away. This is where the Khazar king now resides. The town is divided into three parts by a large river which descends from the high plateaux of the land of the Turks. One branch flows towards the territory of the Bulgars and falls into the Sea of Azov.[38] Itil is built on both banks of the river, in the middle of which is an island which is the centre of government. The royal palace is located on one end of the island, which is linked by a bridge of boats to both banks of the river. The population is made up of Muslims, Christians, Jews and pagans.

Mas'ūdī (1966), § 447

16. Mas'ūdī on the Khazars 943

For Mas'ūdī, see headnote to III: 14.

The king, his court and all those of the Khazar race practise Judaism, to which the king of the Khazars was converted during the reign of Hārūn al-Rashīd.[39] Many Jews from Muslim and Byzantine cities came to settle among the Khazars, particularly since Romanus I,[40] the king of the Byzantines in our own time (332/943), forced the Jews in his kingdom to convert to Christianity. Further on in this volume we will give the history of the rulers of Byzantium, which we will set out in order, and will speak of this king as well as the two other rulers who shared power with him. A great number of Jews, therefore, fled from the land of the Byzantines and sought refuge with the Khazars. This is not the place to speak of the conversion of the Khazar ruler to Judaism, as we have already discussed this subject in our previous works.

The pagans who live in this country belong to many different races, among which are the Saqāliba and the Rūs, who live in one of the two parts of the city. They burn their dead on pyres along with their horses, arms and equipment. When a man dies, his wife is burned alive with him, but if the wife dies before her husband, the man does not suffer the same fate. If a man dies before marriage, he is given a posthumous wife. The women passionately want to be burned, because they believe they will enter Paradise. This is a custom, as we have already mentioned, that is current in India but with this difference: there, the woman is not burned unless she gives her consent.

The Muslims are dominant in the land of the Khazars because they make up the king's army. They are known by the name Arsīyya.[41] They originally came from the region around Khwarazm, and settled in the Khazar kingdom a long time ago, shortly after the appearance of Islam, when they fled the double ravages of famine and plague which devastated their homeland. These are strong, courageous men, in whom the king of the Khazars places his confidence in the wars which he wages. When they established themselves in his kingdom they stipulated, among other things, that they be allowed the free exercise of their religion, that they might have mosques and publicly give the call to prayer, and that the king's chief minister should be chosen from among their number. In our days the one who occupies this post is a Muslim named Ahmad ibn Kūyah. He has made an agreement with the king whereby he and his army will not fight against Muslims, but will march into battle against the infidel. Today, around 7,000 of them serve as the king's mounted archers. They carry a shield and wear helmets and chain mail. They also have lancers equipped and armed like other Muslim soldiers.

They also have their own *qādīs*. It is a rigid custom in the Khazar capital that there should be seven judges, two for the Muslims, two for the Khazars, who make their decisions in accordance with the Torah, two for the Christians, who make theirs according to the Gospels, and one for the Saqāliba, Rūs and other pagans. This last judge follows pagan law, which is the product of natural reason. When a serious case that the judges cannot decide comes up, the parties involved consult the Muslim *qādīs* and obey the decision made in accordance with Islamic law. The king of the Khazars is the only ruler of these eastern countries to have a paid army. All the Muslims who live in the country are known as Arsīyya.

The Rūs and the Saqāliba, who are pagans as we have said, served as mercenaries and slaves of the king. Besides the Arsīyya, there are also a certain number of Muslim merchants and artisans, who have emigrated to this country because of the justice and security with which the king rules. In addition to the congregational mosque, whose minaret towers over the king's palace, there are many other mosques to which are attached schools where the Qur'ān is taught to children. If the Muslims and the Christians united, the king would have no power over them.

Mas'ūdī (1966), § 448

17. Mas'ūdī on the khāqān of the Khazars 943

For Mas'ūdī, see headnote to III: 14.

What we have said so far about the king of the Khazars does not apply to the *khāqān*, whose official role consists of living in the palace of another king, confined in the inner apartments, from which he never emerges. He is not allowed to mount a horse or show himself to the courtiers or to the people. As he lives in the harem, he does not govern or take any part in state affairs. Despite this, the authority of the ruler would not be accepted without the presence of a *khāqān* in his palace in the capital. When the Khazars suffer a famine or some other disaster strikes their country, if the fortunes of war turn against them in favour of an enemy nation, or if any other catastrophe suddenly comes upon them, the people and the leading men go in a body to the king and say: 'This *khāqān* has brought us nothing but bad luck; his reign has brought only disaster. Put him to death, or let us kill him.' Sometimes the king hands him over and they kill him, or he kills him himself. At others, the king defends him, saying that he had committed no crime or fault that deserved such punishment. This is the present custom among the Khazars. I don't know if this institution goes back to ancient times, or is more recent, but the practice of always choosing the *khāqān* from the same family argues that the title goes back a long time.

Mas'ūdī (1966), § 453

18. Mas'ūdī on the Bulghārs 943

For Mas'ūdī, see headnote to III: 14.

The Khazars have ships which they sail on a river that flows, above their city, into the great river[42] which traverses it. This river is called the Burtās, and its banks are inhabited by many sedentary Turkish peoples who form part of the Khazar kingdom. Their settlements are continuous and extend from the land of the Khazars to the land of the Bulghārs. This river, which flows from the land of the Bulghārs, carries vessels from both kingdoms. Burtās,[43] as we have already said, is also the name of a Turkish people who live along the banks of this river, from which they have taken their name. The pelts of black and red foxes called *burtāsī* are exported from their country. Some of these furs, above all the black, are worth 100 dīnārs or more. The red furs are worth less. The black furs are worn by Arab and non-Arab kings, who esteem them more than they do sable, ermine and other similar furs. They make hats, caftans and fur coats out of them. There is no king who does not possess a fur coat or a caftan lined with the black fox fur of Burtās.

The upper reaches of the Khazar River (Volga) communicate by one of its branches with a gulf of the Sea of Pontus,[44] also called the 'Sea of the Rūs' because the Rūs, who are the only ones to sail it, live on one of its shores. They form a numerous pagan nation that doesn't recognize authority or revealed law. Many of their merchants trade with the Bulghārs. In their country the Rūs have a silver mine comparable to the one in the mountain of Banjhīr (Panjhīr) in Khurāsān.

The Bulghār capital is located on the Sea of Pontus.[45] If I am not mistaken, these peoples, who are a kind of Turk, inhabit the Seventh Clime.[46] Caravans continually pass back and forth between the Bulghārs and Khwarazm, which is a dependency of the kingdom of Khurāsān. Because the route passes through the encampments of other Turkish nomads, they are constrained to place themselves under their protection. At the present moment (332/943), the king of the Bulghārs is a Muslim, converted as the result of a dream during the caliphate of Muqtadir, sometime after the year 310/922. One of his sons has made the pilgrimage to Mecca, and when he passed through Baghdād the caliph gave him a standard, a black robe of honour and a gift of money. These people have a congregational mosque.

Their king[47] invaded the territories of Constantinople at the head of at least 50,000 cavalry. From there he dispatched expeditions which reached all the way to Rome, then to Spain, the territories of the Burgundians,[48] the Gallicians and the Franks. In order to reach Constantinople, this king had to travel two months along a route that passed through both cultivated and desert lands. In 312/924 a Muslim expedition set out from Tarsus on the Syrian frontier under the command of the eunuch Thamal, known as al-Dulafī, commander of the frontier. He was admiral of a fleet made up of vessels from Syria and Basra. After having crossed the mouth of the channel that leads to Constantinople and then another gulf of the Mediterranean (Adriatic), which has no outlet, the Muslims reached Venice.[49] A detachment of Bulghārs, who had travelled overland, joined them to reinforce them and told them that their king was a short distance away. This proves the truth of our statement that some units of the Bulghārian cavalry reached the Mediterranean coast. A number of them embarked on the ships from Tarsus and returned with them.

The Bulghārs are a large, powerful and warlike nation, which has subjected all the neighbouring peoples. One of the Bulghār cavalrymen, who had embraced Islam along with their king, held off one or even two hundred infidel horsemen. It is only thanks to their defensive walls that the inhabitants of

Constantinople are able to resist them. It is the same with all
those who live in this country; the only way they can defend
themselves from the attacks of these formidable enemies is by
fortresses and defensive walls.

Masʿūdī (1966), §§ 453–6

19. Mas'ūdī on the Land of
the Midnight Sun 943

For Mas'ūdī, see headnote to III: 14.

In the land of the Bulghārs the nights are extremely short during part of the year. They even say that between nightfall and dawn a man barely has time to bring his cooking pot to the boil. In our previous works we have explained this phenomenon from the astronomical point of view and have shown why, at a point on the earth in the polar regions, there are six consecutive months of darkness, succeeded by six months of daylight. The scientific explanation for this is given by the astronomers in their astronomical tables.

Mas'ūdī (1966), § 457

For Mas'ūdī, see headnote to III: 14.

The Saqāliba are descended from Mādhāy, the son of Japheth, the son of Noah and all the Saqāliba peoples derive their origins and trace their genealogies back to him, or at least this is the opinion of most of those who have devoted themselves to the question. The Saqāliba dwell in the north, whence they have spread westwards.

The Saqāliba are divided into several different peoples who war among themselves and have kings. Some of them belong to the Christian faith, being of the Jacobite sect, while the others are pagans and have no scripture and know nothing of divine law.

Among the different peoples who make up this pagan race, there is one that in ancient times held sovereign power. Their king was called Mājik[50] and they themselves were known as Walītābā.[51] In the past, all the Saqāliba recognized their superiority, because it was from among them that they chose the paramount ruler, and all the other chieftains considered themselves his vassals.

Among the Saqāliba peoples of the second rank should be mentioned in the following order the Istrāna, whose king in our own times is called Basqlābij; then the Dūlāba, whose present king is called Wānjslāf. Next are the Namjīn, whose king is called Gharānd; among all the Saqāliba these are the bravest and the best horsemen. After, come the Manābin, whose king is called Ratīmīr; the Sarbīn,[52] a Saqāliba people much feared for reasons that it would take too long to explain and whose deeds would need much too detailed an account. They have no particular religious affiliation.

Then there is the people called the Murāwa and another known as the Kharwātīn, and yet another called the Sāsīn, then the Khashānīn and the Barānijābīn.[53] The names of some of their kings which we have given are in fact dynastic titles.

The Sarbīn, whom we have just mentioned, have the custom of burning themselves alive when a king or chieftain dies. They also immolate his horses. These people have customs similar to those of the Indians.

Earlier in this work, we briefly mentioned this while discussing the Caucasus and the Khazars, we remarked that in the land of the Khazars there are, as well as the Khazars themselves, a Saqāliba and a Rūs population and that these last also immolate themselves. These Saqāliba and other related peoples extend to the east rather than to the west.[54]

The foremost of the Saqāliba kings is Aldayr,[55] whose domains include great cities and much cultivated land, vast troops and countless armies. Muslim merchants make their way to his capital with all kinds of merchandise.

After this, on the borders of this Saqāliba king, comes the king of Prague [al-afragh], who has a gold mine, towns, extensive well-cultivated lands, numerous soldiers and a large population. He is at war with the Byzantines, the Franks, the Bazkard[56] and other nations besides; the hostilities among them are continuous.

Neighbouring this king is the king of the Turks. These people are the handsomest, the most numerous and the most warlike of all. The Saqāliba comprise many different peoples and are very far-flung, but this work is not the place for a detailed description and classification of them.

I began by mentioning the king whose suzerainty has been recognized by all the other rulers since ancient times, that is to say Mājik, king of the Walītābā, who are the original, pure-blooded Saqāliba, the most highly honoured, and take precedence over all the other branches of the race.

Later, dissent having established itself among these peoples, their original organization was destroyed and the various families

formed isolated groups, each choosing a king, as we have said
above. An account of all these events would take too long, all the
more so, since I have already related them in a general way and
with great detail in my earlier works, the *Historical Annals* and
the *Intermediate History*.

Masʿūdī (1966), §§ 905–9

21. Mas'ūdī on the Rūs 943

For Mas'ūdī, see headnote to III: 14.

Sometime before the year 300/912–913, ships carrying thousands of men reached al-Andalus by sea and raided the Atlantic coasts. The people of al-Andalus claimed that these enemies were one of the nations of the *majūs*, who came to attack them by sea every two hundred years and that they reach their country by means of a channel which communicates with the Ocean.[57] This is not to be confused with the channel upon which is the bronze lighthouse.[58] Personally, I think – but God best knows the truth – that this channel communicates with the Sea of Azov and the Black Sea[59] and that the attackers were those Rūs we have already mentioned, since they are the only people who sail those seas that communicate with the Ocean.

Mas'ūdī (1966), §404

22. Mas'ūdī on a Viking raid
on the Caspian c. 913

For Mas'ūdī, see headnote to III: 14.

The Rūs are many nations, divided into different groups. One of them, the most numerous, is the al-Ludh'āna. They separate and travel far and wide, trading with al-Andalus, Rome, Constantinople and the Khazars.[60] It was just after the year 300/912–913 that some 500 of their ships, each manned by 100 men, entered the Strait of Pontus, which joins the river of the Khazars.[61] Men are posted there by the king of the Khazars and from their well-fortified positions, they are under orders to bar the way to anyone coming from the Sea of Pontus (Black Sea) or by land adjoining any branch of the river of the Khazars that communicates with the Sea of Pontus.

This is because the nomadic Ghuzz (Oguz) Turks set up their winter camps in these parts. As the watercourses that link the river of the Khazars with the Strait of Pontus are often frozen, the Ghuzz cross them with their horses, for there is so much water and it is frozen so solid that there is no danger of its breaking under their weight and thus they raid the land of the Khazars. On several occasions, the guards having failed to repel them, the king of the Khazars has been compelled to march out against them in force, so as to prevent them from crossing the ice, and thus he has saved his kingdom from invasion. In summer, there is no way the Turks would be able to cross.

When the Rūs vessels reached the Khazar checkpoint that guards the entrance to the strait, they sent to ask the king for permission to cross his kingdom and make their way down the river of the Khazars and so enter the Khazar Sea (Caspian Sea), which is also known by the names of the barbarian peoples who live by it – the Sea of Jurjān, the Sea of Tabaristān, and so forth, as we have already explained. The Rūs contracted to give the king half of anything they managed to pillage from the people along the shores of that sea. The ruler agreed to their request and they entered the strait and reached the mouth of the river (Don), continuing upstream until they reached the river of the Khazars. Then they went down the river, passed through the city of Itil, and at last arrived at its mouth, where it flows into the Khazar Sea. From the city of Itil to the mouth of the river [is a distance of . . .].[62] The river of the Khazars is wide and the volume of water it carries very great. The Rūs ships spread out across this sea. Raiding parties then rode against Jīl (Gilan), Daylam, Tabaristān and Ābaskūn on the coast of Jurjān. They invaded the lands of Naphtha [Bilād al-naffāta] and harried as far as Azerbaijan – indeed the city of Ardabil in Azerbaijan is three days' journey from the sea.

The Rūs spilled rivers of blood, seized women and children and property, raided and everywhere destroyed and burned. The people who lived on these shores were in turmoil, for they had never been attacked by an enemy from the sea, and their shores had only been visited by the ships of merchants and fishermen. Fighting ceaselessly with the people of Jīl, Daylam, the Jurjān coast, the frontier region of Bardha'a, Arrān, Baylaqān and Azerbaijan, and also against a general sent by Ibn Abī al-Sāj, the Rūs pushed on to the Naphtha coast, which is known by the name of Baku and forms part of the kingdom of Shirwān.

On returning from these expeditions, they took refuge among the islands only a few miles off the Naphtha coast. At that time, 'Ali ibn al-Haytham (reigned 913–917) was king of Sharwān. Troops were marshalled. They embarked on boats and merchant ships and set out for these islands. But the Rūs turned on them and thousands of Muslims were killed or drowned. The Rūs stayed many months doing the deeds we have described, without any of the peoples who live around this sea being able to oppose them. The inhabitants of these shores, which are very densely populated, did what they could to prepare themselves and remained in a state of high alert.

Gorged with loot and worn out with raiding, the Rūs returned to the mouth of the Khazar River and sent a message to the king of the Khazars together with the share of the spoils they had promised him. This prince has no ships and his subjects are not familiar with the art of navigation, otherwise it would have been a calamity for the Muslims.

Meanwhile, the Arsīyya and other Muslims who live in the lands of the Khazars learned what had happened and said to the Khazars: 'Let us do what we want to these people who have sacked the lands of our Muslim brothers, spilt their blood and dragged their women and children away into slavery.'

The king was unable to stop them, so he sent to the Rūs and warned them that the Muslims had decided to attack them. The Muslims gathered an army and went out to meet the Rūs going downstream. When the two armies were within sight of each other, the Rūs left their boats. The Muslims numbered about 15,000; they had horses and were well-equipped and they were accompanied by a certain number of Christians resident in Itil.

The two sides fought for at least three days and God gave the victory to the Muslims. The Rūs were put to the sword or drowned. The number killed on the banks of the Khazar River numbered 30,000. Some 5,000 managed to escape and crossed to the other side with their boats to Burtās,[63] or else abandoned their boats and entrusted themselves to dry land. Some of them were killed by the inhabitants of Burtās, others reached the Muslim Bulghārs, who massacred them. Some 30,000 were thus slain on the banks of the Khazar River. Since that time, the Rūs have never tried anything of the kind again.

Mas'ūdī (1966), §§ 458–62

23. Miskawayh on the Rūs
raid on Bardhaʿa 943

The Rūs made a number of raids on the Caspian in the tenth century. The philosopher and historian Miskawayh (932–1030) gives this vivid description, clearly based on eyewitness accounts, in his Tajārib al-umam *(Experiences of the Nations), a universal history. Bardhaʿa (Barda) in Azerbaijan was a large and important town, and the Rūs may well have intended to settle permanently there and use it as a base for trading and raids. Although Yaqūt says they occupied Bardhaʿa for a year, it is more likely that the events described below lasted a few months at most.*

In this year (332/943) the army of the Rūs invaded Azerbaijan, attacked and occupied Bardhaʿa[64] and took its inhabitants captive.

They are a formidable nation, the men huge and very courageous. They do not recognize defeat; no one turns back until he has killed or been killed. It is their custom for each to carry his weapons and hang tools on his body, such as an axe, a saw, a hammer and similar implements. The warrior fights with a lance and a shield. He carries a sword and a lance and a knife like a dagger. They fight on foot, especially these invaders. They crossed the sea [Caspian] which adjoins their country and sailed down to a great river called the River Kur, which rises in the mountains of Azerbaijan and Armenia and falls into that sea. The Kur flows through Bardhaʿa, and people compare it to the Tigris.

When they reached Bardhaʿa, they were confronted by

Marzubān [ibn Muhammad ibn Musāfir]'s lieutenant, the governor of Bardha'a, at the head of 300 Daylamites and about the same number of Su'luks and Kurds. He called the people to arms as well, and around 5,000 volunteers came forth to wage the *jihād* against the invaders. They didn't know the strength of the Rūs, and thought they would behave like Greeks or Armenians. An hour after battle was joined, the Rūs launched an attack that routed the army of Bardha'a. The volunteers and the rest of the soldiers turned and fled. Only the Daylamites stood their ground; they were all killed except for those mounted on horses. The Rūs chased the fleeing soldiers to the town. Everyone who could find a horse fled, leaving the town to be entered and occupied by the Rūs.

I was told by Abu al-'Abbās ibn Nudār and many other witnesses how the Rūs hurried into the town and tried to calm the people, proclaiming: 'There is no dispute between us on the matter of religion; we only want to rule. It is our obligation to treat you well and yours to be loyal to us.' The armies nevertheless attacked them from all sides, but the Rūs went out against them and defeated them. When the Muslims attacked the Rūs, the people of Bardha'a cried out *Allāhu akbar!*, and flung stones at the Rūs. The Rūs had ordered the people of Bardha'a not to take part in the battle between them and the government troops. This advice was followed by peace-loving men from the upper classes, but the common people and rabble could not control themselves. They showed their feelings by attacking the Rūs when the supporters of the government attacked.

After this had gone on for some time, the Rūs issued a proclamation that none of the inhabitants was to remain in the town, giving them three days to leave. The small number who had mounts to carry them, their womenfolk and their children left, but the bulk of the population remained. On the fourth day, the Rūs put them to the sword, killing a huge number, beyond counting.

After the massacre, they took captive over 10,000 men and boys with their womenfolk, their wives and their daughters. They held the women and children in a fortress within the city called Shahristān, which they had occupied, manned and fortified. Then they shut the men into the congregational mosque, set guards at the doors and demanded that the men ransom themselves.

A Christian civil servant named Ibn Sam'ūn, who lived in the city, acted as negotiator between the two sides. He made an agreement with the Rūs that each man should be ransomed for 20 dirhams. The more intelligent Muslims agreed to this arrangement, but the rest did not, maintaining that Ibn Sam'ūn was trying to imply that Muslims were of equal value to poll-tax-paying Christians. Ibn Sam'ūn therefore broke off negotiations. The Rūs put off their massacre, hoping to get at least this small amount. When it was not forthcoming, they put them to the sword, and slew them to the last man. A few escaped through a narrow conduit which conveyed water to the mosque, and some were able to buy their lives with valuables they carried.

In some cases a Muslim agreed with a Rūs to buy his life for a stated sum, and went with the Rūs to his house or shop. When he produced his wealth, and it turned out to be more than the amount agreed, the Rūs would not let him keep it, not even if it were many times the agreed payment, but kept raising his demands till he had ruined the man. The Rūs would only give him safe conduct when he was convinced that he had nothing left, no gold, silver, bedding or clothing. Only then would he let him go, giving him a piece of stamped clay as a safe conduct. Thus the Rūs gained a vast amount of booty. They kept the women and boys, whom they raped and enslaved.

When the scale of the calamity was realized, and the Muslims in the different regions heard about it, they demanded a combined expedition. Marzubān ibn Muhammad gathered his troops, and called for a general enlistment. Volunteers joined him from all directions. He marched at the head of 30,000 men, but in spite of the number of troops, he could not prevail against the Rūs or inflict any damage upon them. He attacked morning and evening, and regularly met defeat. The battle continued to be waged like this for many days, and the Muslims were always defeated.

When the Muslims found themselves unable to overcome the Rūs, Marzubān took stock of the situation, seeking some stratagem. Now it so happened that when the Rūs took Bardha'a, they over-indulged in the fruit of which Bardha'a produced numerous varieties. As a result, an epidemic broke out among the Rūs, as they come from a very cold country, where no trees grow, and the little fruit which they have is imported from distant regions. When their numbers began to decline, Marzubān decided on his stratagem, a night ambush. He ordered his army to make a quick attack. When the Rūs charged out, he and his followers would pretend to be routed, encouraging the Rūs to think they could annihilate the Muslim army. When the Rūs passed beyond the place where the ambush lay, Marzubān with his followers would turn around and charge, shouting out an agreed signal to the soldiers lying in ambush. When the Rūs were trapped between their two forces, the Muslims would have them at their mercy.

The morning after this scheme had been arranged, Marzubān with his followers marched out and took up their positions. The usual course of events followed. Marzubān and the Muslims fled, and were chased by the Rūs until they had got beyond the ambush point, but instead of turning around, the Muslims continued their flight.

Marzubān later told how when he saw his soldiers flee and that his desperate entreaties to get them to turn around and fight were unavailing, because of their terror of the Rūs, he realized that the Rūs, when they turned back, could not fail to notice the ambush, which would in consequence be destroyed. 'So,' he said, 'I turned back, with my personal attendants, my brother, my staff and my retainers, having made up my mind to die a martyr's death. Most of the Daylamites were then shamed into doing the same. We charged, crying out the signal to the men lying in ambush. They sprang forth behind the Rūs, fought them bravely and killed 700 of them, including their commander. The survivors retreated to the fortress in the town, where they had established their quarters and where they had stored food and supplies, and held their captives and their loot.'

While Marzubān was besieging them, with no other plan than to reduce them by a protracted siege, news reached him that Abū 'Abd Allāh Husayn ibn Sa'īd ibn Hamdān had entered

Azerbaijan and reached Salmas. There he had joined forces with Ja'far ibn Shakkuyah the Kurd, who was at the head of the Hadāyān tribes. Marzubān was therefore forced to leave one of his officers to fight the Rūs, along with 500 Daylamites, 1,500 Kurdish horsemen and 2,000 volunteers. He himself went to Awrān, where he met Abū 'Abd Allāh. An insignificant engagement took place during a heavy snowfall. The followers of Abū 'Abd Allāh, most of them Arabs, deserted him. He therefore made for one of the fortified cities, but on the way received a letter from his cousin Nāsir al-Dawla, informing him of the death of Tūzūn in Baghdād, and the desertion of Tūzūn's troops to himself, and of his determination to descend with them to Baghdād in order to fight Mu'izz al-Dawla, who had entered and taken possession of the city after Tūzūn's departure upstream. He therefore ordered Abū 'Abd Allāh to evacuate Azerbaijan and rejoin him, which he did.

The followers of Marzubān kept fighting and besieging the Rūs until the Rūs were exhausted. In addition, the epidemic became even more severe. When one of them died they buried him with his arms, clothes and equipment, along with his wife or another of his women, and his slave, if he happened to be fond of him, as was their custom. After they left, the Muslims dug up the graves and found a number of swords, which are in great demand to this day for their sharpness and excellence. When their numbers were reduced, they left the fortress in which they had established their quarters by night, carrying all the loot they could on their backs, including gems and fine raiment, and burning the rest. They dragged the women, boys and girls they wanted with them, and made for the Kur River, where the ships in which they had arrived from their homeland lay in readiness with their crews, along with 300 Rūs whom they had been supplying with portions of their booty. They embarked and departed, and God saved the Muslims from them.

I heard amazing stories from eyewitnesses of the prowess of these Rūs and their little regard for the Muslim forces mustered against them. Thus there was a story current in the region which I heard from many persons of how five Rūs were assembled in a garden in Bardha'a with some captive women. One of

them was a beardless youth with a fair face, the son of one
of their chieftains. When the Muslims found out they were
there, they surrounded the garden and a large number of Day-
lamite and others joined forces to fight these five. They tried
hard to take one of them prisoner, but it was not possible, for
none of them would surrender. The Rūs killed many times their
own number before they could be killed. The beardless youth
was the last survivor. When he saw that he was going to be
captured, he climbed a nearby tree and stabbed himself in vital
organs until he fell dead.

Miskawayh (1921), 62–7

24. Istakhrī on the Khazars and their neighbours c. 951

Little is known of Istakhrī. His name indicates that he came from Istakhr, ancient Persepolis, and it is clear from references in his book that he travelled to Sind, Transoxiana, Khurāsān and other places in the eastern Islamic world before settling in Baghdād, where he lived for many years. He died in Samarkand. He was the author of a 'Book of Roads and Kingdoms', a descriptive geography based on the Kitāb suwar al-aqālīm *(Book of the Configuration of the Provinces) of his slightly earlier predecessor Balkhī (d. 934). All of Balkhī's works have perished, but we know that he cast them as a commentary on a series of regional maps. Istakhrī followed Balkhī's general plan, greatly expanding it and completing his work around 951. The account of the Khazars appears to be composite from three different sources of different dates (indicated by Roman numerals).*

I

Khazar is the name of a region [*iqlīm*] and its capital is called Itil, which is also the name of the river [Volga] which flows to it from [the territories of] the Rūs and the Bulghārs and divides Itil into two parts. The larger part, west of the river, is called Itil, the other part is on the east. The king lives in the western part, and in their language is called *bak* or *bāk*. This [western] part is about a *farsakh* long and a wall surrounds it, although some buildings are outside it. The dwellings are felt tents, except for very few that are of clay. They have markets and baths and many Muslim residents; it is said there are more than 10,000 Muslims. They have about thirty mosques. The king's palace is far from the riverbank, and is of baked brick. No one but the king has a dwelling of baked brick. He does not permit anyone else to build with it.

The wall has four gates. There is a gate leading to the river and one to the desert at the back of the city. Their king is a Jew and it is said that his entourage numbers some 4,000 men. The Khazars are Muslims and Christians and Jews, and among them are a number of idol worshippers. The smallest number are Jews and the largest Muslims and Christians, but the king and his entourage are Jews.

The greater part of their manners and customs are those of the idol worshippers. A man prostrates himself before another to show respect. Their legal rulings are peculiar to themselves, following ancient usages that conflict with those of the Muslim, Jewish and Christian religions.

The king has an army of 12,000 men. If one of the soldiers dies, another takes his place. They are not paid regularly, but are given small amounts at long intervals. When there is war or civil disturbance, he orders them to mobilize.

The revenues of this king derive from customs duties and tithes on the merchandise, imposed, according to their own assessments, on every overland, sea and river route. The people of every place and district must supply the king on a regular basis with whatever food and drink and other such things he requires.

The king has seven judges, appointed from among the Jews, Christians, Muslims and idol worshippers. If a lawsuit arises among the people, they make a judgement on it. The litigants do not go to the king himself, they go to these judges. On the day of the judgement a messenger passes between the judges and the king, informing him of what is happening, and he sends his orders to them, which they then carry out.

This city has no villages, but their cultivated fields are scattered about. They go out in the summer some 20 *farsakh*s to sow. They harvest some of the crop by the river and some from the steppe, transporting the crop by wagon or by the river. Their principal dishes are rice and fish.

The honey and wax that they export is brought to them from the regions of the Rūs and the Bulghārs, and the same is true of the beaver pelts, which are exported throughout the world. They are only found in the rivers that run through the territories of the Bulghār, the Rūs and Kiev [Kūyāba], and as far as I am aware, nowhere else.

The eastern half of Khazar is inhabited by most of the merchants and the Muslims and their warehouses. The western half is reserved for the king and his army and the *khulais*[65] Khazars.

The language of the Khazars is not the same as that of the Turks and Persians; it is unrelated to the language of any other nation.[66]

As for the river Itil, we have been told that it originates near Khirghiz territory and flows between the lands of the Kimaks and the Ghuzz (Oguz), forming the border between them. Then it turns west above Bulghār, then returns east, flowing past the Rūs, then past the Bulghārs, then the Burtās. Then it returns to its course and flows into the Khazar Sea (Caspian). It is said that more than seventy streams branch out from this river, while the main course flows by the Khazars until it falls into the sea. It is said that if its waters were gathered into a single river, its upper reaches would be greater than the Jayhūn (Oxus). The abundance and force of its waters are so great that when it reaches the sea it flows into it for the distance of two days' [sail], and the sweetness and freshness of its water allow it to freeze during the winter. Its colour can be clearly distinguished from the colour of the sea.

II

The Khazars have a city called Samandar between it [Itil] and Bāb al-Abwāb (Darband). It has many gardens; it is said that there are more than four thousand vineyards towards the border with Sarīr [Avars]. Their principal fruit is the grape. There are Muslim inhabitants and they have mosques. Their buildings are of wood, woven together, and they are domed.

Their king is a Jew, related to the king of the Khazars. Between them and the border with Sarīr is two *farsakh*s. There is a truce between them and the lord of Sarīr.

The people of Sarīr are Christians. It is said that their throne, which is gold, once belonged to a king of Persia, and when his rule came to an end it was brought to Sarīr[67] by one of the Persian kings. I have heard that it was one of the sons of Bahrām Chūbīn. Kingship has remained among them down to our own day. It is also said that this throne was made for one of the Khusraws over many years.

There is a truce between the Sarīr and the Muslims.

I know of no concentration of people in Khazar territory aside from Samandar.

The Burtās are a nation on the borders of the land of the Khazars. There is no other nation between them. They are a people scattered along the valley of the Itil.

The Khazars do not resemble the Turks. They have black hair. There are two kinds. One kind is called Qarā Khazar (Black Khazars); they are dark brown, inclining to black, as if they were a kind of Indian. The other kind is white and exceptionally good-looking.

The slaves of the Khazars are idol worshippers, who allow their children to be sold and enslave each other. The Jews and Christians who live among them, like the Muslims, are not permitted by their religion to enslave one another.

Nothing is produced in the land of the Khazars for export to other regions except for isinglass [*gharā*].

As for the mercury and honey and wax and beaver pelts and other skins, they are imported to the Khazars.

The Khazars and their neighbours dress in long coats and tunics. They make no clothing themselves. It is imported from the regions of Jurjān, Tabaristān, Armenia, Azerbaijan and the Byzantine empire.

As for their political system and government, their most powerful man is called the *khāqān* Khazar. He is more exalted than the king of the Khazars, yet it is the king of the Khazars who appoints him. When they want to appoint this *khāqān*, they take this man and strangle him with a piece of silk until he is on the point of death. Then they ask him, 'How long do you wish to reign?' He replies, 'Such and such number of years.' If he dies before the time expires, [fine]; if not, he is executed when he reaches the designated year.

The khāqānate can only be held by a member of a well-known clan. The *khāqān* has no power to command or forbid. Nevertheless, he is held in great respect and anyone who comes into his presence must make a full prostration. No one but an elite group, such as the king and those of his standing, can approach him. The king only enters his presence on special occasions; when he does, he rolls in the dust, prostrating himself, then stands at a distance until given permission to approach.

The *khāqān* is brought out only if some calamity occurs. The Turks and the unbelievers dare not look upon him; they turn away and do not fight him [?], out of reverence for him. When he dies and is buried, everyone who passes his tomb dismounts and prostrates himself. A man remounts only when some distance from his tomb.

Their obedience to their king [*khāqān*] reaches such a pitch that when one of their important men is condemned to death, the king does not have him publicly executed. He orders him to kill himself and he goes to his dwelling and kills himself.

III

The khāqānate is confined to a well-known clan, which possesses neither political power nor wealth. When it is the turn of one of them to rule, he is appointed irrespective of his condition. I was told by someone I trust that he saw a young man selling bread in the market and they said that when the *khāqān* died, he was the worthiest to succeed to the khāqānate. He was, however, a Muslim, and only a man who professes Judaism can become *khāqān*. The throne and the golden canopy [*qubba*] which they have are only set up for the *khāqān*. When he appears in public his tents are pitched above the tents of the king, and his dwelling in the town is higher than the dwelling of the king.

The Burtās, Bashkīrs and Pečenegs

Burtās is the name of a region. The people live in scattered wooden houses.

The Bashkīrs [Bashjirt] are of two sorts. One inhabits the farther reaches of Ghuzz territory, behind Bulghār; it is said that they number some 2,000 men. They occupy a well-defended territory in the forests, where no one can get at them. They are under the authority of the Bulghārs. The other Bashkīrs border the Pečenegs, that is, the Turkish Pečenegs on the Byzantine border.

The Bulghār language is like the Khazar language. The Burtās have a different language. In the same way, the language of the Rūs is not like the language of the Khazars and the Burtās.

Bulghār

Bulghār is the name of a city. The inhabitants are Muslim and in the city is a congregational mosque. Nearby is another city, called Suwār, which also has a congregational mosque. A man who used to preach there informed me that the number of people in these two cities amounts to around 10,000. They have wooden dwellings in which they take refuge during the winter. In the summer they scatter, living in felt tents.

The preacher told me that the night there is so short in summer that a man cannot travel more than a *farsakh*. In the winter the day is short and the night long, to the point that the day in winter is like the summer nights.

The Rūs

There are three sorts of Rūs. One sort lives near Bulghār and their king dwells in a city called Kiev; it is larger than Bulghār. Another sort live further away; they are called Slovenes [Salāwīya]. And there is a sort called Arthānīya; their king lives in Arthā and the people come to trade in Kiev.

It has been reported that no stranger has ever entered Arthā, because they kill any stranger who sets foot in their country.

They descend the rivers to trade and say nothing about their affairs or their merchandise. They allow no one to accompany them or enter their country. From Arthā are brought black sable pelts and lead.[68]

The Rūs are a people who burn their dead. Slave girls are burned with the wealthy of their own volition.

Some men shave their beards and some plait them.

Their dress is a short coat, while the dress of the Khazars, Bulghārs and Pečenegs is a long coat.

These Rūs trade all the way to the Khazars and also to Byzantium and Greater Bulghāria, which borders Byzantium to the north. These people are very numerous. Their power is so great that they have levied tribute on the lands neighbouring Byzantium. The people of Inner Bulghāria are Christians.[69]

Istakhrī (1870), 220–26

25. Mas'ūdī on the fur trade 956

For Mas'ūdī, see headnote to III: 14. This passage is from Mas'ūdī's Kitāb al-tanbīh wa'l-ishrāf (Book of Notification and Revision), completed in 956. This and The Meadows of Gold and Mines of Precious Gems *are the only works of Mas'ūdī's to survive. The* Book of Notification and Revision *is an abridgement and update of the* Meadows of Gold, *and contains a number of important additions.*

The river of the Khazars [Volga] passes by the town of Itil, the present capital of the Khazar kingdom. The former capital was Balanjār. The waters of the Burtās River flow into the river of the Khazars. Burtās is the name of a numerous Turkish people who live between Khwārazm and the kingdom of the Khazars, but who are grouped with the Khazars. Large merchant ships ply this river, laden with the products of the land of Khwārazm and other countries. The pelts of black foxes are exported from Burtās. They are the most sought after and expensive of furs. There are several kinds: red, white – which has the same value as mink [*fanak*] – and that called *khalanjī*.[70] The least valuable is the kind called *'arabī*. Black furs are found nowhere but in this country and neighbouring lands. The rulers of non-Arab peoples delight to wear these furs. They make bonnets and sleeveless tunics of them, and it is the black furs that command the highest price.

This fur is exported to the region of Bāb al-Abwāb (Darband), Bardha'a and other places, such as Khurāsān. Black furs are often exported to the north, the land of the Saqāliba, because the Burtās are near northern lands. From there they are exported to the lands of the Franks and to al-Andalus. Many of these black and red furs are then exported to the Maghrib, which has given rise to the belief that they originate in al-Andalus and the lands of the Franks and Saqāliba.

The nature of these furs is warm and dry; extremely warm as is shown by the bitterness of the flesh of the animals they come from. Their hair retains more heat than that of any other animal. The humours it contains resemble those of fire, both containing a comparable mixture of warm and dry. They are an excellent garment for those of delicate health and for the elderly.

The caliph Mahdī [reigned 775–785], during a stay at Rayy, conducted an experiment to see which was the warmest of furs. He took a number of flagons of water and stoppered them with tufts of different sorts of furs. This took place during a year of intense cold and deep snow. In the morning he had the flagons brought to him. All were frozen solid except for the one stoppered with black fox fur. He thus learned which fur was warmest and driest.

Mas'ūdī (1894), 63

26. Ibrāhīm ibn Ya'qūb
on northern Europe 965

Ibrāhīm ibn Ya'qūb al-Isrā'īlī al-Turtūshī was a Jewish mer-
chant from Tortosa. In 965, the year the Khazar empire was
destroyed by the Rūs of Kiev, Ibrāhīm travelled through north-
ern Europe. In Mainz he was astonished to find that dirhams
struck in Samarkand in 913 and 914 were circulating in the
markets, and that pepper, ginger and cloves from the Indies
were available. He was received at the court of Otto I in
Magdeburg, where he learned something of the Slavic princi-
palities bordering Frankish lands. Most interesting are his
accounts of Mainz, Prague and Cracow; these are the earliest
known mentions of these important cities. His references to the
'Bulqār' [Bulghār] are to the Danube Bulghārs, by now Chris-
tian, rather than to the Volga Bulghārs visited by Ibn Fadlān.
The complete account of Ibrāhīm's travels has not survived.
Qazwīnī (1203–1283) preserves the material on European cit-
ies in his Athār al-bilād wa akhbār al-'ibād *(Monuments of the*
Countries and Histories of their Inhabitants*), while Abū*
'Ubayd al-Bakrī (1040–1094) preserves the Slavic material
translated here, in his Kitāb al-masālik wa'l-mamālik *(Book of*
Roads and Kingdoms*), written in 1068.*

Mainz

Mainz [Maghānja] is a very large city, partly inhabited and
partly cultivated fields. It is in the land of the Franks, on a river
called the Rhine [Rīn]. Wheat, barley, rye, grapevines and fruit
are plentiful.

Dirhams are in circulation there, struck in Samarqand in the years 301 and 302/914 and bearing the name of the director of the mint. [Ibrāhīm ibn Ya'qūb] of Tortosa said: 'I think these coins were struck during the time of the Sāmānid ruler Nasr ibn Ahmad. It is extraordinary that one should be able to find, in such far western regions, aromatics and spices that only grow in the Far East, like pepper, ginger, cloves, nard, costus and galingale. These plants are all imported from India, where they grow in abundance.'

Schleswig

Schleswig [Shalashwīq] is a very large city, on the coast of the ocean. Inside it are many springs of sweet water. The inhabitants worship Sirius, except for a small number of Christians. [Ibrāhīm ibn Ya'qūb] of Tortosa relates: 'They gather together for a religious festival to honour the gods, at which they eat and drink. Those that intend to sacrifice an animal set up a pole in front of their house from which they suspend a piece of the animal whose sacrifice they are offering: beef, mutton, goat or pig. In this way everyone can see how they plan to honour the gods.'

Schleswig is poor in grain and the climate is bad. The inhabitants mostly eat fish, which are plentiful there.

When too many children are born, they throw the surplus into the sea to save the cost of raising them.

[Ibrāhīm ibn Ya'qūb] of Tortosa also says: 'Women take the initiative in divorce proceedings. They can separate from their husbands whenever they choose. Both men and women use a kind of indelible cosmetic to enhance the beauty of their eyes.'

And he also said: 'There is no uglier song than the groans that come out of their throats. It is like the baying of hounds, only worse.'

The Saqāliba are the descendants of Mādhāy, son of Yāfith (Japheth) and they dwell in the north-west.

Ibrāhīm ibn Ya'qūb al-Isrā'īlī says:

'The country of the Saqāliba extends from the eastern Mediterranean to the north Atlantic. The tribes of the north dominate them and now live among them. They are of many different kinds. They were once united under a king named Mākhā, who was from a group of them called Walītābā.[71] This group was of high status among them, but then their languages diverged, unity was broken and the people divided into factions, each of them ruled by their own king.

'At the present time they have four kings: the king of the Bulqārs (Bulghārs); Boreslav, king of Prague and Bohemia and Cracow; Mieszko, king of the north; and Nakon,[72] who rules the farthest west.

'The country of Nakon is bordered on the farthest west by the Saxons [Saksūn] and some Norsemen [Murmān]. His country has low prices and many horses, which are exported to other places. They are well-armed, with shields, helmets and swords.

'From Burgh (Fargh) to Māylīyah[73] is ten miles and from [there?] to the bridge is fifty miles. It is a wooden bridge, a mile long. From the bridge to the fortress of Nakon is around 40 miles, and it is called Grad, which means 'large fort'. Facing Grad is a fort built in a freshwater lake. This is the kind of place where the Saqāliba build most of their forts, in swampy meadows with thick foliage. They trace out a circular or square space the size they want their fort to be, and then dig a trench along the perimeter and heap up the earth into a rampart, which they then reinforce with planks and logs, until the walls of the fort are the height they require. They make a gate wherever they want and build a wooden bridge leading to it.

'From the fort of Grad to the Surrounding Sea is eleven miles. No army can penetrate the lands of Nakon without great difficulty, because the country is all marshy, thickly forested and muddy.

'As for the country of Boreslav, from the city of Prague to the city of Cracow is a journey of three weeks; its length is comparable to that of the country of the Turks.

'The city of Prague is built of stone and lime. It is the principal trading city. The Rūs and the Saqāliba go there from Cracow, to trade, and so do Muslim merchants from the lands of the Turks, as well as Turks and Jews, with *mathāqīl al-marqatīyya*.[74] They carry away slaves, tin and various kinds of furs.

'Their country is the best in the north, the richest in proven-
der. There a man can buy enough flour for a month for a
qinshār,[75] and barley to feed a riding animal for forty days is sold
for a *qinshār*. Ten chickens are sold among them for a *qinshār*.

'In Prague are made saddles and bridles and the leather
shields used in their countries.

'In Bohemia are made small lightly-woven kerchiefs[76] like
nets, embroidered with crescents, which have no practical use.
The value of ten of these kerchiefs is always equivalent to one
qinshār. They trade and exchange them, and have receptacles[77]
full of them. They constitute wealth, and the most expensive
things can be purchased with them, wheat, slaves, horses, gold
and silver and everything else.

'It is surprising that the people of Bohemia are brown, with
black hair; blonds are rare among them.

'The road from Mādhinburgh (Magdeburg? Merseburg?) to
the country of Boleslav [to][78] and from it to the fort of Qalīwa
(Calbe) is ten miles, and from it to Nūb Grad (Novigrad) is two
miles. It is a fort built of stone and lime, and it is on the Saale River
[Slāwah], into which falls the River Bode. And from Nūb Grad to
Mallāhat al-Yahūd ['The saltpans of the Jews', Salzmunde?] which
is on the Saale River, is thirty miles. From there to the fort of
Būrjīn (Wurzen), which is on the River Mulde [Muldāwah] [...]
and from it to edge of the forest is twenty-five miles; from its
beginning to its end is forty miles, through mountains and forests.
From it to the wooden bridge over the mud is about two miles.
From the end of the forest the city of Prague is entered.

'As for the country of Mieszko, it is the most extensive of
their countries. It abounds in food and meat and honey and
cultivated fields. His taxes are levied in *mathāqīl al-marqatīyya,*
and they are used to pay the monthly salaries of his men, each
of whom receives a fixed number. He has 3,000 shield-bearers.
One hundred of his soldiers are the equal of 1,000. The men
are given clothing and horses and weapons and everything they
require. If one of them has a child, he is immediately assigned
an allowance, whether it is male or female. When it grows up,
if it is male, he provides for its marriage and gives a dowry to
the father of the girl. If it is female, he has congress with her

and gives a donation to her father. Dowries are very important to the Saqāliba, and their customs concerning them are like those of the Berbers.

'If a woman has two or three daughters, they are considered a form of wealth. If a man has two sons, it is a cause of poverty.

'Mieszko is bordered to the east by the Rūs and to the north by Prussia. The inhabitants of Prussia live on the shore of the Surrounding Sea. They have their own language, and do not know the languages of their neighbours. They are famous for their courage. If an army comes against them, not one of them waits until his comrade joins him, but each man charges on his own, striking with his sword until he is killed.

'The Rūs raid them in ships from the west.'

West of the Rūs lies the City of Women.[79] They have fields and slaves, and they bear children from their slaves. If a woman has a male child, she kills it. They ride horses and devote themselves to war; they are brave and fierce. Ibrāhīm ibn Ya'qūb says: 'The story of this city is true; Otto, the king of the Romans,[80] told me so himself.'

To the west of this city is a tribe of the Saqāliba called the nation of Walītābā (Veleti). It is in the scrublands of the country of Mieszko to the north-west. They have a great city on the Surrounding Ocean. It has twelve gates and a harbour, with a revetment of wooden pilings.[81] They make war on Mieszko and are very courageous. They have no king and trade with no one. Their judges are their old men.

As for the king of the Bulghārs [Bulqārīn], Ibrāhīm ibn Ya'qūb says:

'I didn't enter his country, but I saw his envoys in the city of Magdeburg when they were sent to Otto the king. They were dressed in tight clothing, cinched with long belts which were set with gold and silver studs. Their king is powerful, wears a crown and has secretaries and officials and scribes, issues edicts and prohibitions, and maintains order as great kings do. They have the knowledge of languages and they have translated the gospels into Slavonic. They are Christians.'

Ibrāhīm ibn Ya'qūb said:

'The king of the Bulghārs converted to Christianity when he

raided the lands of the Byzantines and when he laid siege to the city of Constantinople, until its king conciliated him and gave him splendid gifts. Among the things he bestowed upon him was the hand of his daughter, and it was she who led him to become a Christian.'

The author [Bakrī] said:

'Ibrāhīm's statement indicates that his conversion to Christianity took place after 301/912.[82] Another source says that those among them who converted to Christianity did so in the days of King Basil and they remain Christian to this day.'

Ibrāhīm said:

'Constantinople lies south of the Bulghārs and the Pečenegs border them to the east and north. West of it is the Gulf of Venice, which is a gulf of the Mediterranean between Italy[83] and Constantinople. It [the Mediterranean] surrounds the coasts of Rome and Lombardy and ends at Aquileia. All these places form a single peninsula, surrounded by the Mediterranean on the south, the Gulf of Venice to the east and north, with only one opening, to the west. The Saqāliba inhabit the shores of this gulf from its beginning in the eastern Mediterranean, with the Bulghārs dwelling in the east and other Saqāliba in the west. Those western Saqāliba are the bravest, and the people of those regions seek their protection and fear their power. Their country is mountainous, with difficult roads. To sum up, the Saqāliba are brave and aggressive. If it were not for their disunity and the fact that they are widely dispersed and divided into many tribes, no nation could stand against them.

'They live in fertile, well-provisioned countries, devoting themselves to agriculture and other occupations, in which they surpass all the other peoples of the north. They export their products by land and sea to the Rūs and to Constantinople.

'The major tribes of the north speak the language of the Saqāliba because they have mingled with them. These are such tribes as the Germans, the Hungarians,[84] the Pečenegs, the Rūs and the Khazars.

'In all the northern countries famines occur, not because of lack of rainfall and continuous drought, but because of overabundant rain and continual damp. Drought is not devastating for them, because he who is afflicted by it does not fear it, since their country is so damp and the cold so great.

'They sow during two seasons of the year, in summer and in spring, and harvest two crops. Their principal crop is millet.

'The cold, even when it is intense, is healthful to them, but the heat destroys them. They are unable to travel to the country of the Lombards because of the heat, for the heat there is fierce and they perish. Health among them is only achieved when the elements that make up their constitutions are frozen; when these elements melt and boil, the body desiccates and the result is death.

'Two diseases afflict them all; scarcely anyone escapes at least one of them. The diseases are erysipelas [*rayhān al-humra*] and haemorrhoids. They refrain from eating chicken, asserting that it exacerbates erysipelas, but they eat beef and goose, both of which agree with them.

'They wear ample robes, although the ends of their sleeves are narrow.

'Their kings sequester their women and are very jealous of them. A man can have twenty or more wives.

'The most common trees in their country are apple, pear and peach.

'They have an unusual bird; its back is green and it can imitate the sounds made by men and animals. It has been found [ ] they hunt it and it is called *sabā*[85] in the language of the Saqāliba. They also have a fowl called *tatrā* (wood-cock). Its meat is good and its call can be heard from the tree-tops at the distance of a *farsakh*. The most common are of two kinds, one black and one varicoloured; the latter more beautiful than a peacock.

'They have different kinds of wind and string instruments. They have a wind instrument more than two cubits long, and an eight-stringed instrument whose sounding board is flat, not convex.

'Their drinks and wine are made out of honey.'

Miquel (1966), 1059–60, 1062
Qazwīnī (1848–9), 388, 404
Bakrī (1968), 154–84
Kowalski (1946)

27. Muqaddasī on exports from Bulghār 985–990

Muqaddasī's dates are unknown; his only surviving work, Ahsan al-taqāsīm fī maʿrifat al-aqālīm *(The Best Divisions for the Knowledge of the Provinces) was composed between 985 and 990. He follows Ibn Khurradādhbih, Istakhrī and Ibn Hawqal in the school of descriptive geography, and represents the culmination of their work. This list of items exported from Bulghār is the fullest we have. A number, like 'fish teeth', originated in the far north. Some are Arabic and some are Persian; the latter have an asterisk.*

From Khwārazm:

sable [*sammūr*]
grey squirrel [*sinjāb*]
ermine [*qāqūn]
mink [*fanak*][86]
fox
marten [*dallah*]
beaver [*khazbūst]
spotted hare [*kharkūsh]
goatskins [*bazbūst]
wax
arrows
birch wood [*tūz]
tall fur caps [*qalānīs*]
isinglas [*gharā samak*, fish glue]
fish teeth [probably walrus and narwhal tusks]

castoreum oil [*khazmīyān]
amber
tanned horse hides [*kīmakht]
honey
hazelnuts
falcons [ayūz]
swords
armour
maple wood [? khalanj]
Saqālib slaves
sheep
cattle

All these come from Bulghār, and they also bring grapes and much oil.

Muqaddasī (1906), 324–5

28. Muqaddasī on the land of the Khazars 985–990

For Muqaddasī, see headnote to III: 27.

Beyond the Caspian Sea [*al-buhayra*, 'the lake'] is a large region called Khazar, a grim, forbidding place, full of herd animals, honey and Jews. To the north is the barrier of God and Magog, [to the south-west] it borders the territories of the Byzantines. Two rivers flow through it, and most of the towns are located on their banks. Both rivers flow into the lake [Caspian]. The mountain of Binqishlah is on its border towards Jurjān. The capital is Itil. These are its principal towns: Bulghār, Samandar, Suwār, Baghand, Qayshawa, Khamlīj, Balanjar, Baydā'.

Itil, the large capital city, is situated on a river of the same name [Volga, or Itil] which flows into the lake [Caspian]. I apply the same name to the area on the opposite bank of the river, towards Jurjān. The city is surrounded by trees, which grow even within the [walls]. Muslims are numerous here. Their king used to be Jewish, and made laws [*rusūm*] and appointed judges [from the communities of] Muslims, Jews, Christians and idol-worshippers. I was told that Ma'mūn[87] invaded them from Jurjānīyya, and subdued them, forcing their king to adopt Islam. Later I heard that an army of the Byzantines, called Rūs, invaded them and conquered their lands.[88]

The city is walled, and the houses are scattered about within. It is about the size of Jurjān, or larger. Their dwellings are tents of wood and felt, and large *kharkāhāt* [yurts]; a few buildings are made of adobe. The palace of the ruler [*sultān*] is of fired brick and has four gates, one facing the river, accessible by boat, another leading to the steppe. It is a poor, infertile place, bereft of [agricultural?] prosperity and without fruit. They make barley bread and eat it with fish.

Bulghār is divided into two parts. The houses are made of wood and reeds. The night there is short. The mosque is in the marketplace. Since becoming Muslims, they have been going on raids. The town is on the river Itil, closer to the lake [Caspian] than is the capital.[89]

Suwār is also on this river. The houses here are *kharkāhāt*. They have many fields and bread is plentiful.

Khazar is on another river, towards [the district of] Rihāb, built on just one bank of the river[90]. It is larger and pleasanter than the other towns we have mentioned. People had moved from the town to the lake shore; but have now returned to the town. Formerly Jewish, they have become Muslims.

Samandar is a large town on the lake, located between the river of Khazar [Volga] and Bāb al-Abwāb [Darband]. Most of the dwellings are tents. The majority of the people are Christians; they are poor, welcoming strangers, but thievish. The town is bigger than Khazar, with gardens and many vineyards. Their buildings are of wood interlaced with reeds, the rooffs touch each other. There are numerous mosques.

The Caspian Sea is deep, dark and gloomy, and sailing on it is riskier than on the two seas. Its only useful product is fish. Their boats are waterproofed with pitch, large and held together with nails. The islands are uninhabited. It is possible to circumambulate it, if someone should wish to do so, because the rivers that flow into it are not wide, except for the Kur and the Samūr [*nahr al-mālik*]. Some islands in the lake are wooded, with marshes and animals. There is one island from which madder is gathered. The barrier of Gog and Magog is about two months' travel beyond the lake.

Muqaddasī (1906), 355, 360–62

29. Ibn Hawqal on the trade in eunuchs 988

Ibn Hawqal was born in Nisibis (around 920), and set out on his travels in 943; he was in North Africa 947–951, then in Armenia and Azerbaijan in 955, Khwārazm in 969 and Sicily in 973. He met Istakhrī and with his permission took over his Book of Roads and Kingdoms *and expanded it, adding very valuable and vivid details on agricultural and craft production and other economic matters. He made several redactions of the text of his* Kitāb sūrat al-ard *(*Book of the Configuration of the Earth*), the first before 967, the last, and definitive, version in 988. Like his predecessor, his book is an extended commentary on a series of maps of administrative districts.*

A well-known export from al-Andalus is slaves, boys and girls captured in France and Galicia, as well as eunuchs from the Saqāliba. All the Saqāliba eunuchs in the world come from al-Andalus. They are castrated near this country. The operation is performed by Jewish merchants. The Saqāliba are descended from Japheth. Their country is vast and extends over a very great length. Raiders from Khurāsān reach them through the territory of the Bulghārs. They are led in captivity to that province, their manhood left intact, their bodies unmutilated. The territories of the Saqāliba are immense. The arm of the sea which extends from the Ocean into the lands of Gog and Magog crosses their territory all the way to a point west of Trebizond, then to Constantinople, thus dividing it into two halves. One of these, throughout all its length, is raided by the warriors of

Khurāsān, who live on its borders, while the northern regions are invaded by raiders from al-Andalus via Galicia, France, Lombardy and Calabria. Captives from these regions are still plentiful.

Ibn Hawqal (1938), I, 109

30. Ibn Hawqal on the fur trade and the Rūs attack on Itil and Bulghār 965

For Ibn Hawqal, see headnote to III: 29.

The principal foods [at Itil] are rice and fish. The honey, wax and furs exported from their country come from the territories of the Rūs and the Bulghār. This is also the case with the beaver pelts, exported throughout the world, for they are only found on the northern rivers of the territory of the Rūs, the Bulghār and Kiev [Kūbāya; Kūyāba]. The beaver pelts sold in Spain come from the rivers in the lands of the Saqāliba, which flow into the gulf[91] [*khalīj*] in the lands of the Saqāliba, of which we have already spoken. Most of these furs, and especially those of the best quality, that are found in the lands of the Rūs are actually brought from the country of Gog and Magog; they are sometimes sold to the Bulghārs.

This was the state of affairs until the year 358/969, the date the Rūs destroyed Bulghār and Khazarān.[92] The beaver pelts and best-quality furs are sometimes exported to Khwārazm, despite the fact that the Khwārazmians often attack both the Bulghārs and the Saqāliba, organizing raids against them and taking captives.

The Rūs always trade directly with Khazarān, where they are constrained to pay ten per cent duty on all merchandise.

Ibn Hawqal (1938), II, 393

31. Ibn Hawqal on Khwārazm and its trade 988

For Ibn Hawqal, see headnote to III: 29.

Khwārazm is the name of a district [*iqlīm*] completely separate from Khurāsān and Transoxiana. It is entirely surrounded by desert. To the north and west it is bounded by the lands of the Ghuzz (Oguz), while to the south and east it is bordered by Khurāsān and Transoxiana.

It is a vast region, with extensive districts and many cities. It marks the limit of cultivation along the Oxus; beyond there are no cultivated lands until the place is reached where the river falls into the Aral Sea [*al-Buhayra*]. The district straddles both banks of the Oxus. The capital is located on the northern bank, but on the southern there is an important city called Jurjānīya, the largest in Khwārazm after the capital. It is the commercial centre for the Ghuzz and the place whence the caravans set out for Jurjān. These caravans used in former days to depart regularly for Khazaria and Khurāsān.

The cites of Khwārazm, aside from the capital, are the following: Darghān, Hazārāsp, Khīwa, Ardakhusmīthan, Sāfardiz, Nūzwār, Kardurān, Khwāsh, Kurdur, Qaryat Farātakīn, Madhmīnīya, Mazdākhqān and Jurjānīya.

Its capital was known as Kāth Darkhāsh, and is now fallen into ruins; the population has been dispersed to neighbouring places, such as Jurjānīya. The city of Kāth had a citadel which was flooded by the river at the same time as the rest of the city, and the same fate befell the congregational mosque, which was built against the wall of the citadel. There is no trace of it left.

A river called the Kharakrūr ran through the centre of the city and the market, for the city was built on both its banks. The site was about one third of a *farsakh* long and the same in width. Its markets were crowded and commerce flourished at all times.

Khwārazm is a fertile country, producing many kinds of grain and fruit, but not walnuts. Its cotton and woollen textiles are exported throughout the world. Its people are very wealthy and very manly and brave. They are the inhabitants of Khurāsān most given to emigration and travel. Every large city in Khurāsān has a large number of Khwārazmian inhabitants. Their language is unique to them: no other like it is spoken in Khurāsān. They wear short tunics and their bonnets [*qalānis*] are formed in a characteristic size and style that stands out among the peoples of Khurāsān. They show great courage in their battles with the Ghuzz. They have no gold mines, silver deposits or precious gems in their country. The wealth of the inhabitants comes from trade with the Turks and buying herd animals and, above all, slaves from the lands of the Saqāliba and the Khazars, and Turkish slaves from the borderlands, and furs, such as mink [*fanak*], sable, fox, grey squirrel and other kinds of pelts. These are stored up by them, and the slaves are housed there as well.

Their merchants enter the lands of Gog and Magog to collect beaver and other pelts. It is very rare for a man with a beard to go there; most of the merchants who go there are clean-shaven, without beards or moustaches. The adult men of the land of Gog and Magog are beardless. When a man with a full beard enters their country, the king, who is of the line of Gog and Magog, orders his beard plucked out. After his beard has been plucked, the king treats him very well and allows him to enrich himself.

Ibn Hawqal (1938), II, 477–8, 481–2

32. Ibn Hawqal on the Rūs destruction of Itil 965

For Ibn Hawqal, see headnote to III: 29.

At the present time, the Rūs have left nothing to the Bulghār, Burtās and Khazars but a few worthless ruins. They fell upon them and looted everything, obtaining in their territories more than they could have hoped for. I have been told that many of the Khazars have returned to Itil and Khwārazm with the support of the Sharwān Shāh Muhammad ibn Ahmad al-Yazīdī (reigned 956–981), who helped them with his army and his people. They are hoping to make a pact with him to live under his authority and be assigned lands in which to dwell.

In Jurjān in the year [3]58/969, or thereabouts, I asked a man about the vineyards and he said: 'There is not enough left of a vineyard or garden worth giving to a begger. If a leaf were left on a branch, one of the Rūs would carry it off. Not a grape, not a raisin remains in that country.'

Ibn Hawqal (1938), II, 397–8, 393

33. Bīrūnī on dog sleds, skates and silent barter c. 1030

This extract, from Bīrūnī's Tahdīd nihāyāt al-amākin li-tashīh masāfāt al-masākin *(Determination of the Coordinates of Positions for the Correction of Distances between Cities), occurs in a discussion of the system of the Seven Climes* [iqlīm] *into which some Arab geographers divided the habitable world. Bīrūnī (973–1050) explains that the seventh, the farthest north, has a maximum daylight of sixteen hours. He then describes the region to the north of Bulghār, inhabited by the Finno-Ugrian Īsū [Ibn Fadlān's Wīsū, the Ves] and Yūrā [Yughra], mentioned by both Ibn Fadlān and Abū Hāmid.*

Beyond that [the Seventh Clime], the land is sparsely populated and the inhabitants live like wild beasts. The furthest region [to the north] is that of the Yūrā, whose villages can be reached from Īsū [Wīsū] in twelve days. Men travel from Bulghār in wooden sleighs and reach Īsū in twenty days. They load [the sleighs] with provisions and either drag them over the surface of the snow by hand or use dogs to pull them. They also use skates made of bone, with which they can travel long distances quickly.

The people of Yūrā exchange their products by placing them on the ground in a certain area and then retiring, like shy, wild things. The same thing is done by people from the land of Sri Lanka when they barter cloves.

Bīrūnī (1962), 108

34. The 'Enclosed Nations' of the far north 1118

This account of a strange people of the far north encountered by the Iughra, or Yughra (the Yūrā of Ibn Fadlān and the Arab geographers), occurs in The Russian Primary Chronicle, *or* Povest' Vremennÿkh Let *(The Tale of Bygone Years), written in 1116. Janet Marten observes that according to D. S. Likhachev, the following account was composed in 1118, during the third revision of the Laurentian chronicle, by Prince Mstislav, who heard the tale in 1114 when he was in Staraia Ladoga (Marten (1986), 53, n. 92). The prince then quotes a passage from the pseudo-Methodius, the late-seventh-century author of a popular eschatological work that is one of the earliest sources for the story of Alexander's Wall. Here the 'unclean peoples' penned behind the wall will issue forth, heralding the end of the world, simultaneously with the unleashing of eight tribes from Yathrib (Medina).*

I wish at this point to recount a story which I heard four years ago, and which was told to me by Giuriata Rogovich of Novgorod: 'I sent my servant [or slave],' said he, 'to the Pechera, a people who pay tribute to Novgorod. When he arrived among them, he went on among the Iughra. The latter are an alien people dwelling in the north with the Samoyeds. The Iughra said to my servant, "We have encountered a strange marvel, with which we had not until recently been acquainted. This occurrence took place three years ago. There are certain mountains which slope down to an arm of the sea, and their height reaches to the heavens. Within these mountains are heard great cries and the sound of voices; those within are cutting their way out. In that mountain a small opening has been pierced through which they converse, but their language is unintelligible. They point, however, at iron objects, and make gestures as if to ask for them. If given a knife or an axe, they supply furs in return. The road to these mountains is impassable with precipices, snow and forests. Hence we don't always reach them, and they are also far to the north." '

Then I said to Giuriata, 'These are the peoples shut up by Alexander of Macedon. As Methodius of Patara says of them, "He penetrated the eastern countries as far as the sea called the Land of the Sun, and he saw there unclean peoples of the race of Japheth. When he beheld their uncleanness, he marvelled. They ate every nauseous thing, such as gnats, flies, cats and serpents. They did not bury their dead, but ate them, along with the fruit of abortions and all sorts of impure beasts. On beholding this, Alexander was afraid lest, as they multiplied, they might corrupt the earth. So he drove them to high mountains in the regions of the north, and by God's commandment, the mountains enclosed them round above save for a space of twelve ells. Gates of brass were erected there, and were covered with indestructible metal. They cannot be destroyed by fire, for it is the nature of this metal that fire cannot consume it, nor can iron take hold upon it. Hereafter, at the end of the world, eight peoples shall come forth from the desert of Yathrib, and these corrupt nations, which dwell in the northern mountains, shall also issue forth at God's command." '

Cross and Sherbowitz-Wetzor (1953), 184–5

35. Marwazī on the Rūs c. 1130

Sharaf al-Zamān Tāhir Marwazī was a native of Merv (Mary), in what is now Turkmenistan and served the Seljuk sultan Malik-shāh (reigned 1073–1092) and his successors as a physician, until his death around 1130. The following selections are from his zoological encyclopedia Tabā'i' al-hayāwān (The Nature of Animals), which also includes miscellaneous anthropological information in its initial chapters. The first paragraph is copied almost verbatim from Ibn Rusta, but the information in the second is unique in the Arabic sources, as is the reference to the Rūs acceptance of Christianity, then Islam. Minorsky points out in a note that before his conversion to Christianity in 988, Vladimir (reigned 980–1015) investigated other faiths and sent a ten-man embassy to the king of the Bulghārs, but Islam was rejected because 'drinking wine was a joy of the Rūs'.

The Rūs live in an island in the sea, its extent being a distance of three days in either direction. It has woods and forests, and is surrounded by a lake. They are very numerous, and look to the sword to provide them with a livelihood and profession. When one of their menfolk dies, leaving daughters and sons, they hand his property over to the daughters, giving the sons only a sword, for they say: 'Your father won his property by the sword; do you imitate him and follow him in this.'

And in this way their education was effected, until they became Christians, during the year 300/912.[93] When they entered [the fold of] Christianity, the faith blunted their swords, the door of their livelihood was closed to them, they returned to hardship and poverty, and their livelihood shrank. Then they desired to become Muslims, that it might be lawful for them to make raids and holy war, and so make a living by returning to some of their former practices. They therefore sent messengers to the ruler of Khwārazm, four kinsmen of their king; for they had an independent king called Vladimir, just as the king of the Turks is called *khāqān* and the king of the Bulghārs *yiltawār*.[94] Their messengers came to Khwārazm and delivered their message. The Khwārazmshāh was delighted at their eagerness to become Muslims, and sent someone to them to teach them the religious laws of Islam. So they were converted.

They are strong and powerful men, and go on foot into far regions in order to raid; they also sail in boats on the Khazar Sea [Caspian], seizing ships and plundering goods. They sail to Constantinople in the Sea of Pontus, in spite of the chains in the gulf. Once they sailed into the Sea of Khazar and became masters of Bardha'a for a time. Their valour and courage are well known, so that any one of them is equal to a number of any other nation. If they had horses and were riders, they would be a great scourge to mankind.

Minorsky (1942), 36

36. Marwazī on Bulghār and the far north c. 1130

For Marwazī, see headnote to III: 35.

In the northern direction lies the country of Bulghār; it lies between the west and the north, inclining towards the Pole, and is three months distant from Khwārazm. These [people] have two cities, one called Suvār and the other called Bulghār; between the two cities is a distance of two days' journey, along the bank of a river and through very dense forests, in which they fortify themselves against their enemies. The trees are mostly *khadang*,[95] but there are also hazels. They are Muslims, and make war on the infidel Turks, raiding them, because they are surrounded by infidels. There are in their forests fur-bearing animals, such as grey squirrels, sable and so on. The latitude of their territory is very considerable, so much so that in summer their day is extremely long and their night extremely short, so short in fact that the interval between twilight and dawn is not sufficient for cooking a pot [of meat].

At a distance of twenty days from them, towards the Pole, is a land called Īsū [Wīsū], and beyond this a people called Yūrā; these are a savage people, living in forests and not mixing with other men, for they fear that they may be harmed by them. The people of Bulghār journey to them, taking wares, such as clothes, salt and other things, in contrivances drawn by dogs over the heaped snows, which [never] clear away. It is impossible for a man to go over these snows, unless he binds on to his feet the thigh bones of oxen, and takes in his hands a pair of javelins which he thrusts backwards into the snow, so that his feet slide

forwards over the surface of the ice; with a favourable wind [?]
he will travel a great distance by the day. The people of Yūrā
trade by means of signs and dumb show, for they are wild and
afraid of [other] men. From them are imported excellent sable
and other fine furs; they hunt these animals, feeding on their
flesh and wearing their skins.

Beyond these are a coast-dwelling people who travel far over
the sea, without any [definite] purpose and intention; they
merely do this in order to boast of reaching [such and such a
remote] locality. They are a most ignorant and stupid tribe, and
their ignorance is shown by the following. They sail in ships,
and whenever two [of their] boats meet, the sailors lash the two
together, and then they draw their swords and fight. This is
their form of greeting. They come from the same town, perhaps
from the same quarter, and there is no kind of enmity or rivalry
between them; it is merely that this is their custom. When one
of the parties is victorious, they [then] steer the two ships off
together. In this sea is the fish whose tooth is used in hafting
knives, swords and suchlike.[96] Beyond them is a Black Land
which cannot be crossed. As for the sea route, the voyager sailing towards the Pole reaches a part where there is no night in
the summer and no day in the winter; the sun rotates visibly
over the land for six months, circling the horizon like the revo-
lution of a millstone; the whole year consists of one day and
one night.

Minorsky (1942), 34–5

37. Marwazī on the Saqāliba c. 1130

For Marwazī, see headnote to III: 35.

The Slavs are a numerous people, and between their territories and the territories of the Pečenegs is a distance of ten days, along steppes and pathless country with thick trees and [abounding] in springs. They inhabit these forests. They have no vines, but possess much honey. They tend swine, and burn their dead, for they worship fire. They grow mostly millet, and have a drink prepared from honey. They have different kinds of pipes, including one two cubits long. Their lute is flat and has eight strings but no peg-box, while its pegs are level. They have no great wealth. Their weapons are javelins and spears, and they have fine bucklers. Their head chieftain is called *suwīt*, and he has a deputy called *shrīh*.[97] The king has [riding] beasts and on their milk he feeds. The town in which he resides is called Khazrāt, where they hold a market for three days in every month. Among them the cold is so severe that they dig deep underground dwellings which they cover with wood, and heat with the steam [produced by the burning] of dung and firewood. There they remain during their winter season. In the winter the Majgharī (Magyars) raid them, and as a result of their mutual raidings they have many slaves.

Minorsky (1942), 34–6

38. Yāqūt on Hungary 1228

Yaqūt al-Rūmī (1179–1229) finished the first draft of his famous geographical dictionary, the Muʿjam al-buldān *(Lexicon of Countries), in Aleppo in 1224, and completed the definitive edition in 1228. While in Aleppo he met some Bāshghird soldiers serving in the army of the Hungarian king, and questioned them about their country. The story of the conversion of their fore-bears to Islam by emissaries from the Volga Bulghārs is also found in the* Anonymi gesta Hungarorum, *composed between 1196 and 1203. For Yāqūt, see also p. xxxiv.*

When I was in the city of Aleppo, I ran across a group of men called Bāshghird. Their hair and faces were very brown, and they were studying to become jurisconsults in the Hanifite school of law. Seeking to know something of their country and condition, I questioned one of them, and he told me:

'As for our country, it is beyond Constantinople, in one of the kingdoms of the Franks, called Hunkar (Hungary). We Muslims are subjects of their king, posted on the frontiers of his country in about thirty villages, each of which could be a little town, except that the king of Hunkar does not allow us to wall them, for fear that we might rebel. We live in the middle of a Christian country. North of us is the country of the Saqāliba, while south of us lies the country of the Pope, that is Rome. The Pope is the leader of the Franks; he is the representative [*nāʾib*] of the Messiah, occupying the position of the Commander of the Faithful [caliph] among the Muslims. His authority is absolute among them over everything to do with religion.

'To our west lies al-Andalus, and to our east the lands of the Byzantines, Constantinople and its dependencies.

'Our language is the language of the Franks, and our dress is like theirs. We serve with them in the army and go on raids with them against all nations, for they only fight the enemies of the Muslims.'

I asked him how they came to be Muslims, living in the middle of an unbelieving country. He said:

'I have heard a number of our older people say that a long time ago seven men from Bulghār came to our country and dwelt among us. They pointed out our errors to us and led us to the true path of the religion of Islam, and so God guided us, and thanks be to God, we all accepted Islam and God opened our hearts to the faith. And we have come to this country to become *faqīh*s and when we return to our country, its people will honour us and give us authority in religious matters.'

Then I asked him: 'Why do you shave off your beards like the Franks do?'

He said: 'The soldiers are clean shaven, and we are armed and accoutred in the same way as the Franks. Non-military personnel do not have to shave.'

I asked him: 'How many stages are there between our country and yours?'

He said: 'From here to Constantinople, around two and a half months, and from Constantinople to our country, about the same.'

Istakhrī says in his book that from Bāshghird to Bulghār is twenty-five stages, and from Bāshghird to the Pečenegs, who are a kind of Turk, ten days.

Yaqūt (1866), I, 469–70

39. Qazwīnī on Gog and Magog 1275

Zakarīya ibn Muhammad ibn Mahmūd al-Qazwīnī (1203–1283) wrote two extremely influential books on mirabilia and popular cosmology, the Ajā'ib al-makhlūqāt *(The Wonders of Creation), and the* Athār al-bilād wa akhbār al-'ibād *(Monuments of the Countries and Histories of their Inhabitants). The latter volume, from which the following selection is taken, was written in 1263 and revised in 1275. It is largely a compilation of earlier sources, including Yaqūt, Abū Hāmid al-Andalusī and even Ibrāhīm ibn Ya'qūb. Qazwīnī arranged his material according to the system of the Seven Climes, describing the important cities, geographical features and wonders in each clime in vivid and simple Arabic.*

Gog and Magog [Yājūj and Mājūj] are two Turkish tribes, descended from Japheth [Yāfith], son of Noah – peace be upon him! They dwell to the east of the Seventh Clime.

Al-Shu'bī relates that when Dhū al-Qarnayn (Alexander) came to the land of Gog and Magog a huge crowd of people came before him, beseeching his help against Gog and Magog. They said:

'O Victorious King, beyond this mountain live nations whose number is known only to God. They destroy our dwelling places and our crops and our fruits. They consume everything, even the grass. Like wild beasts, they slaughter our herds. They even eat the vermin that crawl on the earth. No other species multiplies like they do. Not one of them dies without fathering a thousand children.'

Said Dhū al-Qarnayn: 'How many tribes of them are there?'

They replied: 'Only God knows their number. Those closest to us consist of six tribes: Yājūj, Mājūj, Tāwīl, Tārīs, Mansak and Kamādā. Each of these tribes alone is as large as the entire population of the rest of the earth. As for those farther away, we have no knowledge of them.'

Dhū al-Qarnayn asked: 'What do they eat?'

They replied: 'Every year two fish swim across the sea to them. Each of the fish, from head to tail, is ten days' march. In the spring they feed on crocodiles, snakes and sea serpents, for which they beseech the heavens, as other people invoke the heavens for rain. When their invocations are answered, they flourish and grow fat; otherwise they grow thin and weak.'

Dhū al-Qarnayn asked: 'What do they look like?'

They said: 'Short torsos, wide faces. Their height is half that of a man of medium stature. They have fangs like wild beasts, and claws instead of fingernails. Hair grows down their backbones. They have two enormous ears, one of which is exceedingly hairy on the outside, but hairless inside, the other hairy inside but hairless outside. They wrap themselves in one, and sleep on the other. Their bodies are so hairy that they are completely hidden. They call out to one another like pigeons and bay like dogs. They copulate like animals, wherever they meet.'

It is related in some sources that Gog and Magog pick away at the Barrier until they can almost see the sun behind it. Then a voice cries out: 'Enough! Tomorrow you will break through!' and they desist. During the night All-Powerful God restores the Barrier to what it was. The next day they dig and tunnel away again, until they are almost on the point of breaking through. Then the voice once more rings out: 'Desist! Tomorrow you shall break through, if God so wills!'

Only a short time remains before the day comes when they return to their task and break through and descend upon mankind. They will drink up all the water of the earth until it is completely desiccated. Men will take refuge in their hill-top fortresses, while they conquer the earth and destroy all they find. When no one is left, they will shoot an arrow into the sky and it will fall back reddened with something like blood, and they will say: 'We have overcome the people of the earth, and now we have reached the people of the heavens.' Then All-Mighty God will send them a worm called *naghaf*. It will enter their ears and nostrils and kill them. [The Prophet] – prayers and peace be upon Him – said: 'By He who holds my soul in His hand, the beasts of the earth will grow fat on their flesh!'

Qazwīnī (1960), 618–19

40. Marco Polo on dog sleds and the Land of Darkness 1293

Marco Polo (1254–1324) is the best-known of medieval travellers, but it is impossible to establish an exact chronology of his journeys. The following is a clearly second-hand description of the territory of a Tatar chief called Kaunchi, Marco Polo's 'Conci', a name Yule says was borne by two men, both descendants of Genghis Khan. One was the lord of Siberia, the other chief of the White Horde, whose grazing lands lay north-east of the Caspian. The latter sent an embassy to Siyah-kuh, north of Tabriz, in 1293, where Marco Polo could have encountered his informant. The fur he calls 'erculin' has not been identified, and he greatly exaggerates the size of the sled dogs.

You find in their country[98] immense bears entirely white, and more than 20 palms in length. There are also large black foxes, wild asses and abundance of sables; these creatures, I mean from the skins of which they make those precious robes that cost 1,000 bezants each. There are also vairs in abundance; and vast multitudes of the Pharaoh's rat, on which the people live all the summer time. Indeed they have plenty of all sorts of wild creatures, for the country they inhabit is very wild and trackless.

And you must know that this king[99] possesses one tract of country which is quite impassable for horses, for it abounds greatly in lakes and springs, and hence there is so much ice as well as mud and mire, that horses cannot travel over it. This difficult country is thirteen days in extent, and at the end of every day's journey there is a post for the lodgement of the couriers who have to cross this tract. At each of these post-houses they keep some 40 dogs of great size, in fact not much smaller than donkeys, and these dogs draw the couriers over the day's journey from post-house to post-house, and I will tell you how. You see the ice and mire are so prevalent, that over this tract, which lies for those thirteen days' journey in a great valley between two mountains, no horses (as I told you) can travel, nor can any wheeled carriage either. Wherefore they make sledges, which are carriages without wheels, and made so that they can run over the ice, and also over mire and mud without sinking too deep in it. Of these sledges indeed there are many in our own country, for 'tis just such that are used in winter for carrying hay and straw when there have been heavy rains and the country is deep in mire. On such a sledge then they lay a bearskin on which the courier sits, and the sledge is drawn by six of those big dogs that I spoke of. The dogs have no driver, but go straight for the next post-house, drawing the sledge famously over ice and mire. The keeper of the post-house, however, also gets on a sledge drawn by dogs, and guides the party by the best and shortest way. And when they arrive at the next station they find a new relay of dogs and sledges ready to take them on, while the old relay turns back; and thus they accomplish the whole journey across that region, always drawn by dogs.

The people who dwell in the valleys and mountains adjoining that tract of thirteen days' journey are great huntsmen, and catch great numbers of precious little beasts which are sources of great profit to them. Such are the sable, the ermine, the vair, the erculin, the black fox and many other creatures from the skins of which the most costly furs are prepared. They use traps to take them, from which they can't escape. But in that region the cold is so great that all the dwellings of the people are underground, and underground they always live.

There is no more to say on this subject, so I shall proceed to tell you of a region in that quarter, in which is perpetual darkness.

Concerning the Land of Darkness

Still further north, and a long way beyond that kingdom of which I have spoken, there is a region which bears the name of Darkness,

because neither sun nor moon nor stars appear, but it is always
dark as with us in the twilight. The people have no king of their
own, nor are they subject to any foreigner, and live like beasts.

The Tartars however sometimes visit the country, and they
do it in this way. They enter the region riding mares that have
foals, and these foals they leave behind. After taking all the
plunder that they can get they find their way back by help of
the mares, which are all eager to get back to their foals, and
find the way much better than their riders could do.

These people have vast quantities of valuable peltry; thus
they have those costly sables of which I spoke, and they have
the ermine, the erculin, the vair, the black fox and many other
valuable furs. They are all hunters by trade, and amass amazing quantities of those furs. And the people who are on their
borders, where the Light is, purchase all those furs from them;
for the people of the Land of Darkness carry the furs to the
Light country for sale, and the merchants who purchase these
make great gain thereby, I assure you.

The people of this region are tall and shapely, but very pale
and colourless. One end of the country borders upon Great
Rosia. And as there is no more to be said about it, I will not
proceed, and first I will tell you about the province of Rosia.

Rosia is a very great province, lying towards the north. The
people are Christians, and follow the Greek doctrine. There are
several kings in the country, and they have a language of their
own. They are a people of simple manners, but both men and
women very handsome, being all very white and [tall, with long
fair hair]. There are many strong defiles and passes in their country; and they pay tribute to nobody except to a certain Tartar king
of the Ponent, whose name is Toctai; to him, indeed, they pay tribute, but only a trifle. It is not a land of trade, though to be sure
they have many fine and valuable furs, such as sables, in abundance, and ermine, vair, erculin and fox skins, the largest and
finest in the world [and also much wax]. They also possess many
silver mines, from which they derive a large amount of silver.

Yule and Cordier (1903), II, 479–87

41. Ibn Battūta on travel in the Land of Darknesss 1332

Ibn Battūta (1304–1377) claims to have made a flying visit to Bulghār in 1332 'in order to see for myself what they tell of the extreme shortness of the day there'. He gives no details of the journey and says nothing about Bulghār itself, except that he set out from Bishdagh (Pyatigorsk) and reached Bulghār ten days later, which is clearly impossible, for the distance between them is 800 miles. On this basis, Janicsek has shown the section to be a fiction, almost certainly included in the account to show that he has encompassed the world (Janicsek (1929), 791–800). For the same reason, perhaps hoping to rival that other great traveller, the Alexander of romance, he wished to enter the Land of Darkness, but was dissuaded by the difficulty of the journey. He did visit northern lands, however, and spoke with fur traders who had visited the far north. From them he learned of the use of dog sleds in the arctic regions.

I wanted to enter the Land of Darkness. This can be done by passing beyond Bulghār, a journey of forty days. But I gave up my plan because of the great difficulty of the journey, and the small profit it offered. One can only travel to this country by small carts ['*ajala*] pulled by large dogs, for this wilderness is covered with ice and the feet of men and hooves of animals slip and slide, while dogs have claws and their paws do not slip on the ice. Only rich merchants enter this wilderness, men who each have forty or more carts, filled with food, drink and firewood. There are no trees, stones or dwellings to be found. Dogs who have already made the trip a number of times guide the travellers. The price of such an animal can reach more than 1,000 dīnārs. The wagon [*'araba*] is attached to its neck and three other dogs are yoked to it. It is the leader, and the other dogs follow it with the wagon. When it halts, they halt too. The owner of this animal never beats it or reprimands it. When it is time to eat, the dogs are fed before the men. If this is not done, the lead dog gets angry and runs away, leaving his master to perish.

When the travellers have journeyed for forty days, they make camp near the Land of Darkness. Each of them puts down the merchandise he has brought, then retires to the camp-ground. The next day they return to examine their merchandise and find set down beside it sable [*sammūr*], squirrel [*sinjāb*] and ermine [*qāqūn*] pelts. If the owner of the merchandise is satisfied with what has been placed beside his goods, he takes it. If not, he leaves it. The inhabitants of the Land of Darkness might add to the number of pelts they have left, but often take them back, leaving the goods the foreign merchants have displayed. This is how they carry out commercial exchanges. The men who go to this place do not know if those who sell and buy are men or Jinn, for they never glimpse anyone.

Ermine is the most beautiful kind of fur. An ermine [coat] will fetch 1,000 dīnārs in India, equivalent to 250 Maghribī gold dīnārs. The furs are pure white and come from a little animal a span in length. The tail is long and is left on the pelt as it is in life.

The sable is cheaper than the ermine. A sable fur [coat] costs 400 dīnārs or less. One of the properties of these furs is that they repel fleas. This is why the governors and great men of China attach one of these furs to the neck of their fur coats. The merchants of Persia and Iraq do the same.

Defremery and Sanguinetti (1854), II, 99–102

42. Ibn Battūta on a winter journey to New Sarai 1332

Ibn Battūta set out from Constantinople during the winter of 1332 for the Mongol camp at New Sarai, founded by Berke Khan (reigned 1255–1267), 225 miles north of Astrakhan. His description of winter travel in the north is unrivalled. This translation is slightly adapted. See also headnote to III: 41.

This was in mid-winter, and I wore three fur coats and two pairs of trousers, one quilted. I wore woollen boots on my feet, and on top of those a pair of boats of the kind called *bulghārī*, which are made of horse hide lined with bear fur. I would wash with hot water next to the fire and the drops that fell instantly froze. When I washed my face the water would freeze in my beard, and when I shook it something like snow would fall out. When my nose ran, it would freeze on my moustache. Because of the weight of the clothes I was wearing I couldn't mount a horse, and had to be helped into my saddle by my companions ... we journeyed for three nights on the river Itil [Volga] and its tributaries, which were frozen solid. When we needed water, we cut chunks of ice and put it in a cauldron until it melted, then used this for drinking and cooking.

Defremery and Sanguinetti (1854), II, 445–6

43. Ibn Fadl Allāh al-'Umarī on Siberia and Alexander's Tower 1342–1349

Ibn Fadl Allāh al-'Umarī (1301–1349) was an important official in Mamluk Egypt, rising to the position of Head of Chancery. He probably composed his Kitāb al-masālik al-absār fī mamālik al-amsār *(Book of the Paths of the Eye Through the Kingdoms of the Countries) after he left office in 1342. In his day, Bulghār was evidently in the grazing lands of the Kipčaq Turks.*

Among the most renowned cites of the Kipčaq is Bulghār, where the shortest night lasts 4½ hours. Badr al-Dīn Hasan Rūmī assured me that when he was there he questioned Mas'ūd, who among the Bulghārs held the office of official timekeeper for the prayers, and received this answer: 'I learned by precise observation and by means of astronomical instruments that the shortest night was exactly 4½ hours. As for the town of Afīkūn, where I also made observations, I found that the shortest night was 3½ hours, that is, an hour less than in the city of Bulghār. The distance between these two towns is twenty days' march.'

Beyond Afīkūn is Sibir and Abir (Siberia), then comes Julmān (Čoliman River basin). Leaving Julmān and heading east, one comes to Karakorum and from there to Khatā (Cathay), which forms part of China, where the Great Khan resides.

Heading west from Julmān one arrives at the land of the Rūs, then that of the Franks and the peoples who inhabit the shores of the Western Ocean (Atlantic).

The countries of Sibir and Julmān border Bāshkird. In Bāshkird is a Muslim *qādī* who is greatly esteemed. In the lands of Sibir and Julmān the cold is excessive and the mountains, plains and houses are covered with snow every year for six consecutive months. There is very little grazing for animals. These peoples inhabit the farthest north, and are rarely visited by travellers. They have few means of subsistence, and if what is reported is true, each of them collects whatever animal bones he can find and boils them, deriving what broth he can from them. The next day he puts them back on the fire, boiling the same bones seven times, until every bit of sustenance has been obtained from them. Although these people live such miserable lives, the slaves who come from there are the most beautiful in the world. Their faces are perfectly white, their features charming and their eyes are blue. These details have been supplied by Badr al-Dīn Hasan Rūmī who has visited these countries.

Shaykh 'Alā' al-Dīn ibn Nu'mān adds that merchants do not go farther than the town of Bulghār and the province of Julmān. Merchants from Julmān travel as far as Yūghra, which is situated far to the north. Beyond Yūghra there is no trace of habitation except a tall tower, built by Alexander, beyond which nothing is found but the Darkness. The traveller, asked what he meant by this expression, answered that this land consists of deserts and mountains where eternal cold and snow hold sway and where the sun never shines, where no plant grows and no animal lives. These lands border a Black Sea shrouded with fog where the sun never appears.

Quatremère (1838), 277–81

Appendix 1
The Khazars *c. 650–c. 965*

The Khazars were Turkic-speaking pastoral nomads, closely related to the Bulghārs. The Khazar khāqānate, which lay astride one of the main invasion routes between the Eurasian steppe and the Byzantine empire, was the most powerful organized state in the steppes north of the Caucasus. With the Caucasus protecting their back, their territory lay between the Caspian and the Black Seas, and extended across the Ukrainian steppe as far west as Kiev and to the borders of what are now Kazakhstan and Uzbekistan in the east. To the north, at the confluence of the Volga and Kama rivers, lay the lands of their tributary vassals, the Bulghārs. Based in their capital of Itil at the mouth of the Volga, the Khazars controlled access to both the Black and the Caspian Seas, creating a commercial network that spanned much of Eurasia. They ruled over, or received tribute from, some thirty-eight different peoples – including Ghuzz Turks, Alans, Caucasian Huns, Avars, Finno-Ugrian speakers and Slavs – and were powerful enough to enforce a *pax Khazarica*, a forerunner of the thirteenth-century *pax Mongolica*. During the ninth and first half of the tenth century trade flourished on the Eurasian steppe and in European Russia towns, and trading posts sprang up along the major rivers. The overland route to China was open, and we know from Ibn Khurradādhbih that Jewish merchants from Europe were travelling along it, passing through Itil on their way (see p. 111).

Originally the Khazars practised a form of Shamanism, venerating the sky god Tengri and natural phenomena like fire, thunder and lightning. Their warriors were buried with their horses, weapons and food; excavations have revealed that young women and children, probably slaves, were sometimes sacrificed with them.

The Khazars had a curious form of double kingship, in which a sacral ruler, the *khāqān* (see Appendix 2), was chosen from among the members of a royal clan, thought to possess *qut*, or charismatic power. The *khāqān* had a purely ceremonial role, while affairs of state were left to a 'king', given various names in the Arabic sources, including *bak* or *bāk* (*beg*), *shād*, and *yiligh*. Istakhrī describes the simulated ritual strangling of the *khāqān* at his inauguration, his auto-proclamation of the length of his reign, and the sanctity and ritual isolation of his person (see pp. 156-7). The Khazar institution of sacral kingship strongly influenced the Rūs; it was also imitated by the Danube Bulghārs and the Magyars, and traces can even be found among the early Ottomans.

At some point in the early ninth century, the Khazar *khāqān* and the military elite converted to Judaism, although the circumstances and date of the conversion are unclear. (This has been much discussed; the best account is still Dunlop (1954).) A passage in the *Book of the Khazars*, written by the Spanish Jewish poet Yahuda ha-Levi in 1140, places the conversion four hundred years earlier, around 740. Yet the detailed accounts of the eighth-century Khazar wars in the Arabic chronicles never mention Jewish kings, which they surely would have done if such had existed. Mas'ūdī says the conversion of the *khāqān* took place during the reign of Hārūn al-Rashīd (786-809), and this seems more probable. Although Christianity had spread to some of the Caucasian peoples at the hands of Georgian and Armenian missionaries, the conversion of the Khazars, or at least the Khazar ruling caste, was the first major success of Abrahamic monotheism among the peoples of the steppe.

A chance discovery in 1999 at last provided a solid piece of evidence for the date of the conversion when a Viking Age coin hoard, one of the largest ever found, was discovered in a farmer's field in Gotland. Called the Spillings Hoard, it contained 170 lb. (85 kg) of silver, including 14,295 silver coins, of which 14,200 were dirhams. Among them was an imitation dirham, dated to 838, with the inscription *Mūsā rasūl allāh* ('Moses is the Messenger of God') (see Kovalev (2005)). Four more coins from the same die and with the same slogan were also found, along with two variants, one with the legend *ard al-khazar* ('Land of the Khazars'), the other bearing a rune-like trident, apparently a dynastic symbol. The first coins struck in the Principality of Kiev in the tenth century, tributary to the Khazars, bear this device too, and it has also been found scratched on stones. The 'Moses' coins show that Judaism was the official religion of the Khazar empire in 838, but do not necessarily mean that conversion took place that year. Issuing an imitation of an Islamic coin with such a provocative legend must have been a response to some specific event, and as far as is known, no further coins bearing it were struck. Whatever the reason, it is difficult not to relate the spread of Judaism in Khazaria to the

Rādhānīya, the multilingual Jewish merchants who were very active in this period and who travelled from the 'Land of the Franks' to China and back, crossing Khazar territory en route (see Part III: 5 and 6).

The conversion of the ruling elite to Judaism did not affect the composition of the Khazar state, which remained multiconfessional, multilingual and multinational. Muslims, Christians, Jews and Shamanists lived and traded in Itil; each community had its own judges and followed its own laws in its internal affairs. In 861, an attempt was made by the missionary Slav brothers Cyril (Constantine) and Methodius to convert the Khazars to Christianity, when they took part in a debate on the relative merits of Christianity and Judaism in the presence of the Khazar *khāqān*. The brothers were received politely and even succeeded in converting 200 of the *khāqān*'s entourage, but he himself declined the invitation to be baptized.

The active export trade and diversified internal economy of the Khazar empire were its great strengths, and differentiated it from previous, more ephemeral, steppe empires. Just as the population was extremely varied, so were its occupations: agriculture, viticulture, bee keeping, stock rearing and crafts have all been identified by archaeologists, and are confirmed by the few Arabic texts we possess. One telling detail reveals just how dominant the Khazar *khāqān*s were during this period: the Byzantines considered them important enough to merit a gold seal on diplomatic correspondence, weightier and more imposing than those used for either the Pope or the Holy Roman Emperor himself (see Dunlop (1954), ix).

Appendix 2
The Rūs

In 844, the year Sallām the Interpreter returned to Baghdad from his mission to Alexander's Wall, fifty-four square-rigged Rūs longships sailed up the Guadalquivir and sacked Seville. The savagery of the attack was unparalleled: the invaders put the city to the sword and devastated its hinterlands, before finally being slaughtered by cavalry sent from Cordoba. Nobody knew who they were, or where they had come from; the Andalusian chroniclers simply called them *majūs*. This word, familiar to us from the Magi of the Gospels, originally referred to Zoroastrians, but came first to mean 'fire worshippers' and then to be almost synonymous with 'pagan'. It was a ninth-century eastern writer Ya'qūbī (d. 897), who identified the *majūs* that attacked Seville with the Rūs in a little book composed around 880, called *Kitāb al-buldān* (*The Book of Countries*): 'West of the city of Algeciras is a city named Seville on a great river, which is the river of Cordoba. The *majūs* who are called *al-Rūs* entered it in the year 229/844 and looted, pillaged, burned and killed' (Ya'qūbī (1892), 354).

The earliest occurrence of the word Rūs, however, is in Latin. The *Annales Bertiniani* record the arrival, in the year 838, of an embassy from the Byzantine emperor Theophilus at the court of the Holy Roman Emperor Louis the Pious at Ingelheim (see Nelson (1991), 44). They were accompanied by a party of men called *Rhos* who bore a letter from Theophilus, asking that they be given help to return to their homeland. They were unable to do so by travelling through Byzantine territory because of 'cruel and barbarous tribes of extreme savagery', probably a reference to the Magyars. Louis questioned the men and discovered that they were Swedes, and that their ruler was called *chacan*, an old Turkic regal title, rendered in Arabic as *khāqān*, meaning 'Lord of the Steppe'. It was borne by the sacral ruler of the Khazar Turks who, from their capital of Itil on the Volga, controlled access to the Caspian and Black Seas (see Appendix 1). Their use of the title shows that the Rūs were in the orbit of Khazar power, despite the vast distance separating Gorodishche (most probably the 'home' to which they were trying to return) from Itil. The men who sacked Seville and the merchants who passed through Khazar territory on their way to Baghdad were both Rūs; we know them today as Vikings.

Louis was not pleased at discovering the Scandinavian origins of his guests, and placed the men under arrest, writing to Theophilus to discover more about their origins and motives. He suspected them of being spies, sent to assess the wealth and vulnerability of his capital. Indeed, he had every reason to be concerned, for the Atlantic coasts of the Frankish empire had been systematically assaulted by Viking raiders since early in the reign of his father Charlemagne. Every port, from Hamburg south, had been sacked, sometimes repeatedly. The Vikings sailed up the major rivers, looting churches and monasteries, and slaughtering the inhabitants of villages and towns or carrying them off into slavery. Nevertheless, Louis's suspicions of the Swedes in this instance were probably unfounded. The Vikings who harried the British Isles and the Atlantic coasts of Europe between 793 and 850, effectively stripping Europe of its silver supply, were overwhelmingly Danes, with a sprinkling of Norwegians. During these years the Swedish Vikings instead raided and traded in Gotland and along the Baltic coast.

In Atlantic Europe, the Vikings were able to harvest wealth accumulated by others. In Baltic lands and what is now European Russia, there were as yet no monasteries or cities to sack – yet even in these unpromising regions, enterprising men could grow rich. The system of rivers and portages that crisscrossed European Russia extended east to the Black and the Caspian Seas, and these in turn provided access to the markets of Byzantium and the Abbasid caliphate, with their insatiable demand for slaves and growing demand for furs. The Rūs set about taking control of these highways to the lucrative markets of the east. During the eighth and ninth centuries, they established fortified trading posts along the major rivers and organized the collection and export of the natural products of the forest regions, particularly honey, wax, furs and slaves. These were sold in eastern markets for silver dirhams, hundreds of thousands of which have been found in Russian and Baltic lands. The Rūs also imposed tribute on the population, a bewildering mixture of Finno-Ugric-, Baltic- and Slavic-speaking peoples: forest dwellers, farmers and herdsmen. It was levied in furs; the Slavic word for 'marten fur' (*kuna*) is still used for the currency of Croatia, but the term goes back to the ninth century.

*

The opening up of European Russia by Swedish Vikings was closely linked to the growth of markets for slaves and furs in the great cities of Cordoba, Constantinople and Baghdad. The Swedish trading city of Birka was founded around 750; Cordoba became the capital of the Umayyad dynasty of al-Andalus in 756; Baghdad was founded in 763. Meanwhile the town of Staraia Ladoga on the Volkhov River, probably founded at about the same time as Birka, was the first Rūs foothold in what is now Russia. A hoard of silver Islamic coins dating from about 790, and struck in North African and Andalusian mints, has been discovered there, and coins from the same period have also turned up at Birka. Such discoveries show that Staraia Ladoga was in contact with Islamic lands almost from the beginning of its foundation; conversely, they confirm the Arabic sources which speak of products of the north, particularly Saqāliba eunuchs and furs, reaching al-Andalus at a surprisingly early date.

In 860, the Rūs somehow negotiated the rapids of the lower Dnieper with a large fleet and attacked Constantinople, devastating the city's suburbs. The next year, the apostles of the Slavs Cyril (Constantine) and his brother Methodius tried unsuccessfully to bring them into the Christian fold; although they failed, commercial relations were established between the Rūs and Constantinople. Trade agreements were hammered out with the Byzantines in 907 and 911, the texts of which have been preserved in *The Russian Primary Chronicle* (see Cross and Sherbowitz-Wetzor (1953), 73–8; Page (1995), 97–100). By the time of Constantine VII (reigned 945–959) the Rūs were established in Kiev and had begun to meld with the Slavic population. Just as the Danish and Norwegian Vikings were transformed into French-speaking Normans, the Rūs became Slavic-speaking Russians, giving their name to the country and people that had absorbed them. With the conversion of Vladimir of Kiev to the Orthodox faith in 986, the process of assimilation was complete.

Appendix 3
The Sāmānids

In the early ninth century, the Sāmānid dynasty succeeded in creating a huge state in Transoxania, east of the Caspian Sea, with its capital in Bukhārā. The Sāmānids included in their domains practically all of the silver mines in the Islamic world, including Panshīr in the Hindu Kush. They held power in Central Asia from 819 to 1005, and after about 850 produced more than ninety per cent of the Islamic coins found in Russian, Baltic and Scandinavian coin hoards.

The Sāmānids were famous for their wealth, their highly developed agricultural system based on intensive irrigation and their excellent crafts. Their great cities, Samarkand, Bukhārā, Nishapur, Merv and Herat, were cultural and economic centres of the first rank. Included in their domains was Khwārazm, a vassal state that played an important political and commercial role in trade with the north. The Khwārazmians were great travellers, traders and warriors. Ibn Hawqal says Khwārazmian communities were to be found in all major trading cities and describes how merchants from Khwārazm ventured as far as the lands of Gog and Magog, that is, north of Bulghār, in their search for the best-quality furs (see III: 30). Ibn Fadlān mentions the presence of Khwārazmian women in Bulghār (see p. 43); Abū Hāmid al-Andalusī found large contingents of Khwārazmian mercenaries in Hungary in 1150 (see p. 78). Ibn Fadlān set out on the second leg of his journey to Bulghār from the Khwārazmian capital of Kāth, near modern Khiva in Uzbekistan.

The late Thomas Noonan attempted to quantify the number of silver dirhams that flowed through European Russia from Khwārazm and Sāmānid Khurāsān via Khazaria and Bulghār, and he estimated that the Islamic world exported 100,000,000–200,000,000 whole dirhams during the ninth and tenth centuries. The Khazars dominated the trade during the ninth century; the Bulghārs, during the tenth.

Khazar revenues, derived from the ten per cent tax on imports, therefore declined sharply in the tenth century, while those of Bulghār correspondingly rose. The main trade route from the Islamic world to the Baltic clearly shifted in the tenth century to Bulghār. Nevertheless, Bulghār continued to pay tribute to the Khazars at the rate of one sable skin per household, even after the conversion of Almish, the king of the Bulghārs, to Islam, which probably took place around 910. A Persian source, Gardīzī, writing about 1050, says 500,000 hearths paid tribute to the king of the Bulghārs. The figure is impossibly high, but even reducing it to 50,000 would produce a very substantial sum. These estimates are rough, but serve to indicate something of the scale of the northern trade.

Around a third of the more than 300,000 dirhams that have turned up in Eastern European coin hoards have been found in the Oka River basin, the natural route from Bulghār to Kiev and Novgorod (Golden (1982), 93). This was the route followed in the twelfth century by Abū Hāmid on his journey from Bulghār to Hungary (see pp. 74–7).

Appendix 4
The fur trade

Fur was a highly valuable commodity in this period, as several of the texts included here confirm. The upper reaches of the Kama (the hunting grounds of the Yūrā people, discussed by Abū Hāmid al-Andalusī on pp. 70–74) were rich in fur-bearing animals, particularly beaver, and the hunter-gatherers in the subarctic and arctic lands even further north either paid tribute in furs to the Bulghār king or traded them for beads and, probably, weapons if they were beyond his jurisdiction. Muslim merchants who traded with the most northerly peoples found them immune to silver coins and fearful of domination; the merchants could only obtain their furs and other products, such as narwhal and sea lion 'ivory', by silent barter. This region therefore marked the northern limit of the Islamic monetary economy.

The Arab geographers tell similar stories of silent barter in the islands of the Indonesian archipelago and in the gold fields south of the Niger, demarcating the boundaries of Islamic trading networks to the east and south respectively. It is striking how such remote peoples were nevertheless incorporated into the networks and visited by intrepid traders. From their strongholds in European Russia, the Rūs too levied tribute on the northern hunter-gatherers, Finno-Ugrian speakers, who lived in the northern forests and hunted as far north as the White and Barentz Seas. Ibn Fadlān gives the names of two of these peoples besides the Yūrā (Yughra): the Wīsū (Ves) and the Arū.

Archaeologists have found characteristic blunt arrows used from the seventh to the thirteenth centuries in northern Russia for hunting beaver, marten, ermine, squirrel and fox. Tipped with a cylinder of bone, horn, metal or wood, the arrow stunned the animal without damaging its skin until the hunter could reach it and kill it. A wide variety of traps were also used, but these have left little archaeological record. Samoyed hunters in the nineteenth century designed traps that would not tear the skins of the animals and destroy their market value, and similar devices must have been used by early medieval trappers.

Sites where these blunt-tipped arrows have been found also yielded large numbers of beads. Krutik, a Ves (Wīsū) site in the Beloozero region, mentioned by R. N. Kovalev, yielded 491 imported beads. Hundreds of thousands of such beads, made of glass, amber, carnelian, chalcedony, coral and other substances, have been found along with the bones of fur-bearing animals at burial and other sites throughout northern Russia. Ibn Fadlān mentions that the Rūs brought beads to Bulghār, where they sold for a dirham each, a very substantial sum; these must have been used to trade for pelts. Many of the beads found in graves came from the Islamic world, and were probably made especially for trading purposes. Glass beads were made in places like Staraia Ladoga and Kiev, and workshops where they were fabricated have been found by archaeologists.

The scale of the fur trade was huge. In addition to the furs received by the Bulghār king in tribute, middlemen – like the Rūs merchants encountered by Ibn Fadlān – brought the furs they had bought or collected as tribute to the great market on the Volga, where merchants from Khurāsān and Khwārazm gathered to buy them. Ibn Rusta says the Bulghārs paid 2–2½ dirhams a pelt, but the price must have varied considerably according to type, rarity and quality. Kovalev has estimated that more than 500,000 pelts were exported from Bulghār every year (Kovalev (2000–2001), 33). The fur trade also financed the formation of the Kievan Russian principality, which began as a Rūs-dominated trading post feeding slaves and furs first to the Khazars, and later to the Bulghārs. By the end of the tenth century, Kiev had become a Christian, Slavic-speaking principality.

The system of levying taxes in furs persisted in Russia well into the modern era, and the search for new sources of fur-bearing animals eventually led Russian trappers far to the east and across the Bering Strait to Alaska and the Pacific North-west of the North American continent. Ibn Fadlān was therefore a witness to the operations of the early medieval equivalent of the Hudson Bay Company.

Glossary

ajā'ib 'wonders', *mirabilia.*

amīr ruler; military leader.

ansār 'helpers'; the early converts – in the lifetime of the Prophet – to Islam in Medina.

bāk also *bak.* Turkic title (modern Turkish *beg*) used by Khazars for the 'king'/military commander who ruled in tandem with the *khāqān.* Other terms used in the sources for the same office are: *tarkhān, īshā (shād)* and *yiligh.*

barīd the Abbasid system of postal relays, used for official communications and intelligence gathering.

bezant the medieval European term for the Byzantine gold *solidus,* equivalent to the dīnār.

dalaq marten pelt, used as currency; one pelt was equivalent to 2 Bulghār dirhams or 2½ Khazar dirhams. This word also occurs in the form *dallah.*

dānaq a small coin, one-sixth of a dirham; the corresponding weight.

dīnār a gold coin with a canonical weight of 1.4 oz (4.25 g). The gold to silver ratio in Bulghār was 1:12, in Khazaria 1:15.

dirham the Sāmānid dirham and its Volga Bulghār imitation was a stamped silver coin weighing 1.13 oz (3.41 g). The dirhams struck in Khazaria were lighter, weighing .9 oz (2.73 g).

dīwān audience chamber.

fals a small coin of base metal.

faqīh a jurisconsult, a man learned in Islamic law.

farsakh measure of distance, roughly 3½ miles.

ghulām literally, a 'young man'. In Abbasid times generally means a slave soldier or former slave serving the owner who freed him. The slaves were usually of Turkic origin. It can also mean a page (p. 35).

hadīth account of an act or a saying of the Prophet Muhammad.

hajj the pilgrimage to Mecca.

Hanafī one of the four *sunnī* schools of Islamic law, founded by Abū Hanīfa (d. 767).

iqlīm from the Greek *klimata*. Arab geographers influenced by the classical tradition divided the habitable earth into Seven Climes. The Persian, or Balkhī school of descriptive administrative geography used the word to mean 'district'.

īshā see *bāk*.

isnād the chain of reputable authorities authenticating a Prophetic tradition (*hadīth*).

janāba major ritual pollution.

jinn impalpable beings who can be malevolent or beneficent, considered to inhabit ruins and other waste places.

khadank birch (Turkic *kading*); see also Part II, note 16.

khalanj maple wood?

khāqān Old Turkic title meaning 'Lord of the steppes'.

khatīb the man who delivers the *khutba*.

khutba the sermon delivered before communal prayers on Fridays. It was customary, although not prescribed by the *sharʿīa*, to invoke the name of the ruler; failure to do so was often seen as tantamount to rebellion.

kilavuz a Turkic word for guide.

künde Magyar title corresponding to *bāk*; see also Part I, note 88 and Part III, note 23.

majūs originally referred to the Zoroastrians, and came to mean 'fire worshippers'; it was transferred to the Norsemen perhaps because of their custom of burning their dead. See also Appendix 2.

mann a weight of 2 *ratl*; 2.5–4.5 kg.

mithqāl (plural *mathāqīl*) both a measure of weight and a gold coin of that weight (1.4 oz; 4.25 g).

nabīdh wine or other drink fermented for only one day, therefore licit for Muslims.

qādī a judge who administers the Holy Law (*sharʿīa*).

qinshār unidentified coin mentioned by Ibrahīm ibn Yaʿqub and encountered in Prague; 1 *qinshār* purchased 10 chickens.

qubba dome.

ratl in Baghdad it weighed 409.5 g; the measurement varied considerably.

ribāt a defensible caravanserai, or fortress; often used as a base by orders of warriors pledged to *jihad* (see III: 3).

shād see *bāk*.

Shāfiʿī one of the four *sunnī* schools of Islamic law, founded by the imam Shāfiʿī (d. 820).

shar'īa the system of Islamic law, codified in four major schools.

sūra chapter of the Qur'ān.

tāgh unidentified tree, used as firewood; Yaqūt glosses as *ghadā*, a variety of euphorbia. None of the suggested identifications is very plausible.

tarkhān Turkic title, 'noble'; also used for the 'king' in the Khazar system of dual kingship.

tāzja Khwārazmian coin; there were 15 to the dīnār.

tengri Turkic sky god.

tussūj unit of weight: 4 *tussūj* to the *dānaq*, 24 to the dīnār.

yabghū ancient Turkish royal title, which occurs in the Orkhan inscriptions. Among the Ghuzz it seems to have been applied to the sons, brothers and other close relatives of the *khāqān*.

yiligh see *bāk*.

yiltawār Turkic *älteber*, title of the vassal of a *khāqān*.

Bibliography

Ibn Fadlān: Arabic text and translations

Canard, M. (1988) *Ibn Fadlân, Voyage chez les Bulgares de la Volga.* Paris: Sindbad. French translation, with additions to the text from Yāqūt.

Dahhān, S. (1959) *Risālat ibn Fadlān.* Damascus: al-Jāmiʻ al-ʻIlmī al-ʻArabī. Copy-text for this translation.

Fraehn, C. M. (1823) *Ibn Fozlan's und anderer Araber Berichte über die Russen älterer Zeit.* St Petersburg: Akademie der Wissenschaften. First scholarly edition of the Arabic text, based on citations in Yaqūt.

Frye, R. N. (2005) *Ibn Fadlan's Journey to Russia: A Tenth-Century Traveller from Baghdad to the Volga River.* Princeton: Markus Wiener.

Kovalevskii, A. P. (1956) *Kniga Akhmeda Ibn-Fadlana o ego Puteshestvii na Volgu 921–922 gg.* Kharkov. Contains photographic reproduction of the Mashhad manuscript.

Togan, Ahmed Zeki Validi (1939) *Ibn Fadlan's Reisebericht.* Leipzig: Kommissionsverlag F. A. Brockhaus. German translation with edition of Arabic text edited from the Mashhad manuscript.

Studies of Ibn Fadlān

Kowalska, M. (1973) 'Ibn Fadlān's account of his journey to the state of the Bulghārs', *Folia Orientalia*, 14, 219–30.

Montgomery, J. E. (2000) 'Ibn Fadlān among the Rūsīyyah', *Journal of Arabic and Islamic Studies*, 3, 1–25. Fully annotated translation of the passage on the Rūs ['Rusiyyah'], with a discussion of the problems raised by the text, the controversies to which it has given rise, and references to a wide range of anthropological and archaeological sources.

—. (2004) 'Travelling Autopsies: Ibn Fadlān and the Bulghār', *Middle Eastern Literature*, 7, 3–32.

—. (2006) 'Spectral Armies, Snakes, and a Giant from Gog and Magog: Ibn Fadlān as Eyewitness Among the Volga Bulghārs', *Medieval History Journal*, 9, 63–87.

Abū Hāmid al-Andalusī: Arabic texts and translations

Dubler, C. (1953) *Abū Hāmid el Granadino. Relación de Viaje por Tierras Eurasiáricas*, ed. C. Dubler. Madrid: Imprenta y Editorial Maestre. Edition of the Arabic text, commentary and Spanish translation; copy-text for this translation.

Abū Hāmid al-Andalusī [Ibn Abī al-Rabīʿ, Muhammad ibn ʿAbd al-Rahīm] (1925) *Le tuhfat al-albāb de Abū Hāmid al-Andalusī al-Ġarnātī*, édité d'après les MSS.2167, 2168, 2170 de la Bibliothèque Nationale et le Ms. d'Alger par G. Ferrand. Paris: Imprimerie Nationale.

—. (1990) *Tuhfat al-albāb* [*Tuhfat al-albāb wa-nukhabāt al-ajā'ib*] *El regalo de los espíritos*. Presentación, traducción y notas por Ana Ramos. Series: *Fuentes arábico-hispanasa* 10. Madrid: CSIC, Instituto de Cooperación con el Mundo Árabe.

—. (1991) *al-Muʿrib ʿan baʿḍ ʿajā'ib al-maghrib. Elogio de algunas maravillas del Magrib*. Introducción, edición y traducción por Ingrid Bejarano. Series: *Fuentes arábico-hispanas* 9. Madrid: CSIC, Instituto de Cooperación con el Mundo Árabe.

Geographers, Historians and Travellers: texts and translations

Bakrī, al- (ed. A. A. al-Hajji) (1968) *Jughrāfīya al-andalus wa ūrūba*. Baghdād: Dār al-Irshād.

Bīrūnī, al- (ed. Muhammad b. Tāwīt al-Tanjī) (1962) *Tahdīd nihāyāt al-amākin li-tashīh masāfāt al-masākin*. Ankara: Doğus Ltd.

Cross, S. H. and O. P. Sherbowitz-Wetzor (tr. and eds) (1953) *The Russian Primary Chronicle. Laurentian Text*. Cambridge, MA: Medieval Academy of America.

Defremery, C. and B. R. Sanguinetti (eds) (1854) *Voyages d'Ibn Batoutah*. Paris: Imprimerie Royale, Vol. II.

Dimashqī, al- (ed. M. A. F. Mehren) (1866) *Cosmographie de Chems-ed-Din Abou Abdallah Mohammed ed-Dimachqui*. St Pétersbourg: Mehren.

Gibb, H. A. R. (1962) *The Travels of Ibn Battuta, A.D. 1325–1354*. Cambridge: Hakluyt Society, Vol. II.

Ibn al-Faqīh (ed. M. J. De Goeje) (1885), in *Compendium libri Kitab al-Boldan* [*Kitāb al-Buldān*]. Bibliotheca Geographorum Arabicorum V. Leiden: Brill.

Ibn Hawqal (ed. J. H. Kramers) (1938) *Opus geographicum. 'Liber Imaginis Terrae'* [*Kitāb sūrat al-ard*]. 2 vols. Leiden: Brill.

—. (1964) *Configuration de la Terre (Kītab sūrat al-ard)*, tr. J. H. Kramers and G. Wiet. Collection UNESCO d'oeuvres representatives. Série arabe. Paris: G. P. Maisonneuve & Larose. Vol. 1.

Ibn Hayyān [Ben Haián de Córdoba] (ed. J. V. Bermejo) (1999) *Muqtabis II. Anales de los Emires de Córdoba Alhaqém I (180–206 H./796–822 J.C.) y Abderramán II (206–232/822–847). Edición facsímil de un manuscrito árabe de la Real Academia de la Historia (legado Emilio García Gómez)*. Madrid: Real Academia de la Historia.

—. (tr. M. A. Makkī) (2001) *Crónica de los emires Alhakam I and ʿAbdarrahmān II entre los años 796 y 847. Almuqtabis II-1*. Instituto de Estudios Islámicos y del Oriente Próximo. Zaragoza: La Aljafería.

Ibn Khurradādhbih (ed. M. J. de Goeje) (1885) *Kitāb al-Masālik wa'l-Mamālik*. Accedunt excerpta e *Kitāb al-Kharāj*, auctore Kodāma ibn Jaʿfar. Bibliotheca Geographorum Arabicorum VI. Leiden: Brill.

Ibn al-Nadīm (tr. and ed. B. Dodge) (1970) *The Fihrist of al-Nadīm. A tenth-century survey of Muslim culture*. New York: Columbia University Press. Vol. 1.

Ibn Rusta [Ibn Rosteh, Abû Alî Ahmed ibn Omar] (ed. M. J. de Goeje) (1892) *Kitâb al-Aʿlâk an-Nafîsa vii*, auctore Abû Alî Ahmed ibn Omar Ibn Rusteh; *Kitāb al-buldān* / auctore Ahmed ibn abi Jakûb ibn Wâdhih al-kâtib al-Jakûbî. Bibliotheca Geographorum Arabicorum VII. 2nd edn. Leiden: Brill.

Ibn Rusta [Ibn Rusteh] (tr. G. Wiet) (1955) *Les Atours Précieux*. Cairo: Société de Géographie d'Égypte.

Istakhrī, Abū Ishāq al-Fārisī al- (ed. M. J. de Goeje). (1870) *Viae Regnorum. Descriptio ditionis Moslemicae*. Bibliotheca Geographorum Arabicorum I. Leiden: Brill.

Janicsek, S. (1929) 'Ibn Battuta's Journey to Bulghār: is it a Fabrication?', *Journal of the Royal Asiatic Society*, 791–800.

Kowalski, T. (1946) *Relacja Ibrahīma Ibn Jaʿkūba z Podróży do Krajów Słowiańkich w Przekazie al-Bekrīego. Relatio Ibrahīm ibn Jaʿqūb de Itinere Slavico, quae traditur apud al-Bekri*. Monumenta Poloniae Historica. Nova Series – Tomus I. Cracoviae. Edition of the Arabic texts of the surviving portions of Ibrāhīm ibn Yaʿqūb's travels in Slavic lands, accompanied by photographic reproductions of the maunscripts of al-Bakrī in which they are found and translations into Polish, with commentary, and Latin.

Masʿūdī, al- (1962–1997) *Les prairies d'or*. Traduction française de Barbier de Meynard et Pavet de Courteille, revue et corrigée par Charles Pellat. Paris: Société Asiatique. Vol. 1.

—. (ed. C. Pellat) (1966) *Murūj al-dhahab wa ma'ādin al-jawhar*. Beirut: Manshūrāt al-Jāmi'a al-Lubnānīya. Vol. 1.

—. (ed. M. J. de Goeje) (1894) *Kitāb at-Tanbīh wa'l-Ischrāf*, 2nd edn. Bibliotheca Geographorum Arabicorum VIII. Leiden: Brill.

Minorsky, V. (1942) *Sharaf al-Zamān Tāhir Marvazī on China, the Turks and India*. James G. Forlong Fund, Vol. XXII. London: Royal Asiatic Society.

—. (1948) 'Tamīm ibn Bahr's journey to the Uyghurs', *Bulletin of the School of Oriental and African Studies*, 12, 275–305.

Miquel, A. (1966) 'L'Europe occidentale dans la relation arabe d'Ibrâhîm b. Ya'qûb', in *Annales. Historie, Science Sociales*, 21ᵉ année, no. 5 (Sep.–Oct.), pp. 1048–64.

Miskawayh [Miskawihi] (tr. D. S. Margoliouth) (1921) *The Concluding Portion of The Experiences of the Nations*, in *The Eclipse of the 'Abbasid Caliphate. Original Chronicles of the Fourth Islamic Century*, ed. and tr. H. F. Amedroz and D. S. Marogliouth. Oxford: Blackwell. Vol. II.

Muqaddasī, al- (ed. M. J. de Goeje) (1906) *Ahsan al-taqāsīm fī ma'rifat al-aqālīm*. Bibliotheca Geographorum Arabicorum III. Leiden: Brill.

Qazwīnī, al-(1848) (ed. F. Wüstenfeld) *Zakarija ben Muhammed ben Mahmûd el-Cazwini's Kosmographie*. Göttingen: Dieterich. Vol. 2.

Qazwīnī, al- (1960) *Athār al-bilād*. Beirut: Dār al-Sādir.

Quatremère, É. (1838) Notice de l'ouvrage qui a pour titre: Mesalek Alabsar fi memalek alamsar [Kibāb al-masālik al-absār fī mamālik al-amsār], voyages des yeux dans les royaumes des différentes contrées (manuscript arabe de la Bibliothèque du roi). *Notices et extraits des manuscrits de la Bibliothèque du roi*. Paris: Imprimerie Royale. Volume XIII, pp. 277–81.

Qudāma ibn Ja'far (ed. M. J. de Goeje) (1889) *Kitāb al-kharāj wa sinā'at al-kitāba*, in Ibn Khurradādhbih (ed. M. J. de Goeje) (1885), 184–266.

Yāqūt (ed. F. Wüstenfeld) (1866) *Jacut's geographisches wörterbuch* [*Mu'jam al-buldān*]. Leipzig: F. A. Brockhaus, 1866–1873. 9 vols.

Ya'qūbī, Ahmad ibn Abī Ya'qūb ibn Wādih al-kātib (1892) *See* Ibn Rusta.

Yule, Sir H. and H. Cordier (1903) *The Book of Ser Marco Polo the Venetian Concerning the Kingdoms and Marvels of the East*. 3rd edn. London: John Murray.

Zuhri, al-, Muhammad ibn Abī Bakr. *See* Hadj-Sadok (1968).

Further Reading

Bates, D. R. (1974) 'Auroral sound', *Polar Record*, no. 107, 103–8.

Berend, N. (2001) *At the Gate of Christendom: Jews, Muslims and*

'Pagans' in Medieval Hungary, c. 1000–c. 1300. Cambridge Studies in Medieval Life and Thought, 4th series. Cambridge: Cambridge University Press.

Crumin-Pedersen, O. (1997) *Viking-age Ships and Shipbuilding in Hedeby/Haithabu and Schleswig*. With contributions by Christian Hirte, Kenn Jensen and Susan Moller-Wiering. Roskild: Viking Musuem.

Curta, F. (2005) *East Central & Eastern Europe in the Early Middle Ages*. Ann Arbor: University of Michigan Press.

Duczko, W. (2004) *Viking Rus: Studies on the Presence of Scandinavians in Eastern Europe*. Leiden: Brill.

Dunlop, D. M. (1954) *The History of the Jewish Khazers*. Princeton: Princeton University Press.

Franklin, S. and J. Shepard (1996) *The Emergence of Rus, 750–1200*. London and New York: Longman.

Frazer, J. G. (1917) 'The Killing of the Khazar Kings', *Folk-lore*, 28, 382–407.

Golden, P. (1982) 'The Question of the Rus Qaganate', *Archivum Eurasiae Medii Aevii*, 2, 77–97.

—. (1991) 'Nomads and their sedentary neighbours in pre-Činggisid Eurasia', *Archivum Eurasiae Medii Aevii*, 7, 41–81.

—. H. Ben-Shammai and A. Róna-Tas (eds) (2007) *The World of the Khazars. New Perspectives. Selected Papers from the Jerusalem 1999 International Khazar Colloquium hosted by the Ben Zvi Institute*. Leiden: Brill.

Hadj-Sadok. M. (1968) 'Kitāb al-Ja'rāfiyya. Mappemonde du Caliph al-Ma'mūn reproduite par Fazārī (IIIᵉ/IXᵉ s.), rééditée et commenté par Zuhrī (VIᵉ/XIIᵉ s.)', *Bulletin d'Études Orientales*, XXI, 1–346.

Jonsson, K. and B. Malmer (eds) (1990) *Commentationis de nummis saeculorum IX–XI in Suecia repertis*. Nova Series 6. Sigtuna Papers. Proceedings of the Sigtuna Symposium on Viking Age Coinage 1–4 June 1989. Stockholm: Numismatic Institute.

Karjalainen, K. F. (1927) 'Die religion der Jugra-völker', *Suomalainen Tiedeakatemia*. Helsinki, 1921–7. Vol. 3, pp. 34–5.

Kovalev, R. K. (2000–2001) 'The infrastructure of the northern part of the fur road: Between the Middle Volga and the East During the Middle Ages', *Archivum Eurasiae Medii Aevii*, 11, 26–37.

—. (2002) 'Dirham Mint output of Samanid Samarqand and its connection to the beginnings of trade with Northern Europe (10th Century)', *Histoire & mesure*, XVII–n°3/4, 197–216.

—. (2005) 'Creating Khazar Identity through Coins: The Special Issue Dirhams of 837/8', in Curta, *East Central & Eastern Europe in the Early Middle Ages*, pp. 220–51.

Lavers, C. and M. Knapp. (2008) 'On the origin of khutū', *Archive of Natural History*, 38 (2), 306–18.

Levi, Judah [Yehuda], ha- (tr. N. D. Korobkin) (1998) *The Kuzari: In Defense of the Despised Faith*. Northvale, NJ: J. Aronson.

Lewis, B. (2001) *The Muslim Discovery of Europe*. New York: W. W. Norton & Co.

Lieber, A. E. (1990) 'Did a "silver crisis" in Central Asia affect the flow of Islamic coins into Scandinavia and eastern Europe?' in Jonsson and Malmer, *Commentationis de nummis saeculorum IX–XI in Suecia repertis*, pp. 207–12.

McCormick, M. (2001) *The Origins of the European Economy: Communication and Commerce, A.D. 300–900*. Cambridge: Cambridge University Press.

Marešová, K. (1976) Nález předmincovniho platidla na slovanském pohřebiši v Uherském Hradišti-Sadech (Find of a pre-monetary currency unit in a Slavic cemetery at Uherské Sady). Časopis Moravského musea, A61/2, 31–6.

Marten, J. (1986) *Treasure of the Land of Darkness. The Fur Trade and its Significance for Medieval Russia*. Cambridge: Cambridge University Press.

Martinez, P. (1982) 'Gardīzī's two chapters on the Turks', *Archivum Eurasiae Medii Aevii*, 2, 109–217.

Miquel, A. (1966) 'L'Europe occidentale dans la relation arabe d'Ibrâhîm b. Ya'qūb', in *Annales. Historie, Science Sociales*, 21ᵉ année, no. 5 (Sep.–Oct.), pp. 1048–64.

Nelson, J. L. (ed. and tr.) (1991) *The Annals of St-Bertin*. Ninth-century Histories. Manchester: Manchester University Press. Vol 1. Covers the years 830–882.

Noonan, T. S. (1984) 'Why dirhams first reached Russia: The role of Arab-Khazar relations in the development of the earliest Islamic trade with Eastern Europe', *Archivum Eurasiae Medii Aevii*, 4, 151–282.

—. (1986) 'Why the Vikings first came to Russia', *Jahrbücher für Geschichte Österopas*, 34, 321–48.

—. (1987) 'The onset of the silver crisis in Central Asia', *Archivum Eurasiae Medii Aevii*, 7, 221–48.

—. (1990) 'Dirham exports to the Baltic in the Viking Age: some preliminary observations', in Jonsson and B. Malmer, *Commentationis de nummis saeculorum IX–XI in Suecia repertis*, pp. 251–7.

—. (1991) 'When did Rūs/Rus' merchants first visit Khazaria and Baghdād?', *Archivum Eurasiae Medii Aevii*, 7, 213–19.

—. (1997) 'Scandinavians in European Russia', in P. Sawyer (ed.), *The Oxford Illustrated History of the Vikings*. Oxford: Oxford University Press, pp. 134–55.

—. (2001) 'Volga Bulghāria's Tenth-Century Trade with Sāmānid
Central Asia', *Archivum Eurasiae Medii Aevii* (2000–2001), 11,
140–218.

—. (2007) 'Some observations on the economy of the Khazar Khaga-
nate', in Golden, Ben-Shammai and Róna-Tas, *The World of the
Khazars*, pp. 207–44.

Obolensky, D. (1967) 'Commentary on the ninth chapter of Constantine Porphyrogenitus' De Administrando Imperio'. Dumbarton
Oaks Center for Byzantine Studies, 1967, 56–63. Reprinted in *Byzantium and the Slavs: Collected Studies*. London: Variorum Reprints,
1971.

Page, R. I. (1995) *Chronicles of the Vikings. Records, Memorials and
Myths*. London, British Museum Press.

Petrov, N. I. (2005) 'Ladoga, Ryurik's Stronghold, and Novgorod:
Fortification and Power in Early Medieval Russia', in Curta, *East
Central & Eastern Europe in the Early Middle Ages*, pp. 121–7.

Pritsak, O. (1971) 'An Arabic text on the trade route of the corpor-
ation of Ar-Rūs in the second half of the ninth century', *Folia
Orientalia*, 12, 241–59. Important study of the Rādhānīya.

—. (1998) *The Origins of the Old Rus' Weights and Monetary Systems. Two Studies in Western Eurasian Metrology and Numismatics
in the Seventh to the Eleventh Centuries*. Harvard Ukranian Research
Institute, Harvard Series in Ukraninan Studies. Cambridge, MA:
Harvard Ukrainian Research Institute, distributed by Harvard University Press.

Pseudo-Callisthenes (1991) *The Greek Alexander Romance*. Tr. with
an introduction and notes by Richard Stoneman. London: Penguin
Books.

Rapoport, S. (1929) 'On the Early Slavs. The Narrative of Ibrahim-
Ibn-Yakub', *Slavonic and East European Review*, 8, 331–41.

Rispling, G. (1990) 'The Volga Bulgarian Imitative Coinage of al-Amir
Yaltawar ('Barman') and Mikail b. Jafar', in Jonsson and Malmer,
Commentationis de nummis saeculorum IX–XI in Suecia repertis,
pp. 275–82.

Róna-Tas, A. (1999) *Hungarians and Europe in the Early Middle
Ages. An Introduction to Early Hungarian History*. New York:
Central European University Press.

—. (2007) 'The Khazars and the Magyars', in Golden, Ben-Shammai
and Róna-Tas, *The World of the Khazars*, pp. 269–78.

Schjødt, J. P. (2007) 'Ibn Fadlan's account of a Rus funeral: To what
degree does it reflect Nordic myth?', in P. Hermann, J. P. Schjødt

and R. T. Kristensen (ed.), *Reflections on Old Norse Myths*. Turn-
hout, Belgium: Brepols, pp. 133–48.

Shboul, A. (1979) *Al-Mas'ūdī & His World: A Muslim Humanist and
His Interest in Non-Muslims*. London: Ithaca.

Spufford, P. (1988) *Money and its Use in Medieval Europe*. Cambridge: Cambridge University Press.

Notes

PART I

THE BOOK OF AHMAD IBN FADLĀN 921–922

1. *caliph Muqtadir*: Reigned 908–932.
2. *Saqāliba*: Arabic (singular *saqlab*), derived from the Greek *sklabos*, meaning 'Slav': see Appendix 2. In Carolingian times the classical Latin word for slave, *servus*, began to be replaced by *sclavus*, so that 'Slav' became synonymous with 'slave' (for the early medieval slave trade, see McCormick (2001), 733–77). The Arab geographers often used the word Saqāliba in a wider sense, however, simply to refer to any northern people, e.g. Slavs, Scandinavians, Finns, Balts, Saxons, Germans, Franks and other peoples of northern lands, and it is not always possible to tell exactly which people is meant. In this volume Saqāliba is always used, except where context definitely means 'Slav'.
3. *Almish ibn (Shilkī) Yiltawār*: MS reads: *al-hasan bin bltwār*. Further on (f. 202v), the name is given correctly: *almish bin y(i)ltawār*. The element *shilkī* has been added from the full form of the name there, confirmed by the text in Yaqūt.
4. *minbar*: The raised platform in a mosque from which the congregation is addressed by the imam.
5. *his name*: I.e. in the name of the caliph. Including the reigning caliph in the *khutba* was a recognition of his suzerainty.
6. *Nadhīr al-Haramī*: A powerful eunuch at the Abbasid court and organizer of the embassy, but he did not accompany it.
7. *Arthakhushmithān*: Described by Yaqūt as 'a large city with busy markets, the size of Nisībīn'. In MS and in Dahhān's edition, the name is spelled 'Arthakhushmithayn'.
8. *Ibn al-Furāt*: Belonged to a dynasty of viziers, and held this office himself three times (908–912, 917–918, 923–924) under the caliph

Muqtadir. He was a talented administrator, but was twice dismissed and imprisoned for corruption, and finally executed in 924. See also notes 21 and 51.

9. *al-Khazarī*: Apparently a Muslim Khazar. The Bulghār embassy to the caliph sought an alliance against the Jewish Khazars, and this of course was supported by Muslim Khazars.

10. *caliph*: Here called *sultān* in MS, rather than *khalīfa*. *Sultān* was not used as a synonym for caliph in Ibn Fadlān's lifetime. It may be a later interpolation or is possibly used in the sense of 'government'. (It occurs also pp. 10, 20, 45.)

11. *Sawsān . . . Saqlab*: Sawsān (lily) is a typical male slave name. Sawsān al-Rassī was a freedman of Nadhīr al-Haramī. The second element of his name is derived from the Aras River (al-Rass), which runs through Armenia, joins the Kur and falls into the Caspian Sea (*Bahr al-Khazar*) below Baku. Tikīn is the Arabic transcription of *tekin*, a Turkic word meaning 'hero', applied to members of the *khāqān*'s family and a common element in Turkish names. Bārs possibly represents the Slavic name Boris, but there is a Turkic name Bars.

12. *without halting*: MS reads *lā yakūnu 'alā shayin* which Canard emends to *lā nalwī 'alā shayin*.

13. *Qirmisīn*: Qarmīsīn in MS; modern Kirmanshah.

14. *Ahmad ibn 'Alī . . . al-Rayy*: Ahmad ibn 'Alī Su'lūk was the brother of Muhammad ibn 'Alī Su'lūk, appointed governor of Rayy by the Sāmānid ruler Nasr ibn Ahmad. Ahmad ibn 'Alī helped the Abbasid general Mu'nis in a campaign against the ruler of Azerbaijan, and in return was appointed governor of Isfāhān and Qum. When Ibn Fadlān met him, he was governor of Rayy. For more details, see Canard, n. 20. Khuwār al-Rayy was east of Rayy, in the province of Qūmis.

15. *agent of the Dā'ī*: Ibn Qārin's full name was Sharwān ibn Rustum ibn Qārin, a prince of the Caspian Bawand dynasty. The 'Dā'i' refers to al-Hasan ibn al-Qāsim (876–928), governor of Jurjān, whose title, granted him by his father-in-law, the *shi'a* Zaydī *imām* and ruler of Tabaristān, was *Dā'ī āl-Haqq*, 'Propagator of the Truth'. These men were bitterly opposed to the *sunnī* regimes of the Sāmānids and Abbasids.

16. *killed . . . Hamawayh Kūsā*: Laylā ibn Nu'mān, the Isma'īlī governor of Jurjān, was captured and put to death in 921 by Hamawayh ibn 'Ali [Humawayh Kūsā], Sāmānid general and governor of Samarqand', who was commander of the army of Nasr ibn Ahmad ibn Isma'īl.

17. *Qushmahān*: The town of Kushmayhān. Muqaddasī lists the six stages of the journey from Merv (Marw) to Āmul. Interestingly, the fifth stage on this desert route is called Ribāt Bāris, the same form of the name as that of the Slavic envoy.

18. *Afirabr*: This place name occurs as Afrīn in MS, but it should be Afirabr, or Firabr (now Farab). Firabr is mentioned by Muqaddasī, who says it lies about a *farsakh* from the river, has low taxes, excellent grapes and a caravanserai built by the Sāmānid ruler Nasr ibn Ahmad, although this may not have been built when Ibn Fadlān passed through.

19. *Jayhānī*: The famous minister of Nasr ibn Ahmad. His full name was Abu 'Abd Allāh Muhammad ibn Ahmad al-Jayhānī, and he was the author of a *Book of Roads and Kingdoms*, unfortunately lost, but citations from it have been preserved in Muqaddasī and Ibn Hawqal.

20. *Nasr ibn Ahmad*: Nasr ibn Ahmad ibn Ismā'īl (ruled 914–943) was sixteen or seventeen at the time of Ibn Fadlān's visit.

21. *our path*: Although the details of this affair are slightly obscure, the general situation is clear. Ibn al-Furāt was imprisoned for peculation in 918 (see note 8), and the revenues of the town of Arthakhushmithān were transferred from his Christian agent Fadl ibn Mūsā al-Nasrānī to Ahmad ibn Mūsā al-Khwārazmī. This money was intended to defray the costs of the embassy, so Fadl ibn Mūsā naturally resented its loss and instructed his agents to arrest Ahmad ibn Mūsā, which they accordingly did. Meanwhile, Fadl encouraged the envoys to proceed before winter set in, thereby, incidentally, preventing them from learning the fate of Ahmad ibn Mūsā. The Gate of the Turks (*Bāb al-Turk*) was a strategic frontier post on the border of Khwārazm, near Zamjān.

22. *ghitrīfī dirhams*: Named after the early Abbasid governor of Khurāsān, Ghitrīf ibn 'Attāb. His two brothers, Muhammad and Musayyab, both had coins named after them, the *muhammadī* and the *musayyabī* dirhams (see p. 10). This passage on coinage is confusing because Ibn Fadlān uses 'dirham' when speaking of the small base coins of Bukhārā, instead of the more exact term *fals*.

23. *Khwārazm*: Ibn Fadlān uses this term both as the name of the province and its capital. The latter was Kāth.

24. *rented the boat*: The envoys probably hired their boat at Jikar-band (Jiqarwand), rather than retracing their steps to Firabr via Baykand. Jiqarband is one of the twenty-five crossings of the Oxus listed by Muqaddasī.

25. *Khwārazm Shāh Muhammad ibn ʿIraq*: Otherwise unknown.

26. *land of the Infidels*: Tikīn was apparently engaged in the arms trade with the pagan tribes to the north, and the Khwārazm Shāh is accusing him of attempting to establish direct commercial relations between Baghdad and the Slavs, bypassing his own authority and that of the powerful Sāmānid ruler, Nasr ibn Ahmad.

27. *kiʾāb, dāwāmāt*: Probably local names for small coins; however, *kiʾāb* can also mean 'dice' and Yāqūt, in the parallel passage, reads *duwwāmāt*, 'tops' (child's toy). Canard suggests reading the latter word (the initial 'm' is unclear in the MS) as *dāwāyāt* (inkwells).

28. *Ardakuwa ... Kardalīya*: Ardakū or Ardakūwa; Frye (2005) reads Kardalīya as Ardakīwa, from the name of the village.

29. *deny the legitimacy ... prayer*: Indicating that they were not *shiʿa*, but the *sunni* do not curse ʿAlī.

30. *seventeen spans thick*: Yāqūt says that the Jayhūn occasionally freezes to the thickness of 5 spans, but the usual thickness is 2 or 3 spans. He accuses Ibn Fadlān of 'lying' in this passage, and goes on to say that the wagons used to transport firewood could not possibly carry 3,000 *ratl*; their normal load was 1,000.

31. *'bread'*: Yāqūt adds: 'If something is given, he takes it; if not, he departs.'

32. *Shaʿbān ... Shawwāl*: That is, December 921–February 922.

33. *boats ... camel skin*: These must have been collapsible boats made of the skin stretched across a wicker frame.

34. *kilavuz*: Zeki Validi Togan is surely correct in suggesting that the word in MS represents the Turkish word *kilavuz*, simply meaning 'guide'.

35. *ribāt ... Turks*: The Ribāt Zamjān was presumably the fort protecting the Gate of the Turks (see note 21).

36. *'Lords'*: The word used is *rabb* (Arabic for 'lord', cognate with Hebrew 'rabbi' – unusual in this context).

37. *'Their political ... themselves'*: Qurʾān 42:38.

38. *kūdharkīn*: There is no agreement about the origin or exact meaning of this word, which is clearly a title.

39. *[]*: There is a blank the length of a word in MS.

40. *nabīdh*: Usually means 'wine', but here probably refers to mead or *kumis*, fermented mare's milk.

41. *numerous yurts*: Buyūt kathīra, but Dahhān (1959) reads Buyūt kabīra (big yurts).

42. *clothing ... pieces*: Classical authors (Ammianus Marcellus xxxi.2, Herodotus iv.75) mention the same custom among the Huns and Scyths respectively. According to Maqrīzī (fourteenth

century), the Yāsā of Genghiz Khan forbade the washing of garments and stipulated that they must be worn until they rot.

43. *Ināl*: The phrase '*ibn akhima*' occurs after this name; it seems to make no sense and has been omitted.

44. *saddle frames*: This is guess work; the word in the text is *ināth*, which makes no sense.

45. *Yaghindī . . . rivers*: Some of these rivers can be securely identified, others are uncertain. Frye (2005), 97 and Róna-Tas (1999), 223 give the following based on the abundant scholarly literature: Yaghindī = Zhayindi; Jām = Emba; Jākhsh = Saghiz; Udhil = Uil; 'Ardin = Kaldygayti; Wārsh = Olenty ?; Akhtī = Ankati; Wabnā = Utba.

46. *Jāyikh . . . Kunjulū*: The tentative river identifications are: Jāyikh = Ural; Jākhā = Chagan; Arkhaz = Irgiz; Bājāgh = Mocha; Samūr = Samara; Kināl = Kinel; Sūkh = Sok; Kunjulū = Kundurcha.

47. *Bāshghirds*: Also Bashkirs, Bashgird, Bashkurt; a Turkic people, speaking a language close to Kipčaq and inhabiting the Ural mountains on the borders of Bulghār territory. These were known to the Arab geographers as the 'Inner Bāshghirds'; the 'Outer Bāshghirds' inhabited areas of what is now Hungary, and were visited by Abu Hāmid al-Andalusī. At the time of Ibn Fadlān, the Bāshghirds were still shamanists.

48. *God . . . souls*: An echo of Qur'ān 17:42.

49. *Jirimshān . . . Jāwshīr*: The river identifications are: Jirimshān = Cheremshan; Uran = Uran; Uram = Urem; Bāynākh = Mayna; Watīgh = Utka; Nīyāsnah = ?; Jāwshīr = Aqtay or Gausherma.

50. *black*: The official colour of the Abbasid dynasty.

51. *Hāmid ibn al-'Abbās*: The caliph Muqtadir's vizier (918–923), replacing Ibn al-Furāt, who was in jail and whose estate had been forfeited to raise the 4,000 dirhams to build the fortress for the king of the Bulghārs (see also note 8). Hāmid had been a wealthy tax-farmer; he is remembered as the man who signed the death warrant for the famous mystic al-Hallāj, executed in 922 while Ibn Fadlān was en route to Bulghār.

52. *over him*: The parallel passage in Yāqūt reads 'over us', but given the dirhams scattered over the queen below, this must be the correct reading.

53. *[Then . . . table.]*: Supplied from the parallel account by Yāqūt. The copyist of the MS appears to have missed a line describing the serving of the third king.

54. *cup*: Yāqūt adds: 'and we drank a cup'.

55. *caliph*: The surprising term *ustādh* (teacher, preceptor) is used here; Canard points out that it was the normal honorific for the

vizier, rather than the caliph, and it is possible that that is what is intended here.

56. *iqāma twice . . . prayer*: The *iqāma* is almost identical to the *idhān*, differing only by the addition of the words *qad qāmat al-salāt* (now is the time of prayer). It is a shortened form of the call to prayer, recited as the prayers begin, and according to the Shāfiʿī rite, which Ibn Fadlān was anxious to impose on the kingdom of Bulghār, the phrases that make up the *shahāda* (the Muslim profession of faith: 'There is no God but God: Muhammad is the messenger of God') are repeated only once, rather than twice as in the Hanafī rite followed by the Sāmānids and most of Central Asia. The Bulghār ruler, by reintroducing the Hanafī *iqāma*, was seen by Ibn Fadlān to be asserting his independence of the Abbasid caliphate.

57. *Abū Bakr the Truthful*: Abū Bakr al-Siddīq (The Truthful) was the first caliph (632–634), the successor to the Prophet Muhammad as head of the Muslim community. The Bulghār king is not only displaying his knowledge of the early history of Islam, and incidentally reminding Ibn Fadlān of the duty of the good Muslim to tell the truth, but taking a sarcastic dig at his guest, who he thinks is lying about the whereabouts of the 4,000 *dīnārs*.

58. *saw the horizon . . . first created*: Although this is clearly an account of the aurora borealis, Ibn Fadlān's description has roots in the Greek scientific tradition. James Montgomery points out that visions of 'spectral armies' battling are a topos that goes back to classical descriptions of meteorological phenomena (see Montgomery (2006), 76–81).

59. *a seventh part of the Qurʾān*: The Qurʾān was often divided into seven parts, so that it could be read over the period of a week.

60. *[scattered . . . fades]*: Added from Yāqūt.

61. *Wīsū*: The Ves, a Finnic-speaking people who inhabited the White Lake region east of Lake Ladoga. See also Part II, note 15.

62. *[summer] . . . [summer]*: Inserted to clarify the text.

63. *Itil*: Not to be confused with the Khazar capital on the lower Volga (near present-day Astrakhan); Itil here refers to the site on the Volga (Itil) later to be occupied by the town of Bulghār, at this time simply a seasonal marketplace. The Volga has changed course, and the ruins of the town are now found some distance from the river.

64. *snakes*: May have been Amur ratsnakes, *Elaphe schrencki schrenki*, which are semi-arboreal and very large.

65. *berry*: Probably berries of the same family as the blueberry.

66. *Tree sap*: This could well be birch sap, given the latitude, but Ibn Fadlān implies that the tree is new to him, and he must already have seen birch trees.

67. *[of his weapons]*: Added from Yāqūt.
68. *before men*: Yāqūt is more specific: 'To cover themselves when swimming with the men'.
69. *Muhammad*: Ibn Fadlān's given name was Ahmad, a variant of Muhammad.
70. *great market*: Later became the town of Bulghār (see also note 63).
71. *Itil River*: Yāqūt adds: 'and it is a river one day's journey away'.
72. *and Magog*: The king's story implies that some of the Wīsū were literate. As in his explanation of the aurora borealis, the king assimilates the giant into Islamic lore, perhaps seeking to frighten Ibn Fadlān with visions of the apocalypse, always associated with the hordes of Gog and Magog (see also Part III, note 5).
73. *They are naked*: This phrase seems out of place here, and the text may be corrupt.
74. *shoved*: Qadhafanī is clearly written; all editors have emended it to something else (Dahhān (1959) reads *fa-qaddamanī*: 'he made me go in front of him'), apparently on the grounds that it is unlikely the king pushed Ibn Fadlān. But the lack of respect may well be intentional: the king is waging a battle of wits with Ibn Fadlān, and the veiled threats embodied in stories like that of the fate of the particularly clever merchant from Sind are becoming more open.
75. *Jāwshīr . . . Suwāz . . . Wīragh*: MS reads 'Jawshīz', but this is the Jawshīr (Aqtay) River, an affluent of the Kama, previously mentioned. 'Suwan' in MS. 'Wīragh' is not clearly written in MS.
76. *This people*: Dahhān (1959) reads *hadhihi l-umma*, following Zeki Validi Togan, but the word *umma* (the Muslim community) is not legible, and the demonstrative pronoun is clearly *hadhā*: so perhaps *hadhā al-qawm* (this people)?
77. *All around . . . trees*: MS reads: 'around it a tree [blank for one word ending in '*t*'] many of *khadank* trees and others'.
78. *rhinoceros*: Karkaddan. Whatever this was, it was not a rhinoceros. Descriptions of the *karkaddan* are a topos of Arabic geographical literature and wonder books (for an amusing discussion of this topic, see Montgomery (2006), 66–72). Ibn Fadlān's account is notable because it does not conform to the conventional description of the *karkaddan*. It should be noted that the identification as a rhinoceros is by his informants, not Ibn Fadlān.
79. *a woman from Khwārazm*: The corpse must be washed by a Muslim woman and this can only be done if one is present (and if not, not). The main source of Muslim women was Khwārazm. The passage implies that Islam has not extended to Bulghār females.

80. *dark green*: Montgomery ((2000), 6, n. 18) points out that *mukhaddar shajar* here means 'dark green' rather than 'green trees'.

81. *brooch*: MS reads *halqa*, which implies a circular ornament; Dahhān (1959) amends this to *huqqa*, following Yāqūt, which would imply a square container of some sort.

82. *The most . . . boats*: This is an awkward sentence. The puzzling phrase is *al-kharaf alladhī yakūnu ʿalā l-sufun yubālighūna fī-hi*. MS reads *yubāyiʾūna* (they sell), which Dahhān (1959) changes, following Yāqūt, to *yubālighūna* (they value dearly), which makes more sense.

83. *raised platform*: *Sarīr* (throne, couch).

84. *[ribs]*: There are several blanks in MS for this paragraph; these have been filled in from the parallel account in Yaqūt. Some manuscripts of Yāqūt give a longer version of the final sentence.

85. *beg*: Written 'bh' in MS, representing the pronunciation of *bāk/beg*.

86. *[Every*: MS breaks off here; the remainder of the text is taken from Yāqūt (1866), under the entry 'Khazar'.

87. *right of him*: The use of purifying fire when entering the presence of the *khāqān* was common to both Turkish and Mongol peoples.

88. *Kundur . . . jawshīghīr*: *Kundur* is probably an error for *künde*, which exists as a Magyar title (see Part III, note 23); *jawshīghīr* most probably stands for *čavūsh* Uighur, 'marshal of the Uighurs'; see Dunlop (1954) 38 and 111, n. 92.

89. *king of the Khazars*: Ibn Fadlān here clearly means the *khāqān kabīr*, the Great Khāqān.

90. *khaz*: The word has not been convincingly explained.

91. *Dār al-Bābūnaj*: Means 'House of Cammomile'; it was probably in Darband, although some scholars have speculated that it may have been in Pumbedita, the residence of the Gaon near Baghdad, or even in far-off al-Andalus.

PART II
THE TRAVELS OF ABŪ HĀMID AL-ANDALUSĪ AL-GHARANĀTĪ 1130–1155

1. *Abū Hāmid*: This passage (in italics) has been supplied from Qazwīnī, who clearly had a fuller account of the journey of Sallām the Interpreter than that preserved by Ibn Khurradādhbih,

which does not contain the passage about the Island of Sheep in the Caspian.

2. *snakes*: Probably Caspian whip snakes (*Coluber caspius*).
3. *al-Mahāmilī*: Abū al-Hasan Ahmad ibn Muhammad ibn al-Mahāmilī (978–1024), a Shāfiʾite jurisconsult from Baghdad.
4. *Lakzān . . . Arabic*: Not all these languages can be identified, but most were spoken in the Caucasus.
5. *Saqsīn*: Abū Hāmid spells this name: Sajsīn, Sakhsīn and Saqsīn; the last is the accepted form. Its exact location is still undetermined, but Abu Hāmid makes it clear that Saqsīn was on the lower reaches of the Volga; it could well be the successor to the Khazar capital of Itil and may have occupied the same site.
6. *Maghrib . . . thousands*: Abū Hāmid's reference to the large number of Maghribīs is very surprising. Maghribī means 'westerner' and here refers to Muslims from North Africa and al-Andalus, all of whom followed the legal school of the imam Mālik. This community from the far west was clearly established in Saqsīn for commercial reasons; if they were merchants, they were almost certainly trading in slaves and furs.
7. *descendants of the Maghribīs*: This suggests they may have been established in Saqsīn for a long period, possibly since Khazar times.
8. *snow . . . colours*: There was a trade in snow, for cooling drinks, in the Islamic world, but it is hard to believe it could have been shipped from Bulghār to interested markets without melting, so it may have been used in Bulghār itself. The colours are not explained.
9. *beyond the Seventh Clime*: Muslim geographers placed the end of the Seventh Clime, the most northerly inhabited region of the earth, just south of Bulghār.
10. *In Bulghār . . . stones*: This paragraph is from Abū Hāmid's *Tuhfat al-albāb*; see Abū Hāmid al-Andalusī (1990), 78–9.
11. *ʿĀd*: This tribe, repeatedly mentioned in the Qurʾān, peopled the earth after the Deluge (the biblical Flood) and in Islamic folklore were a race of giants. Ancient ruins in Islamic lands are often attributed to them. See also p. 84.
12. *not break*: Mammoth ivory was known as *khutū*, and was much sought after for making knife handles as well as the objects mentioned here. See Lavers and Knapp (2008), 306–18.
13. *al-Bulghārī's own hand*: Yaʿqūb ibn Nuʿmān al-Bulghārī (eleventh century); this work has not survived. The folk etymology is of course incorrect; Bulghār is from a Turkic root meaning 'people of mixed origin'.
14. *Abū al-Maʿālī al-Juwaynī*: Abū al-Maʿālī ʿAbd al-Malik al-Juwaynī

(1028–1085), from Nishapur, was a famous jurisconsult, theologian and extremely prolific author. He was one of the teachers of the philosopher al-Ghazālī.

15. *Wīsū ... Arū*: The Ves of *The Russian Primary Chronicle*, the modern Veps; (see also Part I, note 61); the Arū have not been identified but may be the Arthā in other texts.

16. *khalanj*: Probably maple, but the word is very similar to *khadank* (birch), which seems more likely in this context. Qazwīnī says *khalanj* wood was used in Tabarastān to make various receptacles, including serving platters and large bowls, which were then taken to Rayy to be finished on the lathe and decorated. The wood was also used for arrows (Qazwīnī (1960), 104).

17. '*And ... godfearing*': Qur'ān 91:8.

18. *Yūrā*: Yughra of Russian sources: see Appendix 4.

19. *iron blank ... time*: In the parallel passage in his *Tuhfat al-albāb*, Abū Hāmid says that merchants bought these sword blanks in Azerbaijan at the price of one dirham for four blades.

20. *giant birds ... beaks*: This must be the crossbill, a kind of finch, but it is not a 'giant' bird. The Yughra (Yūrā), however, did have legends of giant birds with huge beaks; see Karjalainen (1921), 34–5.

21. *river of the Saqāliba*: Abū Hāmid must have descended the Oka on his way to Kiev (Ghūrkūmān; to Tatars, Merkuman).

22. '*water sable*': Probably the otter.

23. *juqn*: Probably represents the Old Slavic term *kuna* (squirrel pelt), still used today to denote the currency of Croatia.

24. *Saqlabī*: See Part I, note 2.

25. *Nestorian Christians*: Neither the Byzantines nor the Saqāliba were Nestorians.

26. *Maghribīs*: Clearly not from Spain and North Africa, like those above (see note 6). They are almost certainly Pečenegs, the Turkic nomads frequently mentioned in the Arabic sources as inhabiting the steppe lands around the Dnieper; many of them settled in Hungary. Why Abū Hāmid calls them 'Maghribīs' has not been satisfactorily explained. For Ghūrkūmān, see note 21.

27. *king of Bāshghird*: The Hungarian king was Geza II (reigned 1141–1162); see Part I, note 47.

28. *lord of Constantinople*: Manuel I Comnenos (reigned 1143–1180).

29. *kirālī*: *Kazālī* in MS; it should be read *király*, the Hungarian word for 'king'.

30. *thaytal*: Arabic, referring to the wild cow, *Bos taurus*.

31. *al-Shu'bī*: Unidentified.

32. *In Bulghār . . . instantly*: From *Tuhfat al-albāb*.
33. *'Abd al-Wāhid ibn Fayrūz al-Jawhari*: Perhaps the brother of 'Abd al-Karīm ibn Fayrūz mentioned in 'Return to the land of the Saqāliba' above.
34. *Mahmūd . . . place*: Mahmūd of Ghazna (reigned 998–1030), founder of the Ghaznavid dynasty. The enchanted mosque has not been located.
35. *'Alā' al-Dawla Khwārazmshāh*: No one of this name is recorded; maybe 'Alā' al-Dīn (reigned 1127–1156).
36. *lord of Konya . . . Mas'ūd*: The Seljuk ruler of Konya, Qïlïch Arslan II (reigned 1156–1192).
37. *back to Bāshghird . . . family*: This was a journey Abū Hāmid seems never to have made. His patron, 'Awn al-Dīn, was poisoned by rivals in 1165, which may have precipitated his departure from Mosul that year. In any case, he never returned to ransom his son Hāmid in Hungary and never rejoined his womenfolk in Saqsīn.

PART III

PASSAGES FROM OTHER GEOGRAPHERS, HISTORIANS AND TRAVELLERS

1. *the wall*: Although Alexander's Wall was carefully marked on medieval Islamic maps (including that of Idrīsī on the cover of this volume), such a barrier or rampart did not exist, and the story was probably generated by tales of the Great Wall of China. See Qur'ān 18:92–8.
2. *Ashnās*: A Turk, commander of the Abbasid army.
3. *Ishāq ibn Ismā'īl . . . 'Master of the Throne'*: The ruler of Tiflis (*c.* 830–853); married to a daughter of the 'Master of the Throne', (*sāhib al-sarīr*), the Avar ruler of Daghestan. The latter was said to possess an ancient golden throne. The country itself is usually simply called 'Sarīr' (throne).
4. *tarkhān*: A Turkish title denoting high rank; the title of the Khazar ruler, however, was *khāqān*. This probably refers to his military counterpart, the *khāqān beg*.
5. *Gog . . . a half*: The Arabic sources differ greatly in the size accorded the people of Gog and Magog, some saying they were very small, others that they were giants.
6. *"When the . . . is true"*: Qur'ān 18:98.

7. *Isbīshāb, Ushrūsana*: This must be Isbijāb, now Sayram in Uzbekistan; Ushrūsana was the region just east of Samarkand.

8. *Fleet ... Norsemen*: Ustūl al-majūs min al-urdumānīyīn, literally 'the fleet of the *majūs* of the Nordomanni', i.e. Norsemen.

9. *from the Mediterranean*: This must be an error, although the next phrase clearly reads *bahr al-rūm* ('sea of the Byzantines'= Mediterranean). The following passage from Ahmad's son 'Īsā correctly says the Vikings came from the 'Western Sea', i.e. the Atlantic.

10. *'Abd al-Rahmān ibn al-Hakam*: 'Abd al-Rahmān II (ruled 822–852).

11. *the river*: The Guadalquivir.

12. *Aljarafe*: The hills just north of Seville, overlooking the city.

13. *'Abd al-Rahmān III*: Reigned 912–961.

14. *Samkarsh*: The Phanagoria of the Byzantine chronicles, modern Taman on the east shore of the Kertch strait. See Dunlop (1954), 172.

15. *River Tanais ... Khamlij*: Tanais may be a mistake for 'Volga', or the long portage from the Don to the Volga has been omitted. Khamlij is better read Khamlīkh, the 'business' district of Itil.

16. *yurt*: (MS reads *wurt*); used here in the sense of 'grazing lands, homeland'.

17. *Muhammad ibn Ishāq*: I.e. Ibn al-Faqīh.

18. *from ... the Franks*: At this early date the silk industry had not been established in Italy, and the only possible sources in Europe would have been al-Andalus and possibly Sicily.

19. *Rādhānīya*: De Goeje's text (Ibn al-Faqīh (1885)) reads Rāhdānīya, which some scholars see as the solution to the vexed question of the meaning of Rādhānīya: a Persian compound made up of *rah* (way) and *dan* (knowing), forming a name meaning something like 'knowers of the way'. The Mashhad manuscript of Ibn al-Faqīh, however, reads Rādhānīya, confirming the reading in Ibn al-Faqīh's source, Ibn Khurradādhbih.

20. *īshā*: Probably represents the Turkic *shād*, a military title for a high rank; here it corresponds to *bāk* or *yiligh* of other texts.

21. *Sārighshin ... [Khanbaligh?]*: Respectively, possibly the name later rendered as Saqsīn; see also Part II, note 5. MS reading is *hbnl'*, which some scholars have construed as 'Khanbaligh', 'city of the Khan', but this is unlikely.

22. *[Then ... cash.]*: From Gardīzī, who wrote in Persian c. 1050; see Martinez (1982), 158–9. Gardīzī here followed Ibn Rusta's text on the Bulghārs, with occasional amplifications. See also Pritsak (1998), 24.

23. *jilah*: The nominal, or sacral, ruler of the Magyars was *künde*, while the equivalent of the acting ruler, the *khāqān beg*, was *jila*. After the Magyar conquest of the Carpathian basin, the acting ruler took the title *künde*, while *jila* was used for his second in command. See Róna-Tas (2007), 275.

24. *Wabnīt*: (Wāntīt) may be related to the name of the Eastern Slavic tribe, the Vyatiči.

25. *sūbanj*: Probably the Old Slavic title *zhupan*, of Avar or Turkic origin; it is clear from this passage that the Saqāliba possessed the institution of dual kingship, following the Khazar model.

26. *Svetopolk*: This may be the Moravian king Svetopolk (reigned 870–894); there were several rulers with the name at this time.

27. *Graditsa*: MS reads *jarwāb*; a suggested reading is *jarād.s.t*. Graditsa was the name of Svetopolk's capital (later Gradistsche).

28. *an island in a lake*: This may be Gorodishche, called Holmgarthr in the Icelandic sagas, a trading post near where the Volkhov issues forth from Lake Ilmen. If so, this may have been the 'home' to which the delegation of Rhos who visited Ingelheim was attempting to return, as recounted in the *Annales Bertiniani* (see Appendix 2, p. 204).

29. *sell them in Khazarān*: The district included the slave market in Itil.

30. *'Sulaymān' swords*: These 'Solomon' swords apparently took their name from the Salmān district of Khurāsān.

31. *a quarrel . . . wins*: This seems to have been a sort of ceremonial combat; the man who succeeded in nicking the blade of his opponent won.

32. *trousers . . . knees*: Rock carvings have been found at Scandinavian sites which depict the huge trousers worn by the Rūs.

33. *Darband*: Bāb wa l-abwāb (Gate and the Gates) is more usually called in Arabic 'Gate of Gates'. This extraordinary series of fortifications, which extended into the sea, forming a breakwater that also enclosed the port, entry to which was by an iron gate, seems to have been built in Sāsānian times – Chosroe Anushīrwān was the Sāsānian ruler of Iran (reigned 531–579) – although local tradition attributes it to Alexander the Great.

34. *in peril*: From Qarmatian attacks.

35. *'Party Kings'*: *Mulūk al-Tawā'if*. This expression, used by Muslim historians to refer to the Satrapies that sprang up after the death of Alexander, is also used for the independent emirates that followed the breakdown of the Umayyad caliphate in Spain. Mas'ūdī is thinking of the Ikhshīdids, Fātimids, Sāmānids, Spanish

Umayyads, Hamdānids and other independent states that were formed in the ninth and tenth centuries.

36. The caliph Muttaqī (reigned 940–944).

37. *Salmān ibn Rabī'a al-Bāhilī*: Conquered Samandar – probably near present-day Makhač-kala in the north-eastern Caucasus – in 652, but was killed during the battle. For Itil, see Part I, note 63.

38. *Sea of Azov*: Bahr Māyutis (Sea of Maeotis).

39. *Hārūn al-Rashīd*: It is now generally accepted that the conversion of the Khazar rulers took place sometime during his reign (786–809). The Khazar tribal confederation emerged in the sixth century, when a Turkish ruling elite succeeded in uniting a number of Turkish and non-Turkish steppe nomadic groups under their rule in the Volga–Pontic steppe–Caucasus region. Between the seventh and tenth centuries the Khazars were allied with the Byzantines, first against the Sāsānians, then against the Muslims. The conversion of the ruling class to Judaism did not seem to affect this relationship.

40. *Romanus I*: Romanus I Lecapenus, father-in-law of Constantine VII Porphyrogenitus, usurped power from his son-in-law in 919 and held it until 944, when he was deposed by his sons.

41. *Arsīyya*: Derived from one of the names of the Alan people, Aorsi, another version of which is still borne by their modern descendants, the Ossetes.

42. *great river*: The Volga; the tributary is the Samara, then called the Burtās, which lent its name to the people inhabiting its banks (see next note). The city is Itil.

43. *Burtās*: The ancestors of the Finnish Mordve people, rather than Turks. They inhabited the forest land between the Bulghārs and the Khazars.

44. *Sea of Pontus*: Black Sea (Bahr Buntus), but Mas'ūdī is wrong; he means the Sea of Azov.

45. *Bulghār capital ... Pontus*: Mas'ūdī was mistaken; it is on the confluence of the Volga and Kama rivers.

46. *Turk ... Seventh Clime*: The Bulghārs were originally a Turkish people; their homeland was in the steppes in the vicinity of the Kuban River and the Sea of Azov, and one branch (the 'Black Bulghārs') remained there until the tenth century. Another branch, probably because of pressure from the Khazars, migrated in 678 to the Balkans, where they founded a state among the South Slavonic tribes, by which they were eventually absorbed. These were known to the Arab geographers as the Burjān, a word also applied to the Burgundians (see also note 48). A third group, probably

also under pressure from the Khazars, retreated to the north along the Volga, settling at the confluence of that river with the Kama. They subjected the local Finnish population and founded the Bulghār kingdom, which in Mas'ūdī's time paid an annual tribute in sable and other furs to the Khazars. Mas'ūdī's mention of '310/922' is clearly due to some memory of Ibn Fadlān's mission to the Bulghār king in that year, but Almish had converted to Islam at least ten years earlier.

47. *Their king*: This passage has caused great confusion. Mas'ūdī has confused the Volga Bulghārs with the Balkan Bulghārs, and possibly with the Magyars as well.

48. *Burgundians*: Burjān; here, confusingly, the original appellation of the Bulghārs is applied to the Burgundians (cf. note 46).

49. *Venice*: Fanadīya, representing the Latin Venetia.

50. *Mājik*: Although much discussed, no convincing Slavic etymology has been found for this word. Indeed, most of the Slavic words in this passage are problematical. Some of the suggested identifications can be found in the following notes. The Arabic script does not indicate short vowels and a number of letters are only distinguished by dots above or below them. Faced with unfamiliar foreign words, scribes used their imagination. Further information on these Slavic names may conveniently be found in Shboul (1979), 178–89.

51. *Walītābā*: Wiltzes? Veletians? Those that read Walīnānā have identified this tribal name with the Volinians on the River Bug.

52. *Istrāna ... Sarbīn*: Istrāna: perhaps the Stodorans, near the Oder River; Basqlābij: Vasclav?; Dūlāba: the Western Dulebians, a Bohemian tribe that lived on the banks of the River Laba?; Wānjslāf: almost certainly Prince Wenceslaw I (reigned 916–935); Namjīn: the Germans; the name probably represents Slavic Niemczyn (German); Gharānd: perhaps Conrad I (reigned 912–919), king of the Bavarians; Manābin: variants are *māyin* and *maghānin*, and perhaps a people dwelling on the River Main; Sarbīn: the Serbs.

53. *Murāwa ... Barānijābīn*: Murāwa: the Moravians; Kharwātīn: the Croats; Sāsīn: either the Saxons (Mas'ūdī numbers Germanic peoples among the Slavs), or possibly the Czech (Cacin); Khashānīn: two peoples have been suggested, the Kaszub near the Oder River or the Balkan tribe of the Gadczans; Barānijābīn: the Braniczews, a Balkan Serbian tribe?

54. *to the west*: Mas'ūdī must mean the reverse, that the Slavs extend to the west.

55. *Aldayr*: Unidentified; the name can also be read Aldir.

NOTES

56. *Bazkard*: The Magyars (the Bāshghird of Abū Hāmid al-Andalusī).
57. *the Ocean*: Uqiyānūs; i.e. the Atlantic.
58. *bronze lighthouse*: By this, Mas'ūdī means the Strait of Gibraltar (the Pillars of Hercules), guarded, according to legend, by a bronze statue warning sailors not to pass into the Atlantic.
59. *Sea of Azov and the Black Sea*: 'Sea of Maeotis' and 'Sea of Pontus' (see notes 38 and 44).
60. *trading . . . Khazars*: This seems to be an echo of the journeys of the Rādhānīya. Lu'dhāna has not been identified.
61. *the river of the Khazars*: Nahr al-Khazar (the Khazar River), that is, the Volga, which of course does not flow into the Sea of Azov (what is presumably meant by the 'Strait of Pontus'). Mas'ūdī seems to be thinking of the Don, or perhaps Donetz, but the text is still confusing.
62. *[is . . .]*: A phrase giving the distance is missing from the text.
63. *Burtās*: see notes 42 and 43.
64. *Bardha'a*: Surrounded with orchards and fields and known for its figs, fruit, hazelnuts and silks. It is located about fourteen miles from the Kur River, on the banks of one its tributaries, the Terter. According to Mas'ūdī, it was also a market for furs from the north.
65. *khulais*: This word, variants of which occur in Greek and Hungarian, seems to mean 'Khwārazmian', here probably referring to Khazar Turkish mercenaries from Khwārazm.
66. *unrelated . . . nation*: The Khazars spoke a Turkic language closely related to that spoken by the Bulghārs; the modern descendant of both is Chuvash, spoken today in parts of central Russia.
67. *Sarīr*: See Part III, note 3.
68. *Arthā . . . lead*: The Arthā have not been satisfactorily identified; the region of Sweden facing the Åland Islands was known in the Middle Ages as Rodhen or Rodhs, which may lie behind the Arabic Arthā/Arthānīya; the similarity to the word Rādhānīya is probably fortuitous. Ibn Hawqal, who copies this passage from Istakhrī, adds 'and mercury'.
69. *Greater Bulghāria . . . Christians*: By 'Greater Bulghāria' (Bulghār al-a'zam), al-Istakhrī must mean the Volga Bulghārs visited by Ibn Fadlān. 'Inner Bulghāria' (Bulghār al-dākhil) refers to the Danubian Bulghārs, who officially became Christian in 867.
70. *khalanjī*: A fur of two colours.
71. *Walītābā*: Walīnānā – see Part III, note 51.
72. *Boreslav . . . Nakon*: Boreslav: Bwyslāw; Prague: Farāgha; Bohemia: Bwyma; Cracow: Karakū; Mieszko: Mashaqu; Nakon

(Nāqūn), chief of the Obotrite Slav confederation of Meklenburg-Schwerin, died in 965, the year Ibrāhīm visited Otto.

73. *Burgh ... Māylīyah*: Burgh: this is guesswork, perhaps Merseburg; Māylīyah may not be a place name, but the Arabic phrase for 'what lies nearby it' (*mā yalīhi*).

74. *mathāqīl al-marqatīyya*: Mysterious; one commentator has suggested that it be read *bizantīna* (Dubler (1953), 162), translating the whole phrase as 'Byzantine gold coins'. This seems unlikely, since writers of Arabic at this date invariably use *rūmī*, 'Roman', for 'Byzantine'. It is tempting, but probably unwarranted, to see the Latin *mercatum* lurking behind *marqatīyya*. See Glossary for *mithqāl*.

75. *qinshār*: Clearly the name of a coin of some sort, but what? The most common European silver coin in circulation at the time was the penny (pfennig), but it is difficult to reconcile any of the names by which it was known with *qinshār*, which is clearly written in MSS.

76. *kerchiefs*: *Munaydilāt khifāf*. The use of kerchiefs as currency is archaeologically attested, see Marešová (1976).

77. *receptacles*: *Awʿīya* means 'vase', which seems an odd place to keep kerchiefs.

78. *[to]*: There is a word missing in MS here and below.

79. *City of Women*: The City – or Island – of Women is a topos of Arabic, indeed of medieval geographical literature, inherited from the classical tradition. Idrīsī, the twelfth-century Sicilian geographer, locates it on an island in the Atlantic, Qazwīnī in the China Sea.

80. *king of the Romans*: Malik al-rūm; usually refers to the Byzantine emperor, but here it must be an attempt to render the title *rex Romanorum*. Otto I was crowned emperor in 961.

81. *pilings*: This last phrase is guesswork; the text reads *wa hum yasta 'malūna la-hu shutūran harlan*; the final two words, both in the accusative case, are meaningless. Ibrāhīm is describing the harbour at Schleswig; at the nearby port of Hedeby, marine archaeologists have discovered rows of log pilings, almost certainly revetments of the early medieval harbour (Crumin-Pedersen (1997), 37). We have read *sutūr* ('rows; lines') and taken the meaningless *harl* (with emphatic *h*) to have originally stood for a word signifing a kind of log or wood.

82. *912*: Boris I converted to Christianity in 865.

83. *Gulf of Venice ... Italy*: Buhayra banājīya (the lake of Venice); Ibrāhīm's spelling of Venice is close to the old Italian form 'Venigia', although it is difficult to explain the long ā in the second

syllable. *Al-ard al-kabīra* (the great land), an expression usually used of 'mainland' Europe, but here it seems to refer to Italy.

84. *Germans . . . Hungarians*: Respectively, Tudishkīyīn, cf. Italian 'Tedeschi'; Anqalīyīn, perhaps to be read *unqarīyīn*.

85. *sabā*: There is a word missing from MS at the beginning of this sentence; *sabā* does not resemble any Slavonic bird name, although there is a scholarly consensus that the starling is meant; see Rapoport (1929), 339, n. 3.

86. *fanak*: Normally the fennec, but we think it means 'mink' here.

87. *Ma'mūn*: This must be Ma'mūn ibn Muhammad, who was ruler of Gurganj before becoming Khwārazm Shah in 995; see Dunlop (1954), 246–7.

88. *conquered their lands*: This is a reference to the conquest of the Khazars by the Kieven Rūs and their Ghuzz allies in 965.

89. *closer . . . the capital*: Muqaddasī is confused; Bulghār is some 800 miles upstream from the Khazar capital.

90. *Khazar . . . river*: Thus not another name for Itil.

91. *gulf*: Probably the Caspian Sea.

92. *Bulghār and Khazarān*: They were attacked by the Rūs between 965 and 967. The date given by Ibn Hawqal must be the year he heard the news. Khazarān is the name of one of the two districts into which the town of Itil was divided.

93. *912*: Vladimir converted in 988; probably a copyist's mistake.

94. *yiltawār*: The text reads *b.t.ltw*, Ibn Fadlān's *yiltawār*, the title of the Bulghār king. It is clear from this passage that Marwazī thought 'Vladimir' was a title, not a personal name.

95. *khadang*: This equals *khadank* in Ibn Fadlān (birch).

96. *fish . . . and such like*: Narwhal and walrus horn, called *khutū*, was much prized for its durability and was the preferred material for knife handles; see Lavers and Knapp (2008).

97. *suwīt . . . shrīh*: *suwīt*: must represent the first element in the name Svetopolk (see note 26); *shrīh* (*sh.rīh* in MS) has not been satisfactorily explained, see Minorsky (1942), 117.

98. *their country*: The Tatar lands north-east of the Caspian.

99. *this king*: Conci (Kaunchi), a Tatar. *agent of the Dā'ī*: This was the Isma'īlī agent al-Hasan ibn al-Qāsim al-Hasanī. The *dā'ī* (he who summons') was chief propagandist for the Isma'īlī sect.

PENGUIN CLASSICS

THE PROSE EDDA
SNORRI STURLSON

'What was the beginning, or how did things start? What was there before?'

The Prose Edda is the most renowned of all works of Scandinavian literature and our most extensive source for Norse mythology. Written in Iceland a century after the close of the Viking Age, it tells ancient stories of the Norse creation epic and recounts the battles that follow as gods, giants, dwarves and elves struggle for survival. It also preserves the oral memory of heroes, warrior kings and queens. In clear prose interspersed with powerful verse, the *Edda* provides unparalleled insight into the gods' tragic realization that the future holds one final cataclysmic battle, Ragnarok, when the world will be destroyed. These tales from the pagan era have proved to be among the most influential of all myths and legends, inspiring modern works as diverse as Wagner's *Ring* cycle and Tolkien's *The Lord of the Rings*.

This new translation by Jesse Byock captures the strength and subtlety of the original, while his introduction sets the tales fully in the context of Norse mythology. This edition includes also detailed notes and appendices.

Translated with an introduction, glossary and notes by Jesse Byock

PENGUIN CLASSICS

THE SAGA OF GRETTIR THE STRONG

'The most valiant man who has ever lived in Iceland'

Composed at the end of the fourteenth century by an unknown author, *The Saga of Grettir the Strong* is one of the last great Icelandic sagas. It relates the tale of Grettir, an eleventh-century warrior struggling to hold on to the values of a heroic age as they are eclipsed by Christianity and a more pastoral lifestyle. Unable to settle into a community of farmers, Grettir becomes the aggressive scourge of both honest men and evil monsters – until, following a battle with the sinister ghost Glam, he is cursed to endure a life of tortured loneliness away from civilization, fighting giants, trolls and berserks. A mesmerizing combination of pagan ideals and Christian faith, this is a profoundly moving conclusion to the Golden Age of saga writing.

This is an updated edition of Bernard Scudder's acclaimed translation. The new introduction by Örnólfur Thorsson considers the influence of Christianity on Icelandic saga writing, and this edition also includes genealogical tables and a note on the translation.

Translated by Bernard Scudder

Edited with an introduction by Örnólfur Thorsson

Penguin Classics

EGIL'S SAGA

'The sea-goddess has ruffled me,
stripped me bare of my loved ones'

Egil's Saga tells the story of the long and brutal life of the tenth-century warrior-poet and farmer Egil Skallagrimsson: a psychologically ambiguous character who was at once the composer of intricately beautiful poetry and a physical grotesque capable of staggering brutality. This Icelandic saga recounts Egil's progression from youthful savagery to mature wisdom as he struggles to defend his honour in a running feud against the Norwegian King Erik Blood-axe, fights for the English King Athelstan in his battles against Scotland and embarks on colourful Viking raids across Europe. Exploring issues as diverse as the question of loyalty, the power of poetry and the relationship between two brothers who love the same woman, *Egil's Saga* is a fascinating depiction of a deeply human character, and one of the true masterpieces of medieval literature.

This new translation by Bernard Scudder fully conveys the poetic style of the original. It also contains a new introduction by Svanhildur Óskarsdóttir, placing the saga in historical context, a detailed chronology, a chart of Egil's ancestors and family, maps and notes.

Translated by Bernard Scudder

Edited by Ornulfur Thorsson

PENGUIN CLASSICS

SELECTED POEMS
RABINDRANATH TAGORE

'It dances today, my heart, like a peacock it dances ...
It soars to the sky with delight'

The poems of Rabindranath Tagore (1861–1941) are among the most haunting and tender in Indian and world literature, expressing a profound and passionate human yearning. His ceaselessly inventive works deal with such subjects as the interplay between God and the world, the eternal and transient, and the paradox of an endlessly changing universe that is in tune with unchanging harmonies. Poems such as 'Earth' and 'In the Eyes of a Peacock' present a picture of natural processes unaffected by human concerns, while others, as in 'Recovery – 14', convey the poet's bewilderment about his place in the world. And exuberant works such as 'New Rain' and 'Grandfather's Holiday' describe Tagore's sheer joy at the glories of nature or simply in watching a grandchild play.

William Radice's exquisite translations are accompanied by an introduction discussing Tagore's Bengali cultural background, his social, political and religious beliefs, and the lyric metres and verse forms he developed.

'An important book ... William Radice's introduction is excellent' *Sunday Times*

Translated with an introduction by William Radice

PENGUIN CLASSICS

BUDDHIST SCRIPTURES

'Whoever gives something for the good of others, with heart full of sympathy, not heeding his own good, reaps unspoiled fruit'

While Buddhism has no central text such as the Bible or the Koran, there is a powerful body of scripture from across Asia that encompasses the *dharma*, or the teachings of Buddha. This rich anthology brings together works from a broad historical and geographical range, and from languages such as Pali, Sanskrit, Tibetan, Chinese and Japanese. There are tales of the Buddha's past lives, a discussion of the qualities and qualifications of a monk, and an exploration of the many meanings of Enlightenment. Together they provide a vivid picture of the Buddha and of the vast nature of the Buddhist tradition.

This new edition contains many texts presented in English for the first time as well as new translations of some well-known works, and also includes an informative introduction and prefaces to each chapter by scholar of Buddhism Donald S. Lopez Jr, with suggestions for further reading and a glossary.

Edited with an introduction by Donald S. Lopez, Jr

Penguin Classics

THE COMPLETE DEAD SEA SCROLLS IN ENGLISH
GEZA VERMES

'He will heal the wounded and revive the dead and bring good news to the poor'

The discovery of the Dead Sea Scrolls in the Judean desert between 1947 and 1956 was one of the greatest archaeological finds of all time. These extraordinary manuscripts appear to have been hidden in the caves at Qumran by the Essenes, a Jewish sect in existence before and during the time of Jesus. Written in Hebrew, Aramaic and Greek, the scrolls have transformed our understanding of the Hebrew Bible, early Judaism and the origins of Christianity.

This is a fully revised edition of the classic translation by Geza Vermes, the world's leading Dead Sea Scrolls scholar. It is now enhanced by much previously unpublished material and a new preface, and also contains a scroll catalogue and an index of Qumran texts.

'No translation of the Scrolls is either more readable or more authoritative than that of Vermes' *The Times Higher Education Supplement*

'Excellent, up-to-date ... will enable the general public to read the non-biblical scrolls and to judge for themselves their importance'
The New York Times Book Review

Translated and edited with an introduction by Geza Vermes

PENGUIN CLASSICS

THE DEATH OF KING ARTHUR

'Lancelot has brought me such great shame as to dishonour me through my wife, I shall never rest till they are caught together'

Recounting the final days of Arthur, this thirteenth-century French version of the Camelot legend, written by an unknown author, is set in a world of fading chivalric glory. It depicts the Round Table diminished in strength after the Quest for the Holy Grail, and with its integrity threatened by the weakness of Arthur's own knights. Whispers of Queen Guinevere's infidelity with his beloved comrade-at-arms Sir Lancelot profoundly distress the trusting King, leaving him no match for the machinations of the treacherous Sir Mordred. The human tragedy of *The Death of King Arthur* so impressed Malory that he built his own Arthurian legend on this view of the court – a view that profoundly influenced the English conception of the 'great' King.

James Cable's translation brilliantly captures all the narrative urgency and spare immediacy of style. In his introduction, he examines characterization, narrative style, authorship and the work's place among the different versions of the Arthur myth.

Translated by James Cable

PENGUIN CLASSICS

REVELATIONS OF DIVINE LOVE
JULIAN OF NORWICH

'Just because I am a woman,
must I therefore believe that I must not tell you about the goodness of God?'

After fervently praying for a greater understanding of Christ's passion, Julian of Norwich, a fourteenth-century anchorite and mystic, experienced a series of divine revelations. Through these 'showings', Christ's sufferings were revealed to her with extraordinary intensity, but she also received assurance of God's unwavering love for man and his infinite capacity for forgiveness. Written in a vigorous English vernacular, the *Revelations* are one of the most original works of medieval mysticism and have had a lasting influence on Christian thought.

This edition of the *Revelations* contains both the short text, which is mainly an account of the 'showings' themselves and Julian's initial interpretation of their meaning, and the long text, completed some twenty years later, which moves from vision to a daringly speculative theology. Elizabeth Spearing's translation preserves Julian's directness of expression and the rich complexity of her thought. An introduction, notes and appendices help to place the works in context for modern readers.

Translated by Elizabeth Spearing with an introduction and notes by A. C. Spearing

PENGUIN CLASSICS

THE RUBA'IYAT OF OMAR KHAYYAM

'Many like you come and many go
Snatch your share before you are snatched away'

Revered in eleventh-century Persia as an astronomer, mathematician and philosopher, Omar Khayyam is now known first and foremost for his *Ruba'iyat*. The short epigrammatic stanza form allowed poets of his day to express personal feelings, beliefs and doubts with wit and clarity, and Khayyam became one of its most accomplished masters with his touching meditations on the transience of human life and of the natural world. One of the supreme achievements of medieval literature, the reckless romanticism and the pragmatic fatalism in the face of death means these verses continue to hold the imagination of modern readers.

In this translation, Persian scholar Peter Avery and the poet John Heath-Stubbs have collaborated to recapture the sceptical, unorthodox spirit of the original by providing a near literal English version of the original verse. This edition also includes a map, appendices, bibliography and an introduction examining the *ruba'i* form and Khayyam's life and times.

'[Has] restored to that masterpiece all the fun, dash and vivacity' Jan Morris

Translated by Peter Avery and John Heath-Stubbs

PENGUIN CLASSICS

ON LOVE AND BARLEY: HAIKU OF BASHO

'Orchid – breathing
incense into
butterfly's wings'

Basho, one of the greatest of Japanese poets and the master of haiku, was also a Buddhist monk and a lifelong traveller. His poems combine 'karumi', or lightness of touch, with the Zen ideal of oneness with creation. Each poem evokes the natural world – the cherry blossom, the leaping frog, the summer moon or the winter snow – suggesting the smallness of human life in comparison to the vastness and drama of nature. Basho himself enjoyed solitude and a life free from possessions, and his haiku are the work of an observant eye and a meditative mind, uncluttered by materialism and alive to the beauty of the world around him.

These meticulous translations by Lucien Stryk capture the refined artistry of the originals. This edition contains notes and an introduction that discusses how the life and beliefs of Basho influenced his work.

Translated by Lucien Stryk

PENGUIN CLASSICS

THE CAMPAIGNS OF ALEXANDER
ARRIAN

'His passion was for glory only, and in that he was insatiable'

Although written over four hundred years after Alexander's death, Arrian's *Campaigns of Alexander* is the most reliable account of the man and his achievements we have. Arrian's own experience as a military commander gave him unique insights into the life of the world's greatest conqueror. He tells of Alexander's violent suppression of the Theban rebellion, his total defeat of Persia, and his campaigns through Egypt, India and Babylon – establishing new cities and destroying others in his path. While Alexander emerges from this record as an unparalleled and charismatic leader, Arrian succeeds brilliantly in creating an objective and fully rounded portrait of a man of boundless ambition, who was exposed to the temptations of power and worshipped as a god in his own lifetime.

Aubrey de Sélincourt's vivid translation is accompanied by J. R. Hamilton's introduction, which discusses Arrian's life and times, his synthesis of other classical sources and the composition of Alexander's army. This edition also includes maps, a list for further reading and a detailed index.

Translated by Aubrey de Sélincourt
Revised, with a new introduction and notes by J. R. Hamilton

PENGUIN CLASSICS

THE CONQUEST OF GAUL
CAESAR

'The enemy were overpowered and took to flight.
The Romans pursued as far as their strength enabled them to run'

Between 58 and 50 BC Julius Caesar conquered most of the area now covered by France, Belgium and Switzerland, and invaded Britain twice, and *The Conquest of Gaul* is his record of these campaigns. Caesar's narrative offers insights into his military strategy and paints a fascinating picture of his encounters with the inhabitants of Gaul and Britain, as well as lively portraits of the rebel leader Vercingetorix and other Gallic chieftains. *The Conquest of Gaul* can also be read as a piece of political propaganda, as Caesar sets down his version of events for the Roman public, knowing he faces civil war on his return to Rome.

Revised and updated by Jane Gardner, S. A. Handford's translation brings Caesar's lucid and exciting account to life for modern readers. This volume includes a glossary of persons and places, maps, appendices and suggestions for further reading.

Translated by S. A. Handford
Revised with a new introduction by Jane F. Gardner

PENGUIN CLASSICS

THE PERSIAN EXPEDITION
XENOPHON

'The only things of value which we have at present are our arms and our courage'

In *The Persian Expedition*, Xenophon, a young Athenian noble who sought his destiny abroad, provides an enthralling eyewitness account of the attempt by a Greek mercenary army – the Ten Thousand – to help Prince Cyrus overthrow his brother and take the Persian throne. When the Greeks were then betrayed by their Persian employers, they were forced to march home through hundreds of miles of difficult terrain – adrift in a hostile country and under constant attack from the unforgiving Persians and warlike tribes. In this outstanding description of endurance and individual bravery, Xenophon, one of those chosen to lead the retreating army, provides a vivid narrative of the campaign and its aftermath, and his account remains one of the best pictures we have of Greeks confronting a 'barbarian' world.

Rex Warner's distinguished translation captures the epic quality of the Greek original and George Cawkwell's introduction sets the story of the expedition in the context of its author's life and tumultuous times.

Translated by Rex Warner with an introduction by George Cawkwell

THE STORY OF PENGUIN CLASSICS

Before 1946 ... 'Classics' are mainly the domain of academics and students; readable editions for everyone else are almost unheard of. This all changes when a little-known classicist, E. V. Rieu, presents Penguin founder Allen Lane with the translation of Homer's *Odyssey* that he has been working on in his spare time.

1946 Penguin Classics debuts with *The Odyssey*, which promptly sells three million copies. Suddenly, classics are no longer for the privileged few.

1950s Rieu, now series editor, turns to professional writers for the best modern, readable translations, including Dorothy L. Sayers's *Inferno* and Robert Graves's unexpurgated *Twelve Caesars*.

1960s The Classics are given the distinctive black covers that have remained a constant throughout the life of the series. Rieu retires in 1964, hailing the Penguin Classics list as 'the greatest educative force of the twentieth century.'

1970s A new generation of translators swells the Penguin Classics ranks, introducing readers of English to classics of world literature from more than twenty languages. The list grows to encompass more history, philosophy, science, religion and politics.

1980s The Penguin American Library launches with titles such as *Uncle Tom's Cabin*, and joins forces with Penguin Classics to provide the most comprehensive library of world literature available from any paperback publisher.

1990s The launch of Penguin Audiobooks brings the classics to a listening audience for the first time, and in 1999 the worldwide launch of the Penguin Classics website extends their reach to the global online community.

The 21st Century Penguin Classics are completely redesigned for the first time in nearly twenty years. This world-famous series now consists of more than 1300 titles, making the widest range of the best books ever written available to millions – and constantly redefining what makes a 'classic'.

The Odyssey continues ...

The best books ever written

PENGUIN 🐧 CLASSICS

SINCE 1946

Find out more at www.penguinclassics.com